If you have a home computer with Internet access you may:
- request an item to be placed on hold.
- renew an item that is not overdue or on hold.
- view titles and due dates checked out on your card.
- view and/or pay your outstanding fines online (over $5).

To view your patron record from your home computer click on Patchogue-Medford Library's homepage: **www.pmlib.org**

Television Westerns

Six Decades of Sagebrush Sheriffs, Scalawags, and Sidewinders

Alvin H. Marill

THE SCARECROW PRESS, INC.
Lanham • Toronto • Plymouth, UK
2011

Published by Scarecrow Press, Inc.
A wholly owned subsidiary of The Rowman & Littlefield Publishing Group, Inc.
4501 Forbes Boulevard, Suite 200, Lanham, Maryland 20706
http://www.scarecrowpress.com

Estover Road, Plymouth PL6 7PY, United Kingdom

British Library Cataloguing in Publication Information Available

Library of Congress Cataloging-in-Publication Data
Marill, Alvin H.
  Television westerns : six decades of sagebrush sheriffs, scalawags, and sidewinders /
Alvin H. Marill.
     p. cm.
  Includes bibliographical references and index.
  ISBN 978-0-8108-8132-7 (hardback : alk. paper) — ISBN 978-0-8108-8133-4 (ebook)
  1. Western television programs—United States. I. Title.
  PN1992.8.W4M38 2011
  791.45'65878—dc22   2011005194

∞™ The paper used in this publication meets the minimum requirements of American
National Standard for Information Sciences—Permanence of Paper for Printed Library
Materials, ANSI/NISO Z39.48-1992.

Printed in the United States of America

Contents

Foreword

The television Westerns . . . how we miss them. No one who grew up in the fifties, sixties, or seventies could forget what an impact they had on our young lives. Taming the lawlessness of Dodge City . . . riding along on a cattle drive . . . discovering the diversity of folks on a wagon train crossing the Great Plains . . . following the lives of family members on ranches in Wyoming or Nevada or the Arizona Territory.

The Western speaks to Americans in a particular way: our rebellious spirit, our sense of adventure, our love of the land, our longing to see and traverse those mountains, rivers, and plains that were a part of the pioneer experience—and to imagine what it must have been like in those more primitive and rambunctious times as our young country was finding its way.

The TV Western was our guide. It may not always have been realistic (finding solutions to troubling problems in thirty- and sixty-minute time blocks) or accurate (negative stereotyping of nonwhites that took years to correct), but nobody can say it wasn't entertaining. Just thinking about that era brings literally dozens of great theme songs to mind.

Nobody thinks of the *William Tell Overture* as the start of a Rossini opera anymore. It's now *The Lone Ranger* theme. (Leonard Bernstein himself admitted it in the very first televised *Young People's Concert* in 1958.) And while the song's long radio history is undoubtedly partly responsible, it is the widely seen, televised adventures of Clayton Moore and Jay Silverheels that, more than anything, crystallized those thirty seconds of classical music in the minds of millions as the aural signature of a mysterious masked man righting wrongs in the Old West.

And that was just the beginning. The singing cowboys brought their own tunes to the small screen—Gene Autry's "Back in the Saddle Again," Roy Rogers and Dale Evans's "Happy Trails"—and one frontier adventurer was responsible for the first TV theme to hit number one on the record charts: "The Ballad of Davy Crockett," a clever narrative device suggested by Walt Disney himself for the Fess Parker shows on the series *Frontierland* at Disneyland.

The popularity of those early themes helped to motivate producers searching for just the right song to introduce their Western heroes to television audiences. They encouraged songwriters to create faux cowboy ballads, thus giving us the memorable vocal themes for *Wyatt Earp*, *Bat Masterson*, *Rawhide*, *The Rebel*, *Daniel Boone*, *Branded*, and the Warner Bros. group of *Cheyenne*, *Sugarfoot*, *Maverick*, and *Bronco*, among others.

Just as often, however, producers would opt for an instrumental theme, asking their composers to take the orchestral-Americana approach pioneered by Aaron Copland in the concert hall and Jerome Moross (*The Big Country*) at the movies. The result was memorable big-sky, wide-open-spaces themes like Moross's own *Wagon Train*, Percy Faith's *The Virginian*, Herschel Burke Gilbert's *The Rifleman*, George Duning's *The Big Valley*, and Jerrold Immel's *How the West Was Won*.

Guitars, banjos, and harmonicas were heard so often that one wonders whether their prominent place in TV Westerns was partially responsible for kids getting hooked on folk music and rock 'n' roll. David Rose's arrangement of the *Bonanza* theme—one of the rare instances in which lyrics were written but never heard on the show itself, only later on records—and his own *High Chaparral* theme were among the classic melodies to feature guitars, both electric and acoustic, to suggest the flavor of the Old West.

Later, of course, producers searching for greater degrees of authenticity would trim back their orchestras to feature just a handful of colorful, appropriately Western instruments: the fiddles, bluesy guitars, and Jew's harp of *Paradise*; the guitars and harmonica of *The Young Riders*; and the fiddle, harmonium, guitars, and unusual percussion of *Deadwood*.

And sometimes that desired authenticity extended to the choice of vocalist. Veteran Frankie Laine sang several themes, from *Rawhide* and *Gunslinger* to *Rango* and *The Misadventures of Sheriff Lobo*. Country singers Johnny Cash (*The Rebel*), Johnny Western (*Have Gun—Will Travel*), Ed Bruce (*Bret Maverick*), Waylon Jennings (*The Dukes of Hazzard*), and Clint Black (*Harts of the West*) have all lent their voices—and sometimes, their acting skills—to weekly series.

Al Marill's wide-ranging, nostalgic chronicle ferrets out many obscure Westerns that also had first-rate music—music that is unfortunately forgotten simply because the shows themselves didn't last. Many were penned by some of the most distinguished composers of Hollywood and Broadway: *Riverboat* (Elmer Bernstein), *Outlaws* (Hugo Friedhofer), *The Great Adventure* (Richard Rodgers), *Wide Country* (John Williams), *The Loner* (Jerry Goldsmith), *The Men from Shiloh* (Ennio Morricone), and *Cade's County* (Henry Mancini), to name just a few. The great Bernard Herrmann, who scored numerous Alfred Hitchcock classics, wrote several remarkable dramatic scores for TV Westerns, including *Have Gun—Will Travel*; *Gunsmoke*; *The Virginian*; and *Cimarron Strip*.

What might be termed "revisionist" Westerns boasted some of the more offbeat themes of the genre, starting with the jazz scores of *Shotgun Slade* and extending to the irreverent song of *F Troop* ("where Indian fights are color-ful sights and nobody takes a lickin' / where paleface and redskin both turn chicken"); the lighthearted instrumental *The Wild Wild West*; the mystical *Kung Fu*; and the boldly retro *Adventures of Brisco County Jr.*

Marill also reviews dozens of made-for-TV movies and miniseries in the Western genre, and a surprising number have truly memorable music worthy of concert-hall performance. Chief among them is Basil Poledouris's Emmy-winning effort for the eight-hour *Lonesome Dove*, among the finest folk-influenced Americana scores ever written for the small screen. Several of the best of these scores take on an elegiac tone, as if to mourn the end of the frontier and simpler times: Bruce Broughton's Emmy-nominated *True Women*, Craig Safan's music for the Custer retelling *Son of the Morning Star*, and Jerry Fielding's for-the-frontier-tracker saga *Mr. Horn*. In a more traditional vein were John Addison's *Centennial*, Lee Holdridge's *Buffalo Girls*, and Bob Cob-ert's Western Heritage Award–winning *Last Ride of the Dalton Gang*.

Among movies and minis that focused on Native American themes, Gerald Fried's Emmy-nominated score for the epic *The Mystic Warrior* drew on authentic Sioux chants and instruments for verisimilitude. Patrick Williams's *Geronimo* and Charles Fox's *The Broken Chain* offered similarly dramatic takes on the traditional sounds of those who made the West their home long before the white man. Many of these orchestral scores rank among the most impressive music ever written for television.

So as you pore over the following pages, recalling the great (and some not-so-great) sagebrush sagas of television history, take a moment to remember the music that accompanied them. I'm betting that you'll be humming some of your favorite Western themes.

—Jon Burlingame

Jon Burlingame writes about film and television music for *Variety* and lectures on the subject at the University of Southern California. He is the author of *TV's Biggest Hits: The Story of Television Themes from "Dragnet" to "Friends"* and *Sound and Vision: 60 Years of Motion Picture Soundtracks*.

Acknowledgments

To Vincent Terrace, Jon Burlingame, Mort Chenvenson, Jane Klain and the folks at the Paley Center for Media, and the Broadcast Pioneers of Philadelphia—silver spurs and a tip of the Stetson.

Introduction

From out of the West, in the earliest days of the "flickers," galloped or moseyed a cowboy known as Broncho Billy Anderson. Well, not exactly out of the West, but from the Palisades in northern New Jersey, near Fort Lee. Broncho Billy Anderson (he apparently favored the extra "h" in his nickname) was one of the earliest cowboy actors in the movies. Before him, there were such cinematic items as *The Cripple Creek Bar-room Scene*. Westerns aficionado Don Miller noted in his 1976 book *Hollywood Corral* that this "vignette of frontier life lasting a few seconds was filmed by [Thomas] Edison associate W. K. L. Dickson shortly before the turn of the century." Miller said that "it depicted the inhabitants of a contemporary saloon, and is the first known example of a Western setting on film." A few years later, in 1903, came the first real Western story, *The Great Train Robbery*, also for Edison's company.

We've come light-years away from that—through rootin' tootin' cowboy epics, or sagebrush sagas, and B movies; through hard-ridin' Bill Hart and Tom Mix, Hoot Gibson, Ken Maynard, Tex Ritter, Johnny Mack Brown, Wild Bill Elliott, Charles Starrett, Buck Jones, the Duke, Gene, Roy, Hoppy. Through two-fisted straight-shooting Western heroes, a whole gallery of varmints, loyal sidekicks, range riders, singing cowboys, barroom brawls, masked men, Injuns good and bad. Through *The Big Trail*; *Stagecoach*; *Red River*; *The Virginian*; John Ford's great late forties trilogy; *High Noon*; *Shane*; the James Stewart Westerns with director Anthony Mann; the Randolph Scott Westerns with Budd Boetticher; *3:10 to Yuma*; *The Good, the Bad and the Ugly*;

How the West Was Won; Sam Peckinpah's *Ride the High Country*; and, to close the circle more or less, *Bronco Billy* once again (this time in the persona of Clint Eastwood and his homage).

Arguably, only the New Orleans, Kansas City, and Chicago jazz and the movie Western are purely American—roots in the good old U.S. of A. Certainly the Western would be adopted in the fifties and sixties in Italy, Spain, France, and Germany. What kind of career would Sergio Leone, for instance, have had were it not for his spaghetti Westerns (all but one of his credited films were in that genre)? Or prolific German writer Karl May, who'd never been to America and who was a contemporary of America's Zane Grey (nearly forty of his novels formed the basis for his country's Western movies)? Or France's actor/writer/director Robert Hossein and his relatively few so-called bagetti Westerns?

"The Europeans have always seen the Western as a major contribution to American art and culture, as integral a part of American folklore as the *Odyssey* is of the Greeks'," film authority William K. Everson wrote in his 1992 book, *The Hollywood Western: 90 Years of Cowboys, Indians, Train Robbers, Sheriffs, and Gunslingers and Assorted Heroes and Desperados.* "The Western, whatever its size—grand scale, epic, in color and wide screen, humble 'B' feature, or half-hour television potboiler—has always been one of the enduring staples of movie entertainment."

Once Saturday matinee staples at the local Rialto, B Westerns of the mid to late thirties and into the forties would give way to the top-of-the-bill sagebrush sagas (with far more sophisticated production values) of the Waynes, Scotts, McCreas, Stewarts, and a few decades later, Eastwoods. The television era, from its beginnings after World War II, would bring the Western and the frontier drama into America's living rooms and would be among the cornerstones of what became pop culture—from *Hopalong Cassidy* and *The Lone Ranger* to *Maverick, Rawhide, Gunsmoke, Wagon Train,* and *Bonanza,* to *Lonesome Dove, Broken Trail,* and *Deadwood.*

CHAPTER ONE

Defending Range Justice on the Tube

"The classic Western contains the following ingredients," J. Fred MacDonald wrote in his *Who Shot the Sheriff?* "Heroes and guns, horses and cattle, outlaws and Indians, and the like—usually situated in desert locales on the nineteenth-century U.S. frontier." This fairly comprehensive overview is extended into the early years of the twenty-first century and includes as well some modern-day dramas and comedies that are Western themed.

The cowboy of Saturday matinee and double feature at the downtown movie house ambled over to television in the years after World War II, William Boyd bringing Hopalong Cassidy as one of the first. But before Hoppy, there was Howdy—as in Howdy Doody.

Purists might pause when puppet Howdy Doody and flesh-and-blood pal Buffalo Bob Smith, a real-life radio cowboy, get lumped into a book devoted to TV Westerns and Western-themed children's programs of the day. After all, though, on *Howdy Doody*, which NBC began airing just after Christmas 1947, host Buffalo Bob wore buckskins and Western garb and freckled-faced Howdy Doody himself was dressed for Western success, complete with checkered shirts, jeans, and a John Wayne–style bandana around his neck. Howdy came from Doodyville, Texas (with his twin brother Double), and had such American Indian friends on his show as "kowabunga"-shouting Chief Thunderthud and the positively enchanting Princess Summerfall Winterspring.

And initially there were a number of puppet Western shows airing locally around the time that Hopalong Cassidy came galloping along in his ten-gallon white hat astride Topper.

Through the late forties and early fifties, when the medium was basically local, there aired assorted Western-themed shows aimed at the young 'uns with a host—often a former B-Western actor in full cowboy garb—telling (or making up) tales of the Old West, spinning yarns, and showing in truncated form sagebrush sagas, matinee fodder dating back to the midthirties.

In 1949, on the West Coast, *The Adventures of Cyclone Malone* began airing on KNBC in Los Angeles, an early fifteen-minute daily marionette show with cliff-hanger endings that was about Cyclone Malone, sheriff of Yazoo Junction in Wishbone Hollow. His girlfriend, teacher Cozy Dumond, is there to encourage him in the hunt for the bad guys, along with the Indian chief One Lone Feather and the animals who live with him—like Burgess Cruzzard, a talking buzzard, and Cucamonga, Cyclone's trusty talking horse. Ross Jones voiced Cyclone.

The puppet-powered action series, nominated for an Emmy as Best Children's Show of 1949, was written and produced by Ann Davis and Dorothy Novis (who happens to be actress Helen Hunt's grandmother). More than sixty years later, Yazoo Junction Sheriff Cyclone was resurrected in a one-act children's play, *The Adventures of Cyclone Malone: The Wattalottawatta River Pirates*, by Lane Roisley, a friend of Novis's daughter, Catherine Fries Vaughn. It is performed in elementary schools. Cyclone here is battling a bunch of dastardly scalawags to impress his sweetie, Cozy Dumond.

At the other end of the country, there was, for one, Rex Trailer. He grew up in West Texas in the thirties, learned his cowboy skills on his grandfather's ranch, and was later taken under Gabby Hayes's wing and encouraged to become an on-air personality. In the late forties, Trailer went to work for DuMont Television and soon became host of the network's *Oky Doky Ranch*. Oky Doky was a cowboy puppet with a huge mustache (he was voiced by Dayton Allen), and Rex Trailer became the network's equivalent of Buffalo Bob Smith. When Trailer joined the show in 1949 toward its end, it had already been established in local television, and DuMont put it on the network and shortened it from thirty minutes daily to fifteen. Actress Wendy Barrie was the hostess. Trailer and his horse Gold Rush then went to Philadelphia where, from 1950 to 1956, he had a show called *Ride the Trail with Rex Trailer*, hosting movie Westerns. Ultimately, Trailer moved to Boston and became a television legend there over the next two decades, primarily with his daily Western show for kids, *Boomtown*.

In the months between the premieres of the two seminal TV Western series *Hopalong Cassidy* and *The Lone Ranger*, the network launched two puppet shows with Western themes. On January 9, 1950, CBS began airing live (and, because of this, locally) a kiddy show titled *Life with Snarky Parker*, featuring Bil and Cora Baird's Marionettes. The fifteen-minute, four-times-a-week program that lasted just nine months followed the adventures of Deputy Sheriff Snarky Parker and his horse Heathcliff in the town of Hotrock in the 1850s. One of Snarky's goals: to rid the town of Ronald Rodent, a nasty varmint. Snarky himself kind of resembled later actor/director Richard Benjamin. The show's director was Yul Brynner—in his day job before becoming a notable actor. Brynner was a house director at CBS in New York, who initially helmed the local station's coverage of afternoon proceedings at the United Nations and also later worked on *Danger* and *Studio One* in their early days.

CBS also had *The Buffalo Billy Show*, a live puppet series that ran afternoons for several months beginning in October 1950 and followed Buffalo Billy, a young adventurer, as he journeys West with a wagon train. Buffalo Billy was voiced by Don Messick, a puppeteer who had a long subsequent history as a top voice actor.

And then there was Hopalong Cassidy.

Many of William Boyd's Hoppy movies of earlier days—based on the series of adventures created by Clarence E. Mulford, though in truncated form to fill twenty-seven minutes—were unspooled again on television rather than creating new adventures. (Since at the time we were watching shows on a ten-inch screen, it was easy to find scenes to cut—anything, apparently, that had wide, sweeping chases, for instance.) Defending range justice from his Bar 20 Ranch astride his faithful steed Topper, the now silver-haired Hoppy, dressed all in black, made a fortune for the fading, more than middle-aged Boyd when the *Hopalong Cassidy* series began in syndication in late 1948. From June to September 1949, NBC picked up the series, airing it locally at first on Friday nights at 8:00, and then produced another group of hour-long Hoppy adventures during 1950 and 1951, running Saturday nights from 9:00 to 10:00, at least on the West Coast.

A third batch of Hoppys, this time with heavyset Edgar Buchanan as his TV sidekick Red Connors, was produced for first-run syndication on NBC in a half-hour form in 1952–1953. *Variety*'s review of the NBC series that began airing in September 1952 found that "as long as Hoppy stays on the side of the law, keeps Twin Rivers free of ornery critters, and laughs at danger in the Western version of an Edward Arnold risibility rouser, he will lose none of the idolatrous affection from the country's small fry. It's no reflection that he doesn't hop around like he did 20 years ago. . . . Hoppy will still be head man with the young shavers as long as he can throw a slowing leg across the saddle." (The later NBC show was sponsored by Van Camp Seafoods, leading *Variety* to note, "Sponsor used both an Indian chief and a singing cowboy to sell the tunas in tins.") Boyd had the foresight during the 1940s to buy the rights to the old theatrical Hoppy features—and with television, he became a millionaire. He found gold in them thar Hollywood Hills. *Time* magazine, in this period, wrote in a William Boyd profile that Hoppy really changed Boyd—who had taken to the sauce when his movie career had faded before television beckoned. "As far as the public was concerned, he had virtually assumed a new identity, that of Hopalong Cassidy."

The Hoppys in first run came to an end, but the show (which then went into endless syndication) and its merchandising—bubblegum cards, bed-sheets, wallpaper, kiddy cowboy outfits—made Boyd immensely wealthy, and he eventually sold out his stock of films, along with the rights, for a reported $70 million and retired. A tip of the old ten-gallon hat is found in writer/di-rector Keith Clarke's top-notch hour-long 2001 TV documentary that aired on Starz! and the Western Channel, titled *Hopalong Cassidy: Public Hero #1*, hosted by Dennis Weaver. Among those paying tribute were Grace Bradley, Boyd's widow; film critic Leonard Maltin; and, strangely, Bill Cosby (prob-ably a longtime fan).

Next to the hugely popular *Hopalong Cassidy*, one of the earliest purely Western series on network television was a fifteen-minute show called *Cac-tus Jim*, which aired on NBC, at least in the Chicago area, from October 31, 1949, though October 26, 1951. It basically presented edited versions of theatrical Westerns, hosted initially by Clarence Hartzell—as what was heralded in WNBQ publicity as a yarn-spinning, range-riding old-timer—and later by Bill Bailey. And on ABC, locally, from July to September 1950 cowboy star Ray "Crash" Corrigan hosted *Crash Corrigan's Ranch*, a thirty-minute children's variety show in a Western setting, with music, skits, and exciting clips from B Westerns of the past. (Ray had been one of the trio of cowboys in the *Three Mesquiteers* series for Republic in the thirties and *The Range Busters* for Monogram in the forties.)

Around the same time, in late 1950, old-time cowboy actor Rex Bell hosted a short-lived but rather informative children's show out of Los Ange-les. *Cowboys and Injuns*, originally a local L.A. show but then airing on ABC, told young "pardners" about cowboy and Indian folklore. Bell later went into politics and was Nevada's lieutenant governor in the fifties and early sixties.

Saturday Roundup, an NBC offering featuring Kermit Maynard, former rodeo champion and onetime cowboy star Ken Maynard's brother and often stand-in, aired in the early evening in the summer of 1951 (Saturdays, 8:00–9:00 p.m.). Also on the show occasionally were singing cowboys Tex Fletcher and Smith Ballew. Maynard hosted dramatized versions of James Oliver Curwood's West-erns primarily, but the show failed to generate enthusiasm.

Other children's Western shows in the same vein were *Trail Blazers Theater* on DuMont, *For Cowboys Only* on ABC, *Silhouettes of the West* on CBS, *Sagebrush Theater*, *Bob Atcher and Western Stories* (Atcher was a popular singing cowboy on radio and early TV out of Chicago), and the like, each offering up Western theatrical films of the past, perhaps a musical number or two, and a skit for the youngsters.

Close in the television foot- and hoofprints of Hoppy and Topper were the Lone Ranger and his trusty snow-white steed Silver, along with Indian pal Tonto and his pinto Scout. *The Lone Ranger* television series premiered on September 15, 1949, on ABC, airing Thursdays from 7:30 to 8:00 p.m. and later on Fridays, 10:00–10:30 p.m.—a mite late for the kids. Critic Jack Gould of the *New York Times* couldn't have been more hopelessly wrong when, following the show's premiere, he called *The Lone Ranger* "just another Western, and not a notably good one at that." It was by all standards to be one of the seminal Western shows on television. It also was Emmy nominated in the category Best Film Made for and Viewed on Television (losing to Jackie Gleason's *The Life of Riley*. The following year (1950) it received a nomination as Best Children's Show (along with *The Cisco Kid*).

The Lone Ranger would be ABC's first big hit, galloping through the end of the 1956–1957 TV season—when unlike today there were "official" seasons. "A fiery horse with the speed of light, a cloud of dust, and a hearty Hi-Yo Silver! The Lone Ranger rides again!"—as intoned by announcer Fred Foy, most notably. Cue the first eight bars of the *William Tell Overture*.

The long-famous good guys versus bad guys Western "legend" was created by George W. Trendle and Fran Striker for a Detroit radio station, the writing pair also responsible for *The Green Hornet*. The story told—as all know—about how the only surviving member of group of six Texas Rangers (John Reed), ambushed by the notorious Butch Cavendish gang, is found by a friendly Indian (Tonto) and nursed back to health. After "burying" John in a fake sixth grave alongside his Ranger compatriots (to convince Butch that all the Rangers had died), Tonto and the Lone Ranger became faithful companions searching for bad guys out West. The Lone Ranger wore a black eye mask (as if that would really hide his identity) and rode the mighty steed Silver; his Indian sidekick was astride Scout. And after righting wrongs, the Lone Ranger left a single silver bullet to let folks know he was there as he and Tonto rode off in search of their next adventure— through 221 episodes (the last 39 filmed in color). On radio, Brace Beemer narrated and starred, among others through the years, as the Lone Ranger. (John Todd, a distinguished Shakespearean actor—according to announcer Fred Foy in a taped reminiscence—played Tonto.) The TV version began by retelling the familiar story and ran for eight seasons. Clayton Moore and Jay Silverheels played the leads on television and in the two 1950s theatrical versions. (For a while in the midfifties, a contract dispute kept Moore off the trail and John Hart took the role.)

The hugely popular series aired on both ABC and CBS through much the fifties—ABC in primetime, CBS on Saturday afternoon repeats.

The 1956 big screen production of *The Lone Ranger*, inspired by the success of the popular TV show (and long before that the hit radio version of beginning in 1933 as the cornerstone of the Mutual Radio Network and spanning the 1940s three nights a week), together with assorted theatrical serials through the years, proved one of the hits among younger moviegoers. (There was a theatrical sequel called *The Lone Ranger and the Lost City of Gold* two years later.)

Former screen actress Bonita Granville and her husband, Jack Wrather, had acquired from Trendle and Striker the broadcast rights to *The Lone Ranger* as well as *Lassie*, and she costarred in the 1956 film version of the series. Since Wrather controlled the rights to both *The Lone Ranger* and *Lassie*, it was easy enough, though somewhat incongruent, to have the famed masked man pay a visit to young Jon Provost on the latter series (after Clayton Moore's show left first run) and that's just what happened in a 1959 *Lassie* episode called *The Peace Patrol*.

In the late 1960s on CBS, *The Lone Ranger* rode again for a full season on Saturday mornings as a cartoon character (see later among Western cartoons).

In 2003, an ill-advised TV-movie pilot sought to revive the old Western in a revisionist manner. Its conceit was telling of a young twenty-something Harvard law student (played by Chad Michael Murray, whose claims to fame were starring roles in *The Gilmore Girls* and *Dawson's Creek*) in the many years before and leading up to the traditional Lone Ranger tale, going West to hook up with his Ranger brother, and even having a fling with an Indian maiden named Alapo, whose brother just happened to be Tonto. It was rejected by contemporary audiences.

CHAPTER TWO

The Gene and Roy Era

In 1950, Gene Autry, the greatest of the latter-day screen cowboys (not to tick off Roy Rogers's fans), came to television—courtesy of sponsor Wrigley's Doublemint chewing gum—in a CBS series that would run for six years. For his Flying A Productions, Gene Autry starred as Gene Autry and, as his sidekick, Pat Buttram starred as Pat Buttram, riding the range—Gene, naturally astride Champion the Wonder Horse. Neither Gene nor Pat wore badges but they helped sheriffs, marshals, and locals maintain law and order in the Southwest for 104 episodes (a handful of which were in color). Always white hatted, Gene, of course, got a chance every week to sing a number—other than the title signature song "Back in the Saddle Again," and Pat did the bumptious sidekick stuff. Note that, as with *Hopalong Cassidy* and *The Lone Ranger*, Autry's show had no females along for the ride—at least as regulars.

The Gene Autry Show later spun off two other Flying A series: *Annie Oakley*, starring Autry protégé (and the only female cowboy star on television) Gail Davis—who turned up periodically on Gene's own show—and *The Adventures of Champion*; yes, the handsome steed scored his own series several years later. The show resurrected Gene's singing cowboy career around the time he was becoming a surprising pop star for Columbia Records, with "Rudolph the Red-Nosed Reindeer," "Here Comes Santa Claus," and "Peter Cottontail," all of which (films, records, and later TV) made him a very wealthy man—and subsequently, of course, a television executive and then a baseball entrepreneur. TV maven Vincent Terrace observed, "The series'

episodes were restored in 2000 by Flying A Productions and syndicated—
these are the ones the Western Channel showed, and looked like they were
filmed yesterday. Great job of restoring."

Gene ultimately galloped off to become one of the owners of Los Angeles's KTLA, a West Coast pioneer that went on the air on January 22, 1948.
Autry and associates bought the station from Paramount Pictures in 1964
for $12 million, and in September of that year, he decided to host his own
show, *Melody Ranch*, along with fellow singing cowboy Rex Allen, featuring
Western song and dance. The Cass County Boys and the Melody Ranch
Band provided the musical numbers. In 1980, KTLA offered two specials
honoring Autry on his fifty years in the business as a Western legend. In June
there was *Gene Autry: An American Hero*, with Gene being honored by host
Hugh O'Brian and friends ranging from Glenn Ford to Red Skelton to Ringo
Starr. Then in August, he took part in a nostalgic documentary narrated by
John Ritter (actor son of Autry's onetime two-fisted riding and singing pal
Tex Ritter). The show, *The Singing Cowboys Ride Again*, reunited Autry with
Roy Rogers, Rex Allen, Jimmy Wakely, and others—warbling "Tumbling
Tumbleweeds" for the finale.

In his 1981 book *Saturday Morning TV*, Gary Grossman noted, "Whereas
The Lone Ranger could be produced for $17,000 an episode in 1952, and
$18,000 in 1954, it rose to $20,000 in 1955 and $27,000 a year later. *The
Gene Autry Show* and *Wild Bill Hickok* experienced similar increases. And
though the experience was low by today's standard half-hour price tag [at
the start of 1980] of $150,000 to $300,000, the number of productions that
could earn out their investment was narrowing as costs rose. One of the ways
to keep the budget down was to work where there were crews experienced in
bargain-basement technique."

Interestingly, an "authentic" Lone Ranger mask—which turned out to be
purple rather than black initially since it photographed better on the black-
and-white screen—autographed by Clayton Moore found its way to PBS's
Antiques Roadshow in spring 2010 and was judged to be worth in the range
of $25,000. Compare that to what it cost to produce the show itself during
its heyday.

The Marshal of Gunsight Pass was the next significant (though, in retrospect, primitive and some would say minor) network television Western.
Following the brief radio series at the end of the forties, it moved to ABC-TV
in early 1950 and ran only through September, airing at 7:00 on Thursday
nights—at least on the West Coast, where it was telecast live. It was a low-
budget Western about a marshal (initially played by movie-buckaroo-turned-
TV-producer Russell Hayden for the first few shows, and then by Eddie

Dean, a popular onetime singing screen cowboy) maintaining law and order for thirty minutes a week in the titular town of Gunsight Pass. His deputy sidekick was played by bug-eyed Roscoe Ates, the Don Knotts/Barney Fife of an earlier time; his lady friend, by Jane Adrian. Kinescoped versions of the show played outside of Los Angeles—where it had significance in network TV history as being a very rare Western action series produced live in a studio. How they got the horses to behave on cue against cheap backdrops proved a marvel of very careful staging. Here's what *Variety* wrote about the premiere show that was telecast on Thursday, February 10, 1950: "[It] brought high caliber live Western fare to local television last night. Layout is sparked by the camera direction of Phil Booth and full scale Western set rigged for the show by Herbert O. Phillips." The journal went on to note that: "Russell 'Lucky' Hayden and Roscoe Ates handled deputy marshal and sidekick roles effectively."

A case might be made that another hugely popular series of the day, the filmed (in color) *The Cisco Kid*, had much the same general story concept if not content as *The Lone Ranger*. Both had heroic do-gooders roaming the West with handsome steeds and faithful companions. But *The Cisco Kid*'s genesis was an O. Henry story of 1904 while *The Lone Ranger* was an "original" on radio thirty years later—in fact, some time after *The Cisco Kid* became a popular film star in the persona of Warner Baxter. On television, *The Cisco Kid*, immaculately dressed, dashing in his wide sombrero, was portrayed by Spanish actor Duncan Renaldo, who'd also played him in films (and on and off in radio) in the late forties, following Cesar Romero and Gilbert Roland. With his jovial sidekick Pancho, played by somewhat portly Italian American actor Leo Carrillo (a beloved Hollywood character performer who later had a noted California beach named after him), the ever gallant "Ceesco"—as Pancho normally called him in his fractured English—ranged the old Southwest on his horse Diablo (Pancho's was Loco), running down bad guys, charming the señoritas.

The Cisco Kid, a thirty-minute show (156 episodes), initially ran in syndication from 1950 to 1956, though generally in black and white since there was no color TV transmission until middecade. It was nominated for the 1950 Emmy as Best Children's Show. As has been noted, Renaldo and Carrillo, in their fifties and seventies, respectively, at the time, did most of the hard riding themselves in this surprisingly durable series. It was produced by ZIV, one of the major packagers of television shows of the time. Original Mexican-style music for the entire series was by Albert Glasser, later known for scoring very low-budget drive-in movie classics such as *The Amazing Colossal Man*.

Perennial cowboy sidekick George "Gabby" Hayes landed his own weekly show on NBC from 1950 to 1954 and then for a while on ABC in 1956. *The Gabby Hayes Show*, aimed at little buckaroos—"young whippersnappers," he often called them—had the beloved grizzled old-timer spinning yarns and assorted tall stories about the Old West and about his zany relatives, frequently while whittling a piece of wood, and showing edited versions of rip-roarin' B Westerns from his studio home, the Double Bar M Ranch. The NBC series ran for fifteen minutes, preceding *Howdy Doody*; the one on ABC aired on Saturday mornings for thirty minutes.

The Gabby Hayes Show received an Emmy nomination in 1952 as Best Children's Program (losing to *Time for Beany*). Several DVDs of Gabby's popular show are currently available online.

And then there was *Alibi's Tent Show*, syndicated in 1951. Max "Alibi" Terhune hosted this daily aimed-at-the-kids Western show. It originated from California TV station KNXT, channel 2, and was sponsored by Dad's Root Beer. Terhune, who was an accomplished ventriloquist (his dummy pal was Elmer Sneezeweed), became part of the popular cowboy trio the Three Mesquiteers in the thirties, making twenty-one feature films appearing as Lullaby Joslin, six of them with John Wayne. After that he and costar Ray Corrigan appeared in the Range Busters series, with Terhune doing two dozen of these Saturday matinee sagebrush sagas. He later made cowboy films with Allan "Rocky" Lane, Monte Hale, and Johnny Mack Brown.

Another short-lived Western series aimed at the kids and syndicated in 1951 was *Lash of the West*, in which forties B Western star Lash LaRue demonstrated his cowboy skills, particularly his trademark expertise with the bullwhip; hence Al LaRue's nickname Lash. ABC later ran the show between January and April 1953.

Around the same time the somewhat similar *Tim McCoy Show* was airing in syndication. McCoy's series (fifteen minutes daily)—in color, out of KCAL in Los Angeles in 1952—blended stories of frontier life and Indian lore, about which the veteran cowboy star was a recognized authority. Joining McCoy as cohost was veteran character Iron Eyes Cody, who'd made a career on the screen playing Indians, but near the end of his life, his Sicilian ancestry was made public. He was actually Espera Oscar de Corti of Gueydan, Louisiana. On one show, at least, he had Indian actor Chief Yowlachie as guest, with McCoy interpreting the Native American sign language

Monty Hall, the popular game show host of the much later *Let's Make a Deal*, hosted and narrated, while clad in checkered shirt and jeans, a children's show on NBC on weekends. Called *Cowboy Theater*, the show ran in the early evening during the midfifties. Yes, that's Monty Hall, not Monte Hale, the signing cowboy of matinee Westerns of yore.

Action in the Afternoon aired on CBS during the 1953–1954 season—and it had a history. Broadcast live out of Philadelphia station WCAU, the half-hour show was network TV's first and only daily live Western series. The program, set in the town of Hubberle, Montana (population 486), starred Jack Valentine as (well, Jack Valentine) a guitar-playing, singing cowboy—as he was earlier on local shows in places like Boston and others. The five-times-a-week series aired primarily through its run at 3:30 p.m. opposite pre–Dick Clark's *American Bandstand*—also live out of Philadelphia at the time. (Dick Clark didn't become the host until August 1956.) The fictional Hubberle's outdoor setting was a vast back lot outside of the station that had a wooded area with a large stream running through and a place for a mock-up set—virtually in between the cars of the station's personnel, with indoor shots in one of several WCAU studios.

Here's what *Time* magazine said of the show on its premiere in February 1953: "*Action in the Afternoon* (weekdays, 3:30 p.m., CBS-TV) has a permanent outdoor set: a Western cowtown built by Philadelphia's WCAU-TV on a vacant lot. But, though the TV camera gets outdoors, it has little freedom: there are no long chases on horseback or free-for-all barroom brawls in the movie horse-opera tradition. The dialogue limps even more obviously than the camera. *Action in the Afternoon*, still without sponsor, is an experiment that needs a lot more work."

The station promoted *Action in the Afternoon* in its brochure circa June 1953 as "a spectacular experiment in outdoor television. Adventurous as the West! Alive as America! First live Western on TV." A *Philadelphia Evening Bulletin* review that month referred to the show as "an adventure series of roaring six-shooters and two-fisted brawls . . . one of the most novel TV ideas ever originated." WCAU-TV at the time was owned by the *Bulletin*.

An incident recalled fifty-five years later by Mort Chevenson, scenic designer for the show, involved one of the actors who was playing an outlaw about to be hanged. He was seated atop his horse, his hands tied behind his back, a noose around his neck, when the horse became agitated and began to move, and the guy was very nearly hanged in reality. Another Chevenson memory was an event that made the local papers: a spiffy MG in the parking lot, owned by one of the station personnel, was struck by the show's stagecoach. The employee stunned the insurance company when reporting his car had been damaged by a stagecoach in '53—that's 1953, not 1853.

In addition to the star, Jack Valentine, *Action in the Afternoon* featured Mary Elaine Watts as Red Cotten, the sassy belle of the Copper Cup Saloon;

Blake Ritter, one of the station's staff announcers, who not only narrated the series but also played the editor of the *Hubberle Gazette*; Sam Kressen as Sheriff Sam Mitchell; Jean Corbett as his wife, Amy; Barry Cassell as shady Ace Bancroft; Harris Forrest as Ozzie Matthews, Jack's sidekick; and Creighton Stewart as Grimes, who ran the Hubberle Bank. Stewart, director Bill Bode recalled much later, "was a skilled performer. The negative reaction came from radio fans. Creighton had a luxurious, mellifluous voice. Unfortunately his face, full of lines and wrinkles, didn't match the image he'd created on radio. To protect WCAU Radio's valued talent, we killed Banker Grimes during a bank robbery."

Among the WCAU "insiders" (Valentine was considered an "outsider"), most notable—though not at the time—was the local actor who played Grimy Jones, the local coroner. His name was John Zacherle, and he went on in TV history to be closely associated with cult horror classics, thanks initially to the program out of WCAU, *Zacherley's Shock Theater* (he'd added a final *y* to his name).

Nate Friedman, one of the actors on *Action in the Afternoon* and now, according to the Broadcast Pioneers of Philadelphia, a prominent attorney in the area, recalled, "Just like in the early days of radio, many actors played more than one part, one with a beard and one without. You were two different people. Put a bandanna and you were part of a gang robbing the bank. Who knew? When the station decided to do *Shock Theater* in 1957, they thought of Zacherle." And W. Barry Cassell was the weekend news guy on the station when he wasn't twirling his prop mustache in evil glee.

Another of the local actors on *Action in the Afternoon* was Mark Richman, who later had a career in Hollywood, especially on television. The show's musical director, Dick Lester, later became Richard Lester, went to England, and emerged as one of the screen's influential directors of the 1960s and onward, with the Beatles' films *A Hard Day's Night* and *Help!* and the movies *A Funny Thing Happened on the Way to the Forum*, *Petulia*, *The Three Musketeers*, and one or two of the Superman flicks. Backing up Jack Valentine musically was the Tommy Ferguson Trio, with whom Valentine made a number of Western recordings in the early fifties.

Like *The Lone Ranger*, with its use of Rossini's *William Tell Overture* as its distinctive theme (and earlier *The Goldbergs'* use of Toselli's *Serenade*), *Action in the Afternoon* went to the (contemporary) classics for its song. While the main theme from Aaron Copland's *Billy the Kid* played, the show's characters of the day stood in tableaux and began moving around when the music faded.

In 1952, the concept of the kiddy shows involving the popular "cowboys and Indians" games of the era went back to basics—briefly—in a proposed

Saturday morning program called *The Buckskin Kid* that had youngsters in cowboy getup and lariats running around astride sticks with wooden horse's heads, looking for rustlers and other varmints. The idea was to have a shoot-'em-up Western with children performing all the roles (with voiceover dubbing by adults). The would-be series was to follow the adventures of the Buckskin Kid, a "man" of action, his (wooden) horse Genius, and his side-kicks Hap (a ladies "man") and Whopper (who doesn't lie, but has a knack for stretching the truth). In the pilot episode, Kid, Hap, and Whopper help General Isle of the North Alaska Mounted Police put down an Indian upris-ing when the Alaska Apaches, led by Chief Avalanche (played by a grown-up), go on the warpath. This fifteen-minute pilot, somewhat primitive but available on YouTube, didn't gallop, but was similar in idea to the successful theatrical gangster spoof of decades later in which Jodie Foster and Scott Baio paraded around with a group of fellow actors—teenage and below—as mobsters in *Bugsy Malone*.

The Range Rider, starring former stuntman Jock Mahoney in the title role (no name) and Dick Jones as his youthful sidekick, Dick West, ran in syndica-tion during 1951 and into 1952. Produced by Armand Schaefer—also Gene Autry's producer from Flying A Productions—it followed the exploits of the footloose, hard-riding title character while he defended justice and righted wrongs during the frontier days in California. Like most TV Westerns of the day, this show was aimed at the younger set. In New York, the half-hour syndicated show was sponsored by Chuckles Candy and ran on Sunday after-noons at 4:30. *Variety*'s critic found the Western to be "a topflight sagebrush vidpic series" and the premiere "a traditional hoss opera yarn—involving outlaws raiding gold shipments, Rider tangling with the badmen, suspicion falling on Jones' ex-convict father, etc. It was nicely handled with good pro-duction values, fisticuff action but not much shooting, leaping mounts, and outdoors scenes." Mahoney, *Variety* pointed out, "cuts an attractive figure in his buckskin outfit and with slick horsemanship. Jones is a valuable adjunct, wearing a smart double-breasted shirt. The clothes trademarks are important as part of a licensed-merchandising operation." (Mahoney went on to play riverboat gambler Yancy Derringer in late fifties television and then Tarzan in the movies; Jones was to become Buffalo Bill Jr. in a later series.)

Although most Western stars wanted their shows to be called action packed, they were, to be sure at this point, relatively void of gun violence. Jock Mahoney told author Gary Grossman, "*The Range Rider* was not violent. We had some wing-ding fights where I'd completely demolish some stores and cabinets, but good always won out. That was the message of the TV Western."

Cisco Kid Duncan Renaldo said in a later interview, "We never killed anybody in any of our shows. We shot in self-defense, we shot the guns out of bandits' hands, but we didn't kill."

Gene Autry's success with his TV series doubtless didn't go unnoticed by his movie rival Roy Rogers, who had long been billed as "King of the Cowboys," and thus happy trails led Roy Rogers and Dale Evans to a new career on television beginning in 1951 on NBC. *The Roy Rogers Show* was a half-hour weekly contemporary Western series stressing family values. Rogers and Evans, using their own names, were joined by ranch hand Pat Brady (also using his own name and playing the obligatory bumbling sidekick)—Rogers rode Trigger, of course; Evans had her horse Buttermilk; and Brady tooled around in a cantankerous Jeep named Nellybelle. The musical group of which Rogers had once been part, the Sons of the Pioneers, who on the show hung around as ranch hands, invariably showed up for a musical number with him.

In the series, Rogers and Evans were ranchers (the Double R Bar) who also owned the local diner—when Rogers wasn't off maintaining law and order without a badge. "We were careful to make our villains very repulsive," Rogers told the press. "Too often they were more attractive than the hero. We make certain that doesn't happen with our show." As townsfolk on the show were actors Harry Lauter as Mayor Ralph Cotton and Harry Harvey Sr. as Sheriff Potter, and various roles were played by Denver Pyle, Dub Taylor, Ruta Lee, Gloria Talbot, Minerva Urecal, and Wally West. Roy Rogers Jr. also turned up as a local kid in an episode or two.

The wholesome show was hugely popular and aired on Sunday nights until 1957. Later CBS picked up the reruns and aired them from 1961 to 1964. The couple also had a short-lived musical variety series, *The Roy Rogers and Dale Evans Show*, airing on ABC in late 1962. Brady also was part of that show, along with the Sons of the Pioneers and Cliff Arquette (Rosanna, Patricia, David, and Richmond's grandpa) in the guise of his popular Charley Weaver character.

Two syndicated series dealing with the Old West—*The Adventures of Kit Carson* and *The Adventures of Wild Bill Hickok*—kicked off in the fall of 1951. In the former, broad-shouldered Bill Williams starred pretty competently as the hero, roaming the West, a la *The Cisco Kid*, in fictional exploits with his Mexican sidekick El Toro, played by Brooklyn-born gringo Don Diamond. The real Kentucky-born Christopher Houston "Kit" Carson (December 24, 1809—May 23, 1868) was an American frontiersman. Leaving home at an early age, he became a trapper, gained notoriety for his role as John C. Fremont's guide in the American West, fought in the Mexican-American

War of the mid-1840s, and later became a rancher in New Mexico. During the Civil War, he helped organize the New Mexico volunteer infantry, and afterward was dragooned into the army to help "tame" the Navajo people. (More than eight thousand of them surrendered to the army while an equal number faded into the badlands, it has been written.) The 104-episode *Kit Carson* series ran until 1955.

On the *Wild Bill Hickok* series (113 half-hour episodes), stalwart Guy Madison starred along with beloved, raspy-voiced Andy Devine as his sidekick Jingles. (They also were in a concurrent radio Hickok series on Mutual.) "When we went into production on *Wild Bill Hickok* in 1950," Guy Madison was quoted by author Gary Grossman in *Saturday Morning TV*, "no one knew what the impact of TV was going to be. The one thing it took was guts, because the studios wouldn't let their contract players appear on TV." Madison talked about the fast pace of making not only his show and the other Westerns but also low-budget theatrical oaters. "We couldn't waste any time in TV. We made a half-hour show in two-and-a-half days. That included dialogue, action, everything. At one point we knocked out seven films in seventeen days."

In his *Hollywood Corral*, aficionado Don Miller gave a special tip of his ten-gallon hat to the Hickok show as one of the most popular series of its time, going on to note, "The episodes, and the innumerable TV series that preceded and followed it, were little more than low-budget horse operas accomplished in approximately half the running time of a theatrical feature. . . . Madison's characterization was nowhere near the original Wild Bill Hickok, so the series was merely a traditional batch of short Westerns transposed to another medium." Nevertheless, the weekly hoss opera with Madison and Devine turned out to be extremely popular, not only with the small fry, but also with adults, who were once Saturday matinee small fry. It enjoyed a seven-year run before heading off to TV cowboy heaven and the great syndication pasture beyond.

Like all of their Western hero counterparts, Wild Bill and Jingles saddled up and ranged the Old West, righting wrongs on their horses Buckshot and Joker and beating up on the bad guys. Quite different from the fictional hero played by handsome Madison, the real Hickok of the 1800s was said to be far from a matinee idol. He was variously a Pony Express rider and a Union scout during the War between the States, and he fought with Custer (though not at the Last Stand at the Little Bighorn, of course). Later Hickok was marshal of Abilene, Texas. The website HistoryNet.com refers to James Butler Hickok basically as "a Pistoleer, Peace Officer and Folk Hero," and one of the premier gunfighters of the Old West—a legend in his own time, credited with the deaths of over one hundred bad men and bushwhackers. His exploits, as colorfully described in an 1867 issue of *Harper's New Monthly Magazine*, made him a superstar of the time—at least among the gunman greats, he was regarded as the best pistol shot on the plains. He died in 1876. But then again, it has been noted, kids did not tune in for originality or accuracy. Just action-packed fun, primarily for younger viewers.

Sky King, a contemporary Western, had a great degree of popularity, especially among the youngsters, when aired first on CBS beginning in April 1952 and then on ABC, staying aloft for seventy-two episodes, when production was halted because of a dispute between sponsor and ad agency. Another batch of episodes was filmed in 1955. (It originated as a fifteen-minute, three-times-a-week radio show on ABC in 1946.) *Sky King* remained on television on and off for about seven years. Kirby Grant—actor and aviator—played a former naval flyer turned rancher (the Flying Crown Ranch) who, in a Cessna rather than on horseback, helped maintain law and order in the fictional Arizona ranch community of Grover City; his teenage niece and nephew, Penny and Clipper, were played by Gloria Winters and Ron Hagerthy. The first *Sky King* episodes, made for less than $9,000 each, were made for Peter Pan peanut butter. After the last original episodes of *Sky King* were filmed in 1959, Kirby Grant retired.

Russell "Lucky" Hayden was back with a second Western serial, called *Cowboy G-Men*, costarring Jackie Coogan. This thirty-minute syndicated series that was filmed in color and that aired for a while in 1952 (there were thirty-nine episodes) followed the exploits of undercover government agents Pat Gallagher and Stoney Crockett, who patrolled California during the 1880s, sometimes with an associate named Zerbo. It was truly a low-budget affair, slanted for the kids, and directed primarily by veteran Western directors Lesley Selander and Paul Landres.

Around the same time in 1952, one of the landmark Western anthologies, *Death Valley Days*, premiered. A syndicated series, it began life on the radio, the brainchild of New York ad agency scriptwriter Ruth Woodman, who supposedly never saw Death Valley. She wrote many of the scripts during its fifteen-year run on radio, sponsored, like the durable TV series that would follow, by 20 Mule Team Borax—many episodes of which were filmed on location in Death Valley. The series—Western-based dramas, lighthearted tales alike, in which dozens of familiar film and TV faces regularly appeared—was hosted for the first dozen or so years by Stanley Andrews, who played the Old Ranger. He spun endless yarns depicting incidents in the lives of frontier folk in Nevada and California during the late nineteenth century. One of the more or less fictional tales the Old Ranger told rather wryly was the sixties episode titled "A Calamity Called Jane" that featured Fay Spain as Calamity and Rhodes Reason as Wild Bill Hickok.

When Andrews hung up his boots and spurs in 1964, Ronald Reagan came aboard as host and occasional star (and he invariably did the commercials, too—at least once with daughter Patti) for three years before being elected governor of California, then Robert Taylor (for about 77 episodes), then Dale Robertson, and finally country star Merle Haggard. The trail ended in 1975 after 558 episodes. Episodes of the show, which was produced for Gene Autry's Flying A Productions, have turned up in reruns, along with various hosts—retitled syndicated series like *Call of the West* with John Payne, *Frontier Adventures* with Dale Robertson, *The Pioneers* with Will Rogers Jr., *Trails West* with Ray Milland, and *Western Star Theater* with Rory Calhoun. If *Death Valley Days* hadn't had the longevity, there might never have been *Wagon Train* years later, another Western anthology.

A word or two should be said here about Ronald Reagan, who hosted for a time two hugely popular TV anthology series—one exclusively Western, the other with occasional Western dramas. Whatever else is said about Reagan, his acting career, at least post–World War II, made him a prolific Western movie star, if not quite up there with Randolph Scott, star of thirty-nine Westerns from 1946 onward (although Scott never acted on television), and Joel McCrea, who starred in thirty-one (plus two before the war). At least Reagan was in the same cowboy star league with big-screen colleagues Jimmy Stewart, Dick Powell, and Robert Taylor. In addition to hosting *Death Valley Days* from 1965 to 1968, Reagan starred in eight episodes; on *General Electric Theatre*, which he hosted and was the company spokesman for its entire 228-drama run, Reagan starred in at least a dozen stories—nearly all Westerns. (He also did cowboy star turns in one episode of the *Zane Grey Theatre* in 1961 and in one *Wagon Train* in 1963.)

In addition to *Death Valley Days* and, later, *Dick Powell's Zane Grey Theatre*—both exclusively airing tales, fanciful and not, of the Old West—and *Wagon Train*, there were a handful of anthology drama series that frequently showcased Western stories, most notably *General Electric Theatre* with Ronald Reagan and *Schlitz Playhouse of Stars* hosted by Irene Dunne. It was on *Schlitz* that two of the major Western series—*Tales of Wells Fargo* with Dale Robertson as Jim Hardie and *The Restless Gun* with John Payne as Vint Bonner—were born. (More about these later.)

Gene Autry's cowgirl protégé, pint-size Gail Davis (who made a handful of theatrical features with him and appeared occasionally on Autry's series) was given her own show for Flying A, a fictional version of the exploits of *Annie Oakley* (syndicated 1953–1956). The *New York Times* singled this show out as "above average," reporting that "featuring a gal as the individual who preserves law and order is a refreshing twist . . . and it stars the personable Gail Davis in the title role." The *Times*'s Jack Gould also found that "*Annie Oakley* supplements the routine gun play with some substantial story material that holds interest and boasts some good characterizations." This series made Davis the first of only a handful of female Western stars—if you don't count Dale Evans, who always worked on TV with Rogers. Born Phoebe Ann Moses in Darke County, Ohio, the real-life, and far from pretty, sharpshooter Annie Oakley (portrayed earlier in features by Barbara Stanwyck and Betty Hutton) was best remembered as having worked with Sitting Bull and Buffalo Bill in the latter's Wild West Show around the world. She lived from 1860 to 1926.

On the series, number two in the 1954 list of top kids' shows, Annie was pictured, all petticoats and pistols, as the scourge of rustlers and varmints around her hometown of Diablo in the company of the local sheriff (played by towering Brad Johnson). There were eighty-one episodes of the show, with many being rerun on Saturday and Sunday afternoons on ABC in the late fifties and again in the midsixties. After the series stopped filming in 1956, Gail Davis did an unsold pilot for Autry, *Melody Ranch*, a television adaptation of Autry's radio show of the forties. Then she went on to do a walk-on as Annie Oakley in Bob Hope's *Alias Jesse James* on the big screen. Her only other TV work appears to have been a single episode of *The Andy Griffith Show* in 1961.

The half-hour syndicated Western series *Stories of the Century* (1954–1955) had Jim Davis and Mary Castle playing a pair of detectives working for the fictional Southwestern Railroad (later there was a second female detective, played by Kristine Miller). They weekly tracked down one famous outlaw after another suspected of holding up trains—Belle Starr (Marie Windsor), in the premiere episode; Billy the Kid (Richard Jaeckel); Jesse James (Lee Van Cleef); Black Bart; Doc Holliday; John Wesley Hardin; Black Jack Ketchum; Ella "Cattle Kate" Watson; the Daltons, including a pre–Davy Crockett Fess Parker as Grat Dalton; Geronimo; and other bad guys and girls of the Old West.

The series spanned a thirty-year period (the 1870s through the 1890s), although the leads never seemed to have aged. *Stories of the Century* had the distinction of being an Emmy winner in 1954 as Best Western or Adventure Series.

One of the major stars in thirties films happened to be a German shepherd named Rin Tin Tin. The dog barked his way through radio in the forties and then returned to the (small) screen in *The Adventures of Rin Tin Tin* (ABC

1954–1959). The show related the tale, in the opening episode, of how a youngster named Rusty (played by Lee Aaker) and his dog, the only two survivors of an Apache raid on a wagon train, were found during a patrol of members of the 101st Cavalry. Succeeding thirty-minute stories—over the next five TV seasons—followed the exploits of the boy (made an honorary corporal) and his talented four-legged friend, who got his name in the show's title. And with the help of Lieutenant Rip Masters (James L. Brown), who unofficially adopted them, they pursued their efforts to assist the 101st in maintaining the peace around Fort Apache. Herbert B. Leonard produced the series of 164 episodes for Screen Gems; William Beaudine directed. Rinty, as the dog affectionately was known, reappeared three decades later in a TV series of contemporary adventures.

Besides these series Westerns that premiered between 1948 and late 1954, the Old West on television was a recurring theme of assorted anthology shows, like the popular *Four Star Playhouse*, with rotating stars Dick Powell, Ida Lupino, Charles Boyer, and David Niven. A 1953 Western episode, "Trail's End," was written by Blake Edwards and starred Powell as a gunslinger, which, *Variety* reported at the time, "relies more on mood and suspense than action. . . . Virtually the entire affair takes place in one setting as a stranger on horseback meets up with a man and his wife on the trail." (Lee Van Cleef and Jean Howell played them.) And things proceed from there. Powell is actually a feared marshal who's tracking a killer known as the Sonora Kid. Moving on to be an important producer in television—and sometime star—Powell was remembered in this period for both this anthology show and his subsequent one, *Dick Powell's Zane Grey Theatre*, a generally top-notch filmed Western series of the late fifties dramatizing, primarily, the works of author Zane Grey.

One of TV's earliest Western spoofs was live (from New York) on NBC's *Armstrong Circle Theatre* in late December 1953, when Peter Lind Hayes and wife, Mary Healy, in their first television play, starred in the send-up "The Marshal of Misery Gulch." The marshal, of course, is pictured as hopelessly hapless. "Satire, to be effective, demands a sharp, overdrawn characterization, that pokes fun without either becoming slapstick or turning into straight melodrama," wrote the *Variety* critic in reviewing the show. "James Sheldon, who directed, managed to get a lot of movement into the show—cowboys kept riding past the camera—but didn't manage to convey the sense of satire that could make such a takeoff hilariously funny."

Arguably a Western of sorts, *Satins and Spurs*, television veteran Max Liebman's landmark NBC musical "spectacular" (Liebman is credited with coining the word for this type of show) aired live on September 12, 1954.

Betty Hutton headed the cast in her television debut, along with Kevin Mc-Carthy and French chanteuse Genevieve. The ninety-minute show, about a rodeo rider (Hutton) who falls for a magazine writer (McCarthy), had a musical score by Jay Livingston and Ray Evans, who previously had written "Buttons and Bows," among others. The program was glitzy but did not get especially good reviews, prompting Hutton to announce her (first) retirement from show business.

CHAPTER THREE

The Western Disney-
Style and the Pivotal Years

In 1954, Walt Disney came to ABC television and brought with him "Frontierland," among others, that featured over the next seven years such newly made Western films and series as *Davy Crockett*, that made a star of Fess Parker, brought vaudeville hoofer Buddy Ebsen back to the fore as Crockett's pal George Russell, and created a national craze for coonskin caps. The unprecedented popularity of *Davy Crockett* was said to have caught the folks at Disney Studios by surprise, and four more hour-long adventures were quickly developed. All five aired at intervals between October 1954 and December of the following year. *Davy Crockett* was truly a pop culture phenomenon of the time. Many television historians have claimed erroneously that this was the medium's first miniseries. They were wrong in that the individual Crockett adventures were self-contained stand-alones. Several different ones were spliced together to make a theatrical feature of Davy's fictional exploits: "Davy Crockett, Indian Fighter," in December 1954; "Davy Crockett Goes to Congress" five weeks later; "Davy Crockett at the Alamo" four weeks after that; then "Davy Crockett's Keelboat Races" and "Davy Crockett and the River Pirates" in late 1955. Although the real Davy Crockett died at the Alamo, for Disney he survived and moved on to more fictional adventures. The Davy Crockett mania of the time, with its merchandising and bubble gum cards, was topped by a multi-million-selling record of the show's theme song, "The Ballad of Davy Crockett," written by Disney staff composer George Bruns. It was a hit for both Bill Hayes, later to be a popular soap star, and even Fess Parker himself.

Author and media historian Neal Gabler wrote about Fess Parker in the *Los Angeles Times*, a day or so after Parker's death in March 2010: "Parker was not only present at the creation of modern mass culture, he was smack dab in the middle of that creation. Before Elvis Presley, Beatlemania, *The Simpsons* and *SpongeBob SquarePants*, there was Davy Crockett, the buckskin wearing frontier hero whom Parker portrayed on Walt Disney's Disneyland . . . and who within weeks had invaded the American imagination as well as the pocketbooks of American parents succumbing to their children's pleas for Crocket paraphernalia, especially Crockett's coonskin cap. Crocketmania surged across the country." Gabler felt that "[Parker's] character embodied courage and common sense in the uncertain '50s. . . . He is not only a big part of baby boomer memory as television's first mega star in television's first case of mass hysteria. He is a big part of American iconography as the man who embodied the best of who we once were and who we like to think we still are."

There was another *Davy Crockett* series—a brief one—on a later Disney program. In 1988–1989, Davy returned for several episodes in Disneyland, with Tim Dunigan as Crockett, Johnny Cash (in the first one) as the reminiscing elderly Davy, and Gary Grubbs as Crockett's sidekick George Russell. These were titled "Davy Crockett: Rainbow in Thunder," "Davy Crockett: A Natural Man," "Davy Crockett: Guardian Spirit," "Davy Crockett: A Letter to Polly." It must be assumed that these episodes all occurred before Davy lost his life at the Alamo.

Disney tried duplicating the success of *Davy Crockett* but none even came close. All, though, were fictional exploits of actual Western heroes. First there was *The Saga of Andy Burnett*, with Jerome Courtland as a pioneer who traveled to the Rockies from Pittsburgh in the 1820s. His buddies were rough-and-ready trappers Joe Crane (Jeff York), Old Bill Williams (Slim Pickens), and Jack Kelly (Andrew Duggan). Premiering October 2, 1957, the show ran for six episodes intermittently. The series was adapted from several novels by Stewart Edward White; Courtland went on to become a prolific TV director.

Next multipart Disney Western series was *The Nine Lives of Elfego Baca* starring Robert Loggia as a (real-life) peace-loving but determined lawman in Tombstone, Arizona. It ran six episodes in 1957–1958.

After that was *Tales of Texas John Slaughter* (ABC, 1958–1961) with actor-turned-best-selling-author Tom Tryon playing the famed Louisiana-born Texas Ranger and later a cattle baron on the frontier. The real Slaughter was said to have worn a pearl-handled .44 and to have carried a 10-gauge, double-barreled, sawed-off shotgun.

The other series in Disney's Frontierland group was *The Swamp Fox*, played by Leslie Nielsen. This really wasn't a Western but a series of adventures of a Revolutionary War hero (ABC, 1959–1961).

In that general period, in the late fifties, Disney's *Mickey Mouse Club* aired a number of multi-episode youth-oriented tales that were, in one way or another, Western themed. *Corky and White Shadow*, for one, was a teenage-girl-and-her-German-shepherd adventure (they are the title twosome), living in the town of Beaumont with Corky's widowed dad, the sheriff (Buddy Ebsen), and helping him track down a varmint named Durango Dude, an outlaw who had robbed the local bank. All in all there were seventeen afternoon Corky episodes that ran periodically beginning in January 1956.

Spin and Marty, another *Mickey Mouse Club* series in late 1955, was a contemporary Western of sorts about two boys (Tim Considine and David Stollery) and their adventures on a dude ranch run by Jim Logan (Roy Barcroft) while training for a local rodeo (there were thirty episodes). This was followed in late 1957 by *The Further Adventures of Spin and Marty*, in which they vied for the affection of cute Annette Funicello. And this one was followed by *The New Adventures of Spin and Marty* (late 1958) in which the two stage a variety show with Annette, Darlene Gillespie (of *Corky and White Shadow*), and Kevin Corcoran (Moochie on yet another *Mickey Mouse Club* series of the day), to pay for the damages caused when Marty's jalopy crashes into the ranch house.

In the midsixties, on *Walt Disney Presents*, there was the three-part *The Tenderfoot*, inspired by author James H. Tevis's *Arizona in the '50s*. Captain James Henry Tevis was one of the original Arizona Territorial Rangers when the organization was first founded. In *The Tenderfoot*, Brandon de Wilde portrayed young Jim Tevis, who with nothing more than a Stetson, a gun, and three buddies, headed West to seek his destiny. Along the way, he befriended Kit Carson's black-sheep brother Mose (Brian Keith), a crusty army dragoons captain (James Whitmore), and an itinerant musician turned trooper (Paul Durand). Tevis's adventures, Disney-style, include the roundup of wild mustangs and a climactic horse race.

The Kit Carson story was retold fictionally in a two-part episode of *Walt Disney's Wonderful World of Color* on NBC in early 1977. In "Kit Carson and the Mountain Men," with Carson (played by Christopher Connelly) teaming up with pals John Fremont (Robert Reed) and Jim Bridger (Gregg Palmer), their exploits on a Far West expedition was dramatized.

On the ABC anthology series airing biweekly under the moniker *Motorola Television Hour*, there was what veteran television producer Herb Brodkin, who oversaw the program, maintained was the first *live* outdoor Western produced indoors for network television. Airing on November 3, 1953, and titled "Outlaw's Reckoning," it starred Eddie Albert, Lee Marvin, and Jane Wyatt, and had a brace of six horses crossing a forty-foot bridge built inside a TV studio especially for the production. The drama was based on a story by Ernest Haycox, best remembered for John Ford's *Stagecoach.*

Pall Mall Playhouse (a summer 1955 anthology of unsold Western pilots on ABC) starred many notable television and motion picture actors, including Irene Dunne, John Ireland, Stephen McNally, and Will Rogers Jr. Sponsored by Pall Mall cigarettes, this series aired for eight weeks on approximately one hundred affiliate stations of the ABC network from 8:00 to 9:00 p.m.

Several original Western tales turned up during the fifties on live drama anthology shows like *Philco/Goodyear Playhouse, Kraft Television Theatre, Studio One, Climax!, Cavalcade of America, Robert Montgomery Presents,* and most notably *Playhouse 90. Philco* offered, among others, the 1952 "A Cowboy for Chris" with Buster Crabbe as an itinerant cowpoke who ends up at a frontier boardinghouse and becomes the idol of the youngster whose mom owns the place (Brandon de Wilde, in a part similar to his one in *Shane*). This one was restaged several years later on *NBC Matinee Theatre.*

On the *United States Steel Hour* on ABC, in April 1954, for one, Jeff Morrow and Richard Jaeckel starred as fast guns in playwright Frank Gilroy's "The Last Notch." Later it would be filmed as a big-screen Western, *The Fastest Gun Alive* with Glenn Ford. On *Philco* in 1955, there was Gore Vidal's "The Death of Billy the Kid," starring Paul Newman. Several years later, Newman repeated the role in the big-screen version of Vidal's story, now called *The Left-Handed Gun. DuPont Show of the Week,* in October 1962, aired Sidney Carroll's lighthearted Western drama about a card game, "Big Deal in Laredo," with Walter Matthau, Teresa Wright, and Zachary Scott. A couple of years later the episode was transferred to the big screen as *Big Hand for the Little Lady* with Henry Fonda, Joanne Woodward, and Jason Robards. Fielder Cook directed both versions.

Richard Boone starred as John Wesley Hardin, the notorious outlaw and gunfighter of the Old West (glorified here, making him a college-educated lawyer gone wrong) in a live Western, "Dead of Noon" on *Studio One* in early 1957. Hardin, according to Western legend, claimed at one point he had killed forty-two men. And on *Goodyear Playhouse,* Robert Preston played Jesse James in a 1956 drama by noted television writer Ernest Kinoy titled "Missouri Legend," adapted from E. B. Ginty's 1938 Broadway play that starred Dean Jagger. Additionally on *Goodyear,* Errol Flynn starred as a rascally Old West con artist, Doc Boatwright, in a filmed drama for Screen Gems titled "The Golden Shanty"—the name of the saloon, the bricks of which he finds to be loaded with gold. So he romances the unhappily married wife of the saloon's proprietor, who offers Doc the gold to get the missus off his back. This tale, directed by Arthur Hiller, aired in November 1959, a month after Flynn's death.

On *Kraft Television Theatre*, there were these Western-themed episodes: "A Long Night in Forty Miles" (October 1952) starred TV drama veteran John Baragrey as a Klondike gold rush gambler who craps out. To hide losses from his wife (played by Hildy Parks), however, he robs a pair of miners of a couple of bags of ore. "The Stake" (May 1954), again with Baragrey, along with Joe Maross and Louisa Horton, had Baragrey playing an army lieutenant on a frontier outpost in the 1870s. He has an affair with the wife of a corporal and, with an Indian attack at hand, finds that his troops have abandoned him to save the corporal's life. And then, in October 1954, Kraft staged a live version of Bret Harte's "The Luck of Roaring Camp."

Kraft's 1959 (filmed) adaptation of Harte's "The Outcasts of Poker Flat," airing on CBS, starred George C. Scott and Larry Hagman, among others. Harte's tales of frontier California earned him acclaim during the 1860s, and his stories helped establish the foundations of western American fiction as the predecessor of Zane Grey, who was the predecessor of Max Brand (Frederick Schiller Faust) and then Louis L'Amour and then Larry McMurtry.

Robert Montgomery Presents aired these Western-themed episodes: "The Drifter" (May 1955), starring Zachary Scott as a footloose Old West cowpoke who hooks up with a dance hall girl from San Francisco; "The Return of Johnny Burro" (August 1955), dealing with a former outlaw (Eric Sinclair) who attempts a reunion with his long ago sidekick (Charles Drake) and the girl he once loved (Augusta Dabney), who's now the sidekick's sweetheart; and "Along Came Jones" (October 1955), a low-key modern-day Western, played for smiles if not laughs, starring Charlton Heston, based on the Gary Cooper forties movie.

David Niven, looking a bit out of place in Western garb, starred on an *Alcoa/Goodyear Theater* drama "The Tinhorn" in late 1957, playing a cheating gambler who masquerades as a traveling preacher on a wagon train to outrun a man who vows to kill him. Niven's touch with the Old West was limited to producing on the *Zane Grey Theatre* for Four Star Productions, where he was one of the partners (although he did star in at least two stories on that series).

Among the myriad of half-hour dramas during its long run, first on radio going back to 1935 and then on TV (NBC, 1952–1953, and ABC, 1953–1957), *DuPont Cavalcade of America* offered an occasional original Western: "The Arrow and the Bow," "Riders of the Pony Express" (about a young Mark Twain in the West), "Duel at the O.K. Corral," "The Texas Rangers."

The anthology series documented historical events using stories of individual courage, initiative, and achievement. Each show opened with DuPont's legendary (now politically incorrect) motto "Maker of better things for better living through chemistry." Similarly there was *TV Reader's Digest* on ABC, with family-oriented fare from the pages of the famed monthly. For instance, its very first drama was "The Last of the Old-Time Shooting Sheriffs" in January 1955, and later "Child Pioneer," that dealt with an adventurous boy who is befriended by Kit Carson. And in 1956, the *Reader's Digest* series aired "Cochise: Greatest of the Apaches." Richard Gaines played the lead, along with Rhodes Reason as Tom Jeffords and John Howard as General Oliver Otis Howard. The half-hour weekly anthology show aired on ABC and ran for thirty-nine episodes.

A ninety-minute musical version of *Ruggles of Red Gap*, starring Michael Redgrave, Jane Powell, Peter Lawford, Imogene Coca, and David Wayne, was televised on *Producers' Showcase* (February 1957). With a score by Jule Styne and Leo Robin, it was based on Henry Leon Wilson's oft-filmed novel about a very proper English butler who goes to the Wild West to work for a crude nineteenth-century frontier family. It wasn't especially well received critically. ("The evening was a mostly disappointing one," wrote the *New York Times's* Jack Gould.) *Ruggles of Red Gap* had been made before in 1918, 1923, and 1933, and then in 1950 as *Fancy Pants* with Bob Hope and Lucille Ball.

Playhouse 90, which became the gold standard for the golden era of live anthology drama on television—although toward the end of its run, *Playhouse 90* featured original dramas on tape and film—aired several interesting television Westerns. One was "Invitation to a Gunfighter" (1957) about the terrorization of a town by a professional gunman. Hugh O'Brian played a homesteader. The town wants his property, and when he resists, a hired gun is brought in to persuade him otherwise. But then the gunfighter decides to grab the entire town for himself. Anne Bancroft played O'Brian's sweetie and Pat O'Brien was her father, the inept sheriff. Later, this drama would be the basis for the Yul Brynner film of the same name.

A year or so later, *Playhouse 90* aired Rod Serling's original "A Town Has Turned to Dust," directed by John Frankenheimer. "Rod Serling poured out a fiery, spellbinding attack on racial discrimination in his 90-minute dramatic effort," *Variety* stated in its review. "He told the profoundly disturbing story that took place on a long and arid street in a Southwestern frontier town in the 1880s when the sheriff stepped aside to let a violent mob reach into the jail and lynch an innocent young Mexican." Rod Steiger starred as the cowardly lawman, and William Shatner was pure evil as the mob ringleader. Decades later when Serling's story was remade as a cable movie, it was in a more contemporary setting located in the South, with a black man the target of the mob.

In December 1957, *Playhouse 90* also had Kathryn Grayson playing an Indian princess, the lead character in a drama called "Lone Woman," who marries a white trader in the 1870s. Costarring were Vincent Price, Raymond Burr, Scott Brady, Jack Lord, and Harry Carey Jr.

Errol Flynn and Helen Hayes also starred (separately) in live Western dramas on *Playhouse 90.* In "Without Incident" (1957), Flynn worked together again with Ann Sheridan—years after they were both Warner Bros. stars—he as a cavalry captain and she as one of two women held by hostile Indians who his unit is sent out to rescue—until faced with a mutiny by his men. Noted writer Charles Marquis Warren, creator of *Rawhide* and producer of *The Virginian, Gunsmoke, The Iron Horse,* and other popular TV Westerns, directed. (Initially, according the *New York Times* at the time, this episode was to be a pilot for a weekly Flynn series called *Cavalry Patrol.*) Hayes played a nun in the Old West in "Four Women in Black" (also 1957), journeying across the desert from Santa Fe to Tucson with three others and having to depend upon a fleeing outlaw (Ralph Meeker) for survival when their horse is stolen.

At the start of 1958, John Frankenheimer directed writer Aaron Spelling's offbeat (filmed) Western "The Last Man" on *Playhouse 90.* It starred Sterling Hayden as a reluctant deputy sheriff—reluctant since he was bent on destroying a frontier town because the locals refused to help his dying wife (played by Carolyn Jones, best known at the time as Mrs. Aaron Spelling).

And there was *Playhouse 90*'s "Bitter Heritage" (1958), which dramatized a fictional Frank and Jesse tale. Franchot Tone starred as Frank James; James Drury (later of *The Virginian*) as his nephew Jesse James Jr.; Elizabeth Montgomery as a banker's daughter who has evidence to save them from a necktie party; and grand dame of the theater Eva LeGallienne in a rare, nonclassic role as Grandma James. "Well peopled with characteristically cast performers out of the front chute," the *Variety* critic backhandedly wrote of the show filmed by Screen Gems, "it offered up a new threat to the cowboy heroes, James Drury, who played Jesse James Jr. like he just came out of a Sunday School class."

A couple of months after the Frank-and-Jesse (Jr.) drama was one of the lesser *Playhouse 90*'s productions, one of the first that the anthology show offered on film—a standard-issue Western called "Massacre at Sand Creek," directed by Arthur Hiller, written and produced by William Sackheim, and starring John Derek as a young cavalry lieutenant at odds with his self-serving commanding officer (Everett Sloane) and refusing to obey orders to gun down a band of unarmed Cheyenne.

NBC offered up, in May 1960, an hour-long drama based on Mark Twain's autobiographical book *Roughing It*, in which Twain, at seventy, reminisced about the days when he was a greenhorn in the Wild West, beginning with a stagecoach trip to the Nevada Territory. Twain was played by James Daly and several decades later, when the tale was retold as a made-for-TV movie, by James Garner.

Western-themed dramas produced by *United States Steel Hour* included "Shadow of Evil" and "Old Marshals Never Die." "Shadow of Evil" (early 1957) had a stellar cast, including Lee Marvin, Jack Cassidy, Shirley Jones, Rip Torn, and Joseph Campanella. The tale was about an outlaw-hating town sheriff who kills a young man, claiming that the youngster had made an attempt on his life. "Old Marshals Never Die" aired in 1958 and followed a former marshal of a New Mexico town—old-timer Cameron Prud'homme as Bat Bethune—who is, in old age, given to shooting at imaginary bad men and endangering the inhabitants, and is finally, though politely, urged to leave town. Both dramas were broadcast live. Another *United States Steel Hour* (February 1960) featured a Max Liebman revue, *The American Cowboy*, with Carol Burnett, Fred MacMurray, and others in humorous skits spoofing, well, the American cowboy.

A couple of months later, a May 1960 CBS special, done like a movie (with a laugh track), had Phil Silvers playing Fletcher Bissell III, aka the Silver Dollar Kid, "the yellowest man in the Arizona Territory and [as the spoof was titled] the slowest gun in the West." Bilko-like Phil is so cowardly that no self-respecting outlaw will gun him down. So the people of Primrose City hire him as their sheriff, figuring his cowardice will help achieve law and order. Jack Benny was along to play Chicken Finsterwald, the most spineless gunslinger west of the Mississippi. The two stumble into encounters with the likes of outlaws Sam Bass (Lee Van Cleef), Black Bart (Ted DeCorsia), and Ike and Jake Dalton (Jack Elam and Karl Lukas). Also in the cast were Marion Ross, Bruce Cabot, and Jack Albertson. The special was written and produced by Nat Hiken, who had created Sergeant Bilko for Silvers.

On a *Jack Benny Show* in early 1962, Benny, returning from a show in Phoenix with Gisele MacKenzie, gets lost and stumbles into a café in what appears to be a Western ghost town. While the pair dines on peanut butter sandwiches, the owner spins a story from the town's history, where a black-hearted villain named Tombstone Harry (Gerald Mohr) tries to force Tess, a beautiful saloon girl (MacKenzie), to marry him, or he'll foreclose on her mortgage. A black-garbed hero, the Cactus Kid (Benny), attempts to stop the varmint. (It's been noted that Jack's once-in-a-while Buck Benny character used in many of his early radio sketches and in one of his forties flicks was the model for his rather cowardly Cactus Kid character—like Red Skelton's familiar Sheriff Deadeye, the not-so-straight Old West lawman, wearing a ten-gallon hat and sporting a handlebar moustache, from both radio and his twenty-year stint on television.)

In 1967, on *Bob Hope Presents the Chrysler Theatre*, there was the good-natured sagebrush spoof that unspooled with the unwieldy title "The Reason Nobody Hardly Ever Seen a Fat Outlaw in the Old West Is as Follows." Its plot had comical Sheriff Tinsley (Arthur Godfrey, in a rare acting role) up against the Swine Gang (Herb Edelman and Jack Lambert as Seth and Sid Swine) and mighty frightened of Curly the Kid (Don Knotts). Another Hope special on his *Chrysler Theatre*, "Have Girls Will Travel," a Western send-up, had him portraying fast-talking itinerant marriage broker Horatio Lovelace, traveling the frontier peddling his lovelies to prospective husbands. But in the town of Golden Gulch, he found himself in a jam with some (humorously) tough local hombres—played by Rod Cameron, Aldo Ray, and Sonny Tufts—when three of his girls (Rhonda Fleming, Marilyn Maxwell, and Jill St. John) change their minds about marrying three mean and unkempt brothers. And no-nonsense sheriff Bruce Cabot doesn't cotton to this either. (Jack Benny, Lucille Ball, and others were along for the romp.)

In his *Chrysler Theatre* anthology series of the sixties, Hope also hosted several other more traditional Westerns, including Rod Serling's "A Killing at Sundial," with Stuart Whitman as a newly rich Native American named Billy Cole who seeks to avenge the years-earlier lynching of his father; "March from Camp Tyler," which featured Peter Lawford as a cavalry officer ordered to take some misfit soldiers across Indian country, including a murderer who hates him (Broderick Crawford and Ben Johnson were among the troops); and the fact-based "Massacre at Fort Phil Kearny," in which a feud between a captain (Carroll O'Connor) and his commanding officer (Richard Egan) was the spark that led to the slaughter by Sioux Indians of eighty-one soldiers in the Old West of 1866.

In NBC's sterling *Our American Heritage* series of early sixties specials—a number of docudramas about notable people and events in American history—there was at least one Western. Jeffrey Hunter starred as explorer John Charles Fremont in the live, hour-long January 1960 episode "Destiny West," with Susan Strasberg as his wife and James Daly as saddle pal and guide Kit Carson. It was written by William Altman and directed by Jack Smight.

Over its many years on CBS from 1953 to 1962, the *General Electric Theater*—the half-hour weekly (Sundays at 9:00 p.m.) dramatic anthology hosted by and sometimes starring Ronald Reagan—presented an assortment of Westerns. Most of the guests gravitated to this show because it was filmed, and it was on film where most made their careers.

James Stewart, for one, made his TV acting debut in "The Windmill," playing a down-and-out rancher trying to keep his days as a former gunslinger a secret (even from his wife, played by Barbara Hale). But to save his bone-dry spread with needed irrigation from a windmill, he must choose whether to expose his past and enter a six-shooter contest for the money.

Stewart starred, too, in a *General Electric Theater* cowboy version of Dickens's *A Christmas Carol*, in which he also made his directing debut. In "A Trail to Christmas," he played a cowpoke Christmas Past and storyteller. (John McIntire was Ebenezer Scrooge.)

Likewise, Alan Ladd did his only TV acting on a couple of *General Electric Theater* dramas, including the Western "The Silent Ambush," playing a sheriff struggling to keep his job even as he loses his hearing. Robert Cummings, in "Too Good with a Gun," starred as a cowboy trying to live down his reputation as a gunman by taking a job as a ranch hand.

Host Ronald Reagan starred periodically in original Western dramas: in "The Coward of Fort Bennett," he's a cavalry officer suspected of abandoning his troops in an Indian raid. Neville Brand and John Dall are a pair of junior officers under his command.

In "A Question of Survival," Reagan's a cavalry captain whose small band is outnumbered by the surrounding Comanche, and he wrestles with a difficult decision when the company surgeon offers to tend the fatally wounded son of the attacking chief.

Reagan did the comedy Western "War and Peace on the Range," playing a producer of low-budget oaters who must contend with a big-name actor's incompetent relative assigned to costar in a sagebrush version of Tolstoy. And, most notably, Reagan starred with his wife, Nancy Davis, along with oddly cast Ward Bond playing a wise old American Indian named Grey Eagle on their turkey ranch in a contemporary Thanksgiving 1958 Western drama entitled "A Turkey for the President." *Variety* wrote of this episode that "even though this turkey G.E. [General Electric] cooked up was light on the stuffing, it was offbeat enough to be mildly diverting."

Climax!, CBS's memorable live anthology drama series of the 1950s, offered an original Western or two. One was "The Mojave Kid," from a frontier short story by Louis L'Amour, with Ward Bond as Ab Kale, aging sheriff of the town of Hinkley, warning the troublesome Mojave Kid (John Lupton), a gunslinger, to stay out of town but knowing he'll be back for a showdown of sorts. Ricardo Montalban got top billing as the lawman's friend, a peace-loving gambler.

On the weekly *20th Century Fox Hour* on CBS, in January 1957, there was a truncated (vest-pocket, as it was referred to) version of Gregory Peck's *The Gunfighter* from 1950. This hour-long adaptation, called "End of a Gun," starred Richard Conte in Peck's role, along with John Barrymore Jr., Marilyn Erskine, and a young Michael Landon. Other Westerns in this series of condensed films from 20th Century Fox include the following:

- "The Still Trumpet," based on the Joseph Cotten–Cornel Wilde Western *Two Flags West* (during the Civil War, imprisoned Confederate soldiers are paroled to help protect pioneers from Indians). Dale Robertson and Victor Jory were the stars of the TV adaptation.
- "The Lynch Mob," from the Henry Fonda–Dana Andrews classic mob violence Western *The Ox-Bow Incident*. Robert Wagner, Cameron Mitchell, and E. G. Marshall starred.
- "Gun in Hand," with Robert Wagner. *TV Guide* described this one: "An outlaw's son is torn between affection for his father and his own belief in law and order. While riding with the outlaw band, he is captured and imprisoned, then learns the gang abandoned his wife to die, leaving his newborn son homeless. Furious, he turns against the gang and joins forces with the law."
- "Man of the Law," from Robert Ryan's *The Proud Ones*, with Wendell Corey in Ryan's role of a marshal who is run out of town for being trigger-happy.
- "Apache Uprising," with Ricardo Montalban as Cochise, from *Broken Arrow* (see discussion that follows).

Tellingly, the casting of non-Indians at the time to play Native Americans is best illustrated with *Broken Arrow*—the film, the TV adaptation, and the series. On the big screen, it was a chiseled, square-jawed Jewish actor from Brooklyn, a radio personality named Ira Grossel with a commanding voice who later changed his name to the nonethnic sounding Jeff Chandler, who initially played Cochise (also in two sequels, one of which had Rock Hudson, in his early acting career, darkened up to play Cochise's son!). In the television version, the part was played by Mexican actor Ricardo Montalban and later Michael Ansara of Syrian/Lebanese extraction. Cochise's squaw opposite Montalban, Sonseeahray, was played by Puerto Rican Rita Moreno. Later, sometime after playing a half-breed named Tina Starbuck in an episode of *Trackdown*, Moreno said in a 1983 interview with *TV Guide*, "If you were a Latina, you played poor, brown-skinned princesses: Mexican, Spanish, Indian, we all looked alike. Or so they seemed to think."

And for CBS's *Schlitz Playhouse of Stars*, as well, hosted by actress Irene Dunne, there was a smattering of Western dramas on film. One of the earliest *Playhouse of Stars* Westerns, "Pussyfootin' Rocks" (November 12, 1952) starred Joan Blondell as Calamity Jane.

In addition to some pilots to later Western series (*A Tale of Wells Fargo* in December 1956, and *The Restless Gun* several months later), there were perhaps a dozen other cowboy-themed dramas that were part of the *Schlitz* TV legacy, for example,

- "No Compromise" (November 11, 1953). Stephen McNally played a Texas Ranger who must bring an outlaw to justice on a train.
- "Pearl Handled Gun" (January 16, 1954). Zachary Scott was a colorful outlaw who, because of his fancy pistol, is idolized by a young boy.
- "Delay at Fort Bliss" (September 3, 1954). Sterling Hayden starred as a strong-willed army officer at a lonely army outpost in Arizona who has a choice to make: turn over an Apache chief's son who is being held prisoner or lose his command.
- "The Long Trail" (November 19, 1954). Anthony Quinn was a Texas Ranger who chases a suspected killer all the way to Oregon.
- "Mister Schoolmarm" (February 11, 1955). Martin Milner played a young Civil War vet who takes a job in Oregon teaching frontiersmen the ways of peace and democracy.
- "Switch Station" (May 10, 1957). Charlton Heston was a footloose cowpoke who gets a job at a stagecoach station's switch station and then has to face a band of stagecoach robbers led by John Carradine.
- "The Way of the West" (June 6, 1958). John Forsythe played a starchy young doctor from Boston headed for California who, in a frontier town along the way, teams up, rather improbably, with lawless Belle Starr (Abby Dalton) to fight a local smallpox epidemic. This subsequently became the pilot (unsold) for a new Belle Starr series.
- "A Ballad to Die For" (July 31, 1959). William Joyce played a singing cowboy named Johnny Guitar who roams the West helping people. This was based rather loosely on the character Sterling Hayden played in Joan Crawford's 1957 cult Western *Johnny Guitar*. The *Schlitz* episode, produced by Jack Webb's Mark VII Productions, was the final *Playhouse of Stars* show and an unsold TV pilot for a *Johnny Guitar* series.

And there were others.

Ford Television Theater, like *Schlitz Playhouse of Stars*, offered a number of half-hour filmed Western dramas after its new 1952 premiere on NBC (then

ABC) as Columbia Pictures was launching its Screen Gems TV subsidiary. (Originally, the anthology series aired hour-long live dramas on CBS between 1948 and 1951.) Early on, there were "The Sermon of the Gun" (January 22, 1953) with Macdonald Carey as an ex-gunfighter turned preacher who takes up his guns once again to save his flock, and "Gun Job" (December 17, 1953), featuring Phil Carey as an ex-marshal turned homesteader with his wife (Ellen Drew), but he clashes with a tough cattleman (played by Ward Bond) who refuses to recognize the law.

A few years later on *Ford Theater* there were "The Face" (March 1956) starring Dale Robertson as a man trying to hunt down the varmint who he remembers as a kid gunned down his mother and father; "Black Jim Hawk" (October 1956) with John Derek as the notorious Old West outlaw, who was obsessed with killing Texas patriot Sam Houston; and "Sudden Silence," an unsold pilot starring Barbara Stanwyck (her 1956 TV acting debut), who, as the wife of small frontier town sheriff (Jeff Morrow), watches its growth amid a scarlet fever scourge.

Stanwyck, it should be noted, went on to host and occasionally star in, and even win an Emmy for, her own (single-season) anthology drama series *The Barbara Stanwyck Show* in 1960–1961. A couple of episodes had Western themes: "The Key to the Killer," in which, as a sheriff's deputy, she finds herself handcuffed to a fleeing outlaw (Vic Morrow), and in "Little Big Mouth," playing the real-life Nellie Bly, a noted journalist in the Old West. One of the premier big screen actresses (along with Loretta Young, Irene Dunne, and June Allyson) to host and star in an anthology drama series, Stanwyck—according to her biographer, Ella Smith—pushed to be able to do women's Westerns on a regular basis on television. She told *TV Guide* in 1958, "I wanted a Western series. But the Brain Boys [her agents] said no, Westerns were on their way out. Way out? Not around my house they're not. From six o'clock on it sounds like the last frontier around there."

Stanwyck already had starred in episodes of *Zane Grey Theatre* and others—she did at least four on that series, written by Aaron Spelling, who'd later produce *Dynasty* and *The Colbys* and a couple of TV movies in between for her. On *The Barbara Stanwyck Show*, one of the Westerns she "slipped into" the lineup was "A Man's Game," written by David Harmon and Albert Beich. She introduced the show this way: "Tonight we place our tongue in cheek and present a gentle spoof of the Old West. You know the West I mean. Where every man is a fast-draw gunslinger and every lady works in a saloon. My role? Well, believe it or not, I play the sheriff—but don't take it all too seriously." She's actually a saloonkeeper in a town that somehow has trouble keeping sheriffs, so she takes the job when reluctantly offered it.

Jimmy Stewart narrated and costarred with George Gobel in *Cindy's Fella*, a folksy Western take on the traditional story of Cinderella, directed by Gower Champion on *Ford Startime* in 1959. In this hour-long filmed comedy-drama, Stewart is an itinerant Yankee peddler named Azel Dorsey who is lured to a local homestead by a "fairy godmother" in the guise of a guitar-strumming roamer (the words of *TV Guide* in its "close-up"), played by Gobel, and there meets the widow-owner's three daughters, one of whom is named Cindy (then waif-like actress Lois Smith), and accompanies her to a barn dance. Jameson Brewer wrote this Western reimagining of the tale. Actually this had been written for Stewart for his early fifties radio Western series, *The Six Shooter*, the genesis of sorts for John Payne's *Restless Gun* TV show. Stewart told *TV Guide* at the time, "This is an un-Western Western. Which is to say, there are no shoot-outs in the middle of a deserted street."

The venerable *Hallmark Hall of Fame* occasionally offered an original Western drama through the show's pre-television movie history. Two of them, at least, were "The Court-Martial of George Armstrong Custer" in 1977, based on Douglas C. Jones's book, and veteran writer James Lee Barrett's genial "Stubby Pringle's Christmas" in 1978.

The speculative Custer drama explored the possibility that he survived the Little Bighorn massacre and was put on trial for insubordination and putting his men in harm's way. James Olson played Custer, but it was the courtroom battle of opposing lawyers Brian Keith (for the defense) and Ken Howard (as the prosecution) that gave sparks to this drama. It was written by prolific John Gay and included an early performance by Blythe Danner as Elizabeth "Libbie" Custer.

The Stubby Pringle tale, which starred Beau Bridges, Julie Harris, and Kim Hunter, was set in Montana in 1910 and concerned a lonesome cowboy with a generous heart (Pringle) who brings some Christmas happiness to an impoverished homesteader, her sick husband, and their two small children, and lights up a young girl's dance.

The Twilight Zone presented a number of Western tales through the years. Three of the most famous episodes, arguably, were "Showdown with Rance McGraw," "Mr. Denton on Doomsday," and "The Grave." In the first, Larry Blyden plays a modern-day Western TV star who time travels back to frontier days and finds himself facing down Jesse James (Arch Johnson).

In the second, Al Denton (Dan Duryea), once a feared gunslinger and now the town drunk, is goaded into a gunfight by Dan Hotaling (Martin Landau), a sarcastic bully. Then a mysterious peddler called Mr. Fate turns up in town to offer Denton a second—and last—chance with his six-gun. Getting back his self-respect and giving up alcohol, Denton learns very quickly that there is a significant downside—when a young hotshot (Doug McClure) with a fast gun challenges him to a showdown, and they learn that fate has stepped in for both of them. Rod Serling, who wrote the morality tale, says in his closing narration, "Mr. Henry Fate, dealer in utensils and pots and pans, liniments and potions. A fanciful little man in a black frock coat who can help a man climbing out of a pit—or another man from falling into one. Because, you see, Fate can work that way . . . in *The Twilight Zone*."

In the third, Lee Marvin is Old West lawman Conny Miller, who, upon arriving in a flea-bitten town for a showdown with outlaw Pinto Sykes, is told that Sykes is already dead. Miller, whom Sykes had belittled as a coward, goes to visit the grave of the man he failed to track down to prove he (Miller) was never afraid of him but gets more than he bargained for when he ventures into the graveyard in the dead of night. Western-movie regulars Strother Martin and Lee Van Cleef appear in key supporting roles.

And between 1953 and 1957, on the series *You Are There*, Walter Cronkite would dispatch noted CBS correspondents to cover notable events, such as the capture of Jesse James (a young James Dean played Bob Ford, the "coward" who gunned down Jesse), the defense of the Alamo (and later the burning of the Alamo), the trial of Belle Starr, the death of Stonewall Jackson, the gunfight at the O.K. Corral, and the end of the Dalton Gang (David Janssen was one of the brothers).

CHAPTER FOUR

Coming of Age on the TV Frontier

The television hoss opera, in retrospect, came of age in 1955 when so-called adult Westerns began replacing those which to that time were generally considered fare for kids—like television itself, when with live anthology drama, and in some cases Westerns, the change was under way from live to filmed programming. In 1955, out of the twenty-five or so new primetime series on the schedules of the three networks, twenty-one were on film, and the remaining four would switch to film before the season's end. It began—on the Westerns front—with two landmark series, premiering within days of one another.

First to air was ABC's *The Life and Legend of Wyatt Earp* (more legend than life, as one critic put it), starring stalwart Hugh O'Brian; beginning September 6, 1955; and establishing itself as the Tuesdays-from-8:30-to-9:00 rock on the network, for its entire six-year run.

Four nights later came what has gone on to become the granddaddy of all Westerns on the tube—one that ran, until 2010 and *Law and Order*, an unprecedented (for a dramatic series) twenty seasons—CBS's *Gunsmoke*, with sturdy James Arness, riding tall in his signature role of Marshal Matt Dillon, on September 10, 1955, Saturday at 10:00 p.m.

Wyatt Earp was based more or less on fact—about the colorful real-life marshal from Ellsworth, Kansas, then Dodge City, then Wichita, and later Tombstone on the frontier. This show developed into thirty-minute somewhat romanticized sagebrush dramas that mixed standard Western action with tales involving family relationships as well as local politics. Ex-marine drill instructor O'Brian as the impeccably dressed—at least on the long-running series—gun-toting lawman was joined on the show by Douglas Fowley (and briefly Myron Healey) as real-life Doc Holliday and Morgan Woodward as fictional Deputy Shotgun Gibbs. Mason Alan Dinehart III, grandson of the veteran cowboy actor who died in 1944, was there for a couple of years as Earp's fellow lawman, Bat Masterson. The final episodes of the series—a five-part drama—concluded with the famous shootout at the O.K. Corral.

The theme music for the hit series was notable as the only TV theme written by Hollywood composers Harry Warren (the guy who wrote the music to "Jeepers Creepers" and "You Must Have Been a Beautiful Baby") and Harold Adamson as a team. "Wyatt Earp. Wyatt Earp. Brave, courageous, and bold. Long live his fame, long live his glory, and long may his story be told." Music historian Jon Burlingame noted in his book *TV's Biggest Hits*, "The Warren-Adamson collaboration produced the first memorable Western tune specifically written for television. . . . Perhaps the most unusual aspect of the music of Wyatt Earp was the fact that most of the score, like the title song, was performed a capella by [veteran vocal arranger Ken] Darby's quartet." It was a robust, all-male chorus known as the King's Men.

Earp's story, in one form or another, would be told over and over again on television through the years.

Gunsmoke's genesis, meanwhile, was the radio show that began three years earlier and featured William Conrad as the voice of Matt Dillon. Radio show and the TV series ran concurrently for a while in the fifties, but with different stories. Legend has it that John Wayne was the original choice for the lead on television, but he did not want to tie himself down to a weekly grind. So the Duke suggested to the producers his strapping young protégé, Arness, who'd made a couple of films with him. Wayne, however, did appear at the beginning of the premier show to introduce Arness. *Gunsmoke* initially was a half-hour show in black and white. (In 1966 it was first broadcast in color; in 1967 it was expanded to one hour.)

Stalwart—though sometimes conflicted—Matt Dillon's television family included Milburn Stone as crusty Doc Adams (whose existence seemed to be solely to dig out the bullets Matt pumped into the bad guys); Amanda Blake as Kitty Russell, who ran the Long Branch Saloon and was a shoulder for Matt (on the radio Kitty was clearly established to be a working girl, the town tramp, but she was "cleaned up" for television); and Dennis Weaver as obsequious, gimpy Chester Goode, Matt's well-meaning deputy for the first nine seasons, to be replaced by Ken Curtis as scruffy Festus Haggen. Also on board for a couple of seasons in the sixties was a young Burt Reynolds as Quint Asper, the town's half-breed blacksmith. Glenn Strange was

Sam the bartender for thirteen years, beginning in 1961, and cowboy old-timer Buck Taylor played Newly O'Brien from 1967 to 1973. Like *Wyatt Earp*, *Gunsmoke* was set in Dodge City. (Did the fictional Dillon and the real-life Earp ever cross paths, since both were marshals there at around the same time?)

In February 1967, with its rating sagging, *Gunsmoke* was announced for cancellation by CBS. But public outcry and the personal intervention of CBS head William S. Paley, who loved the show, saved it. The show was moved to Monday nights, where it rose in the ratings once again and stayed for another eight years.

The popularity of *Gunsmoke*, CBS's Saturday night show for the first twelve seasons, encouraged CBS to rerun simultaneously the original half-hour versions on Tuesday evenings as *Marshal Dillon*, from 1961 to 1963. *Gunsmoke* had 156 half-hour episodes and 350 hour-long ones.

A couple of weeks after launching the Wyatt Earp series, ABC introduced *Cheyenne*, starring Clint Walker. Rugged Walker, as frontier scout Cheyenne Brodie, the strong, silent type, roamed the West in the 1880s, taking on one job after another (he seemed to have a different one in each episode before moseying on). He has showdowns with assorted bad guys, charming the ladies he meets on the trail, turning up as a deputized lawman, engaging in and invariably winning gunfights. (Walker engaged in headline-making contract "shootouts" with Warner Bros. and went on suspension for a while, but that's a whole 'nother story.)

Cheyenne originated as part of a rotating cycle of shows under the umbrella title of "Warner Bros. Presents" when the studio chose to get into TV big-time. Several of the others fell by the wayside, and the studio went with this handsomely produced Western. Other than the title in this Warner Bros. series produced by William T. Orr, this had nothing to do with Warner Bros.' 1947 Western of the same name that starred Dennis Morgan and Jane Wyman. The hour-long *Cheyenne* lasted for eight years, despite the behind-the-scenes contractual battles between star and studio.

Cheyenne actually was the first television film Warner Bros. made and was shot completely on location. For the first season, when the Western was part of Warner Bros.' rotating group of dramas, Cheyenne Bodie had a partner named Smitty, played by L. Q. Jones, fighting all the standard Western varmints. During the second season, *Cheyenne* alternated with *Sugarfoot* and with *Bronco* after that. There'd be 108 episodes, and on the first one, James Garner—then a young Warner Bros. contract player—guest starred. (He would later make several other appearances on *Cheyenne*, each time in a different role.) So did a number of the young Warner Bros. contract players of the time: Connie Stevens, Dennis Hopper, Angie Dickinson, Edd "Kookie" Byrnes, Roger Smith, and Peter Breck.

Three weeks after *Gunsmoke* hit the television trail, CBS rolled out *The Adventures of Champion*, a boy-and-his-horse Western. Gene Autry's famed steed was given his own show (under the aegis of Autry's Flying A Productions). Set in the 1880s, the Western aimed at the kid audience. It was scheduled for Friday at 7:30 p.m., opposite ABC's *Rin Tin Tin*, a boy-and-his-dog Western, and had the popular stallion looking after a twelve-year-old youngster in a series of thirty-minute adventures that lasted only until mid-season. CBS replaced Champion with another animal star, a handsome black stallion, in *My Friend Flicka*, another boy-and-his-horse (semi) Western.

None other than (who else?) Frankie Laine (Mr. Theme Song Balladeer for TV Westerns) was engaged by Autry to croon in his not-too-subtle way the opening over the *Champion* titles:

Like a streak of lightning flashing 'cross the sky
Like the swiftest arrow whizzin' from a bow
Like a mighty cannonball he seems to fly
You'll hear about him ever'where [sic] you go
The time will come when everyone will know
The name of Champion, the Wonder Hoooorse.
(Courtesy of composer Norman Luboff and lyricist Marilyn Bergman.)

My Friend Flicka was set on the fictional Goose Bar Ranch in Coulee Springs, Wyoming, around the turn of the century. It was based on Mary O'Hara's horse stories and the film with Roddy McDowall in 1943. Sharing adventures with Flicka was young Johnny Washbrook (in Roddy's old role). Crusty Gene Evans and lovely Anita Louise were the boy's loving parents.

Interestingly, the half-hour *Flicka* was shot in color but shown on CBS in black and white (Colgate-Palmolive was its sponsor). But when it later moved over to NBC on Sunday nights (sponsorless, for some reason, and odd since this show was aimed at youngsters and shown in the early evening, pre-primetime), it aired in color. Both *Champion* and *Flicka*, despite having young preteen boys at the show's core, were scheduled by CBS for early evening showing rather than on the weekends in the afternoon—between February 1956 and August 1957, *Flicka* was first on Friday evening, then on Saturday, then on Sunday, and finally on Wednesday.

In September 1955, at 7:30 p.m., NBC weighed in with *Frontier*, a high-class filmed anthology of supposedly fact-based Western stories, produced by TV drama pioneer Worthington Miner, created and mainly written by Morton S. Fine and David Friedkin. It was hosted/narrated by Walter Coy, who also acted in occasional episodes, of which there were thirty-one. "This is the West," McCoy would intone at the start of each episode. "This is the land of beginning again. This is the story of men and women facing the frontier. This is the way it happened." The *New York Times* TV reviewer found the premiere episode, directed by Don Siegel, to be "about a timid soul who was persuaded to masquerade as a killer, a superior adventure yarn." The paper felt that "with the other recent arrivals, *Gunsmoke* and the *Wyatt Earp* series, *Frontier* should provide Western fans with enough action to carry them nicely through the winter."

A la Walter Cronkite's familiar *You Are There* closing, "And that's the way it was," narrator Coy ended each show in the *Frontier* series with "It happened that way . . . moving West." *Frontier*, though, had to face off against *The Jack Benny Show*—and was doomed to just a single season.

For the Western crowd in 1955, there also were these half-hour syndicated hoss operas: *Steve Donovan, Western Marshal*, set in the 1870s, and *Buffalo Bill, Jr.*, aimed at the younger set. The former came from producer Jack Chertok, who also produced *The Lone Ranger*, and had veteran Douglas Kennedy in the title role, and Eddy Walter as Rusty Lee, the marshal's younger sidekick and deputy—upholding order in Wyoming Territory. "Lashing out of the pages of American history come the exciting tales of the early Western frontier. A primitive land torn by primitive conflicts and boiling with the feuds and lawless strife of frontier days. Here, on the rugged edge of civilization, some of the most desperate outlaws the world has ever known swarmed like a black plague, looting and robbing," the narrator intoned as each episode unfolded. "But here too, determined to bring peace and justice to this turbulent region of six-guns and sudden death, was another breed of men. The courageous officers appointed to wear the proudest badge of all, the badge of the Western marshal."

Buffalo Bill Jr. was from Flying A Productions and told of the exploits of an orphan (Dick Jones, once *Range Rider*'s young sidekick), adopted with sister Calamity (Nancy Gilbert) by a judge (Harry Cheshire) and subsequently named marshal of the fictional Wileyville, Texas, the town founded by the judge.

Also beginning around the same time were *Brave Eagle* (CBS, 1955–1956), *Tales of the Texas Rangers* (CBS, 1955–1957), and *Fury* (NBC, 1955–1960). One of the few Westerns told from the Indian viewpoint, *Brave Eagle* starred ruggedly handsome Keith Larsen, a paleface actor in Indian makeup playing the titular Cheyenne chief, along with Kim Winona, a real-life Sioux, as Morning Star, and another real Indian, Keena Nomkeena, as Brave Eagle's adopted son. Veteran vaudevillian Bert Wheeler played the obligatory comic role of Smokey Joe, a half-breed. Stories told in the half-hour series that aired on Wednesdays at 7:30 p.m. detailed the struggles of the Cheyenne with nature, other tribes, and encroaching white man. The series was developed by Roy Rogers's Frontier Productions.

Tales of the Texas Rangers was a series that basically showed the Indians' struggle and the white man's dominance, in the beginning at least. The show was unique, it has been noted, because its featured players—Texas Rangers Jace Pearson and Clay Morgan (played by Willard Parker and Harry Lauter)—covered 120 years of Western history and fiction, Old West bad guys, and more or less contemporary villains. The show debuted on CBS, Saturday morning, September 3, 1955. Its sponsors were General Mills' Trix and Tootsie Roll. The series moved to ABC in October 1958 for broadcast Thursdays at 5:00 p.m. Not long afterward, ABC began airing it later, on Monday evenings at 7:30. All told, it ran for sixty-two episodes.

Fury (later to be known as *Black Stallion*), another half-hour NBC Western, was about a rambunctious orphan boy and his horse. The popular series starred Peter Graves—older brother of *Gunsmoke*'s James Arness—playing Jim Newton, adoptive father of the kid (Bobby Diamond). Enterprising young Joey and four-legged companion Fury embarked on adventures in and around Newton's Broken Wheel Ranch. There were 113 episodes filmed between 1955 and 1960 airing on Saturday mornings. NBC kept the show going in reruns for another six years. The main theme, incidentally, was written by Ernest Gold, who'd go on to write the Academy Award-winning score to *Exodus*.

The 1955–1956 season had nine Westerns in primetime, excluding the syndicated shows. In the 1958–1959 season, there would be a record thirty-one Western series spread among the three networks.

In 1956, besides *My Friend Flicka*, CBS rolled out *Dick Powell's Zane Grey Theatre*, one of the tube's top Western anthology series of thirties crooner–turned forties screen tough guy–turned fifties TV producer. Powell hosted and frequently starred in episodes of this long-running anthology. Regularly cast with top-name guest stars, this well-appointed and well-written early Aaron Spelling production for Four Star dramatized in thirty-minute dollops most of the works of famed Western writer Zane Grey. Stars like Jack Lemmon, Jack Palance, Ida Lupino, John Payne, Danny Thomas, and Claudette Colbert acted in the many assorted dramas. "On the basis of the first show," the *New York Times* wrote on the Zane Grey premiere, "those who are addicted to Westerns should find this to their liking. Robert Ryan gave a convincing performance as a rancher who fought off a party of vigilantes bent on hanging him." The initial episode, "You Only Run Once," costarred Cloris Leachman.

Later, many of the episodes turned up in summer reruns under the umbrella title *Frontier Justice*, hosted first by Lew Ayres, then Melvyn Douglas, then Ralph Bellamy.

ABC's new Western lineup in 1956 featured both *The Adventures of Jim Bowie* and *Broken Arrow* (based on the 1950 James Stewart movie). The former, a half-hour weekly drama set in 1830s New Orleans (not exactly the West), followed the fictional exploits of legendary frontiersman/pioneer—and inventor of the Bowie knife—as he crusades for justice. The lead was played by Englishman Scott Forbes, who did not, for some reason, appear in every episode, although he played the title character. (The theme for the show was by Ken Darby and performed by his group the King's Men.) The real Jim Bowie, of course, took a prominent role in the Texas Revolution and died at the Alamo on March 6, 1836. ABC initially took a great deal of flack for the frequent use of the trademark knife, and this led to a cutback of violence on the show.

The *Broken Arrow* series, another thirty-minute Western, was one of those that cast the Indian in a sympathetic light. Before the series, there was a truncated version of the original film—under the title "Apache Uprising"—on the *20th Century Fox Hour*, with Ricardo Montalban in the lead. Michael Ansara got top billing on the series as Apache Chief Cochise (played in the feature film by Jeff Chandler) and John Lupton as Indian agent Tom Jeffords (the Jimmy Stewart role). Assigned to track down stolen guns used in Indian attacks on Pony Express riders, Jeffords endeavored to come to a mutual understanding with the Apache leader, and from this came respect for this particular white man. Jeffords became a blood brother and was bestowed the Indian symbol of friendship, the broken arrow, and they worked in harmony fighting both renegades from the local reservation and elements of the U.S. Army for the rest of the series, which lasted two seasons as a Tuesday-at-nine staple. Its theme was written by Paul Sawtell (music) and Ned Washington (lyrics).

Ansara had professed to having unhappy memories of playing his role in the series several years after it left the network and was sent into syndication (under the title *Cochise*) by ABC on Sunday afternoons. The series more or less typecast him. "Cochise could do one of two things—stand with his arms folded, looking noble, or stand with arms at his side, looking noble," he later said in a *TV Guide* interview.

ABC also brought back Gabby Hayes in 1956 for the young 'uns, at least for eight weeks on Saturday mornings, and the old-timer spun new Old West yarns and showed old cowboy clips as he did on *The Gabby Hayes Show* on NBC nearly six years earlier.

Veteran Western actor Edgar Buchanan had the title role in *Judge Roy Bean*, syndicated in 1956. Set in Langtry, Texas, the show was a half-hour Western—in color but only shown in black and white, like *The Cisco Kid*. Bean was known far and wide as the "Hanging Judge" and, as legend has it, referred to himself—as did others—as "the law West of the Pecos." He held court in a saloon-convenience store in a dusty town along the Rio Grande, so his biography notes, and he died in 1903. In the fictionalized series, Jack Buetel (best remembered for starring as Billy the Kid opposite Jane Russell in Howard Hughes's *The Outlaw* over a decade earlier) played Bean's right-hand man, Jeff Taggart. Cowboy star Russell Hayden produced the series and also turned up periodically as a Texas Ranger who had run-ins with the judge.

Legend also has it that the real judge became so enamored of British actress Lily Langtry, who toured the West in traveling stage shows, that he arranged for his town to be renamed for her. Heavyset Edgar Buchanan, of course, was no Paul Newman, who'd play the self-aggrandizing man of the law years later on the big screen, in *The Life and Times of Judge Roy Bean*. Walter Brennan won an Oscar for his portrayal of Bean in *The Westerner* in 1940. And several decades later, Bean was played by Ned Beatty in Larry McMurtry's *The Streets of Laredo* (among other Roy Beans on television).

Also in 1956, in syndication, *Red Ryder* rode across the plains maintaining law and order, as he had done to the delight of the small fry in films and comic books of the forties. Allan "Rocky" Lane was the stalwart star and Louis Lettieri was his young Indian sidekick, Little Beaver. Lane had the role in a handful of Red Ryder flicks in the midforties along with Bobby Blake. An earlier *Red Ryder* TV pilot, in 1953, featured Jim Bannon, who had played the part in several theatrical Red Ryder adventures in the late forties.

Circus Boy, a Western aimed at the kids that aired on NBC during the 1956–1957 season, followed a traveling circus playing the frontier in the late nineteenth century. It starred Robert Lowery as the circus boss, Big Tim Champion, but the title role was played by young Mickey Braddock as twelve-year-old circus orphan Corky, water boy to Bimbo the elephant in the show. (His parents had died in a high-wire accident, and now Big Tim is his guardian.) A number of veteran actors also were regulars, including Noah Beery Jr. as Joey the Clown; Guinn "Big Boy" Williams as Pete, chief roustabout; grizzled Andy Clyde; diminutive Billy Barty; and others. The filmed show was produced for Screen Gems by Herbert B. Leonard, who previously was associated with *The Adventures of Rin Tin Tin* and later went on to produce *Naked City* and *Route 66*. *Circus Boy* was dropped at the end of the season by NBC but picked up the following one by ABC. Mickey Braddock, the show's kid star, grew up to become Micky Dolenz of the Monkees.

With sturdy Dale Robertson riding tall in the saddle as Jim Hardie (actually the only regular cast member for its first few seasons), *Tales of Wells Fargo* was given a midseason premiere in March 1957 by NBC (initially Mondays from 8:30 to 9:00 p.m. into September 1961). Wells Fargo agent Hardie—and company troubleshooter—was an unofficial lawman tracking down varmints preying on his outfit's shipments and stage passengers.

Variety, at the time, referred to *Wells Fargo* as a lowbrow Western, and found it inconceivable that it could succeed against the new "adult" Western trend. "This Revue (MCA) series is strictly formula, with none of the characterization or human values that have embellished the better class of TV Westerns to date." How wrong. *Wells Fargo* became the second-highest rated Western series of the 1957–1958 season. The stalwart star told *Time* magazine, "The adult Westerns are dishonest. All that conversation is just a cheap, underhanded way of makin' up for the lack of a good story." *Wells Fargo* was all gunfights and fistfights, barroom brawls and shoot-outs, and the audiences lapped them up.

The show altered its format somewhat in late 1961 when it changed nights to Saturday (opposite *Perry Mason*), went to a full hour and color, and made a number of cast additions. (Composer Harry Warren wrote the musical theme to the show when it was expanded to sixty minutes minus commercials.) Jim Hardie now owned a ranch outside of San Francisco, run with the help of his young assistant Beau McCloud (Jack Ging) and his crusty foreman Jeb Caine (William Demarest). Several females also were added to the cast: Virginia Christine as a widow who owned the neighboring spread, and Mary Jane Saunders and Lory Patrick as her pretty daughters and sometimes distractions for Hardie and McCloud. Although Hardie continued taking an assignment or two from Wells Fargo, most of the action was confined to the ranch and its environs. Audiences, it has been pointed out, didn't cotton to Hardie's settling down to domestic life. NBC sent the show to Boot Hill. The pilot for this series aired as "A Tale [singular] of Wells Fargo" in 1956 on *Schlitz Playhouse of Stars*.

And Leon Ames starred in the relatively obscure 1956 syndicated series *Frontier Judge*. Ames was John Cooper, a circuit-riding judge of the Old West. Jack Chertok, who produced all of the original *Lone Ranger* TV Westerns, as well as *Sky King* and *Steve Donovan, Western Marshal*, produced this one that aired on ABC (according to a publicity brochure from Chertok Productions reproduced on the Web).

Sugarfoot and *Colt .45* were, like *Cheyenne* before them, from the Warner Bros. stable of Westerns. Each had a title appropriated from—but had nothing to do with—an earlier Warner Bros. film with Randolph Scott.

And like *Cheyenne*, both were produced by William T. Orr in the Westerns sweepstake in the new 1957 season. *Sugarfoot*, an hour-long series premiering in mid-September, starred amiable Will Hutchins as Tom Brewster, a fun-loving correspondence school lawyer from the East who loves his sarsaparilla and who for adventure wanders across the frontier of the 1860s, doing good where he can for people in distress. Somewhat inept as a laid-back cowboy and rather naïve—and, frankly, a lousy shot—Brewster acquired as a traveling companion a deceptively tough-looking hombre named Toothy Thompson (played by Western veteran Jack Elam), at least for the first season. In the premiere episode, "Brannigan's Boots," Brewster is made sheriff by a crooked mayor who happens to have a young hothead named William Bonney as one of his henchmen. Dennis Hopper guest starred as Billy the Kid. *Sugarfoot* lasted four seasons, alternating with *Cheyenne* for its first two and with the later *Bronco* for one. Will Hutchins later went on to play Dagwood Bumstead in the single-season *Blondie* series.

Colt .45, a thirty-minute weekly series that debuted a month after *Sugarfoot*, revolved around the efforts of Christopher Colt (Wayde Preston), a government agent posing as a gun salesman, to help stem lawlessness on the frontier during the 1880s. Colt was introduced in several episodes of *Sugarfoot*. The series itself was sold even before it was created ("You give us a half hour," William T. Orr reportedly told ABC when it alerted him that a national beer company wanted to sponsor a television program, "and we'll give you a show"). The series itself contained a plethora of action. Not all of it was on the screen, though. It's been noted that during its three seasons on the air, *Colt .45* was a hodgepodge of uncertain sponsorship, a walkout by its star, many repeat episodes, and an abrupt change in its lead actor—with no explanation.

Unfortunately as with Clint Walker in the earlier *Cheyenne*, Warner Bros. began encountering troubles with Wayde Preston, and ultimately another actor, Donald May, was brought in to play Christopher's cousin, Sam Colt Jr. (The real Sam Colt, father of this particular character, was the founder of the legendary gun company.) Preston, who had a thin résumé going into this role, had an even thinner one afterward—except in Europe, where he later went for filming.

One week after *Sugarfoot* premiered and two weeks before *Colt .45* began airing, ABC hit the mother lode with the hour-long lighthearted *Maverick*, which went on to become one of the best remembered shows of the Western genre. This one differed from most of the others in that its leads were devious brothers and semi-swindlers who'd rather be fleecing at the card table than chasing down bad guys. And they were cowards when it came to confronting bad guys (except that they invariably bested the varmints by their wits).

James Garner, awash with charm and already relatively known from the big screen, shot to TV stardom as Bret Maverick. He initially was to do the show alone but once the producers got into it, they decided that more help was needed to lighten Garner's load. Jack Kelly thus was introduced as the equally crafty Bart Maverick, and the two more or less alternated shows and stings. The show was riffing with clever dialogue and humorous situations. Through the years, other family members were brought in for relief, scoundrels all—such as Roger Moore, as English cousin Beau Maverick, and Robert Colbert as another brother, Brent. Diane Brewster became one of the few female cast regulars as adept swindler Samantha Crawford, one of Bret and Bart's pals. Garner also turned up in the series as his and Bart Maverick's own sly grandpa. (Garner's first role in Western duds was in a December 1956 episode of *Zane Grey Theatre*; the first as Bret Maverick, in an episode of *Sugarfoot* just about a year later.)

In his book *Maverick: Legend of the West*, Ed Robertson enlisted the famed show's creator Roy Huggins to provide the foreword. Huggins recalled (in 1997) that, among other things, "I never intended *Maverick* to be a satire on Westerns, because I didn't think that satire would work on a weekly basis. I never intended it to be an 'anti-Western,' either, although I *did* use that term for publicity purposes. But describing *Maverick* as an anti-Western is misleading because *Maverick* was a Western: it had to be confined to a certain period and geographical area, which limited the kinds of stories we could tell."

Huggins as creator/producer worked with executive producer William T. Orr and a core battery of directors, starting with Budd Boetticher, who called the shots on the first episode that aired on September 22, 1957 (opposite Steve Allen on NBC and *The Ed Sullivan Show* on CBS!). *Daily Variety*'s TV critic wrote, following the premiere, "*Maverick*'s well-staged action, leavened by nice touches of humor, serve to make a better than fair TV entry. . . . James Garner impresses as a fresh and rugged young personality, with a strong future in pictures." The trade reviewer's caveat: "However, with the video landscape a-crawlin' with adult Westerns, producer Roy Huggins will have to come up with better scripts to survive in the rating race."

The premiere episode, "The War of the Silver Kings," was adapted by writer James O'Hanlon from C. B. Glasscock's nonfiction 1935 book *War of the Copper Kings* (dealing with the perennial battle between Western miners and the money men back East). Reportedly, studio mogul Jack Warner mandated against paying royalties to writers for the creation of series based on their own original material. Thus Huggins, who had written the pilot, had to dump the original plotline to adhere to studio policy and use a property that Warner Bros. owned. (The score to *Maverick* was by the studio's David Buttolph with lyrics by Paul Francis Webster.)

James Garner was another of Warner Bros.' stars who had run-ins with the studio, and he walked out of the show in December 1960. For years afterward, he grumbled about the terms of his contract and, of course, residuals. Garner famously said (as reported years later in *TV Guide* on the eve of his comeback show, *Nichols* [more later]): "I thought I had some interest in the *Maverick* gold mine—but all Warners gave me was the shaft."

He and the studio never did come to what he considered equitable terms, although the courts found in his favor, and he never did return to the show. Meanwhile the studio had the other various Maverick relatives to pick up the slack. The original series left the air in July 1962, going to that big syndication market in the sky, but occasionally through the years it (and James Garner) returned to Maverick territory under other guises.

Ed Robertson wrote in his book on *Maverick*, "The lure of the legend that became Maverick explains why all three major television networks attempted to bring back [the show] in the late 1970s and early 1980s—and also accounts for the production of the 1994 *Maverick* feature." There was *The New Maverick* on ABC in 1978 (Garner starred, with his name above the title, while Jack Kelly's Bart was below in half the size. Garner's old pal Stuart Margolin directed the two-hour premiere episode "The Lazy Ace" and reprised his role of Philo Sandeen). Next, *Young Maverick* appeared on CBS in 1978 and finally *Bret Maverick* aired on NBC in 1982 (none of the three lasted long). And in the nineties big-screen version of the landmark show, Mel Gibson starred as Bret, and James Garner turned up as a marshal.

Garner and Kelly, as Bret and Bart, managed to cross paths on *Sugarfoot* in a Warner Bros.' Western crossover. For the record, of the 124 episodes of the original show, Garner starred in 59, Kelly in 79, and Moore in 17. Incidentally, Robert Redford made his acting debut (film or television) in a February 1960 episode of *Maverick*, entitled "The Iron Hand." (Of all the TV stars, few were able to move back and forth from the tube to the big screen as easily and consistently as A-lister James Garner.)

Tombstone Territory was one of ABC's lesser entries for the 1957 season, following the exploits of Tombstone newspaper editor Harris Clayton, who did his thing to preserve peace in the Old West through the power of the press and his editorials. Richard Eastham had the lead in the series that ran for a season and a half, with Pat Conway as Sheriff Clay Hollister and Gil Rankin as Deputy Charlie Riggs. This was never among the more notable television Western series of the era.

Erudite actor Richard Boone as Paladin, a suave West Point–educated, high-priced gun for hire, was introduced on CBS at the start of the 1957–1958 season in *Have Gun—Will Travel*, a refreshingly different take on the standard Western. Paladin, an immaculately clad man of culture who quoted poetry by Keats and Shelley and collected chessmen, operated as an Old West troubleshooter out of a fancy San Francisco hotel, the Carlton, in the late 1850s. He offered his services (bodyguard, courier, detective) by way of a calling card with the symbol of a chess knight and the simple legend "Have Gun, Will Travel. Wire Paladin, San Francisco." As has been noted, Paladin could shoot a villain and recite a Shakespeare soliloquy over the corpse. Black clad, intimidating, a loner, Paladin was a man of the West to be reckoned with. Richard Boone directed a number of the episodes and exercised firm control over every one of them. (Composer Bernard Herrmann wrote the show's atmospheric score—at least for the pilot episode. A singer-actor named Johnny Western came up with the title lyrics: "Paladin, Paladin, where do you roam / Paladin, Paladin, far, far from home." Pop star Duane Eddy would have a top-40 version of it in 1962.)

An overnight hit and hugely popular, the show aired for six seasons in its first run on Saturday nights from 9:30 to 10:00. Between 1958 and 1961 it was the number three program on television—following *Gunsmoke* and *Wagon Train* (three Westerns in the top three). There were 226 episodes. Subsequently it aired in syndication under the title *Paladin*.

Trackdown was CBS's other Western, a thirty-minute show premiering in late 1957 and running for two seasons (seventy episodes). With Sam Peckinpah as director (of at least the first story), Robert Culp starred as legendary Texas Ranger Hoby Gilman, ranging the West of the 1870s and hunting down bad guys. Gilman, it has been noted, looked for the moral justice behind each situation in which he found himself. True this might have been considered a formulaic Western, but it was not just a half hour of chase 'em and shoot 'em. Young Steve McQueen got his shot of subsequent TV stardom playing Josh Randall in what was to be a *Trackdown* spin-off, *Wanted: Dead or Alive*. Culp's Gilman was basically a loner—no sidekick—although one veteran actor, Norman Leavitt, played a character named Ralph in at least a third of the episodes, and Ellen Corby (later Grandma Walton) played a local named Henrietta Peters.

Exploits in the series were adapted from cases in the Texas Rangers file—and (as Jack Webb's *Dragnet* for the Los Angeles Police Department) Culp's show was given official approval from the (modern day) Rangers and the state of Texas. Vincent M. Fennelly produced for Four Star Productions.

NBC's entrée into the parade of TV Westerns in the fall of 1957 started with *The Restless Gun*, with John Payne, and *The Californians*, set in the gold rush days (each one ran for two seasons) and culminated with the huge hit *Wagon Train*. The Payne series (the pilot of which, called "Sixshooter," had aired earlier on *Schlitz Playhouse of Stars*) had the forties Fox leading man playing yet another itinerant, idealistic loner named Vint Bonner. A sympathetic working cowhand of sorts, Bonner roamed the post–Civil War Southwest, astride his mount Scar, trying to do good pragmatically without resorting to his more-than-proficient gunslinging.

Rugged John Payne never passed himself off as the similar in name and equally as recognizable John Wayne. Payne was one of the journeyman movie stars of the forties and fifties who was not a screen cowboy hero—he'd frequently be the leading man opposite musical stars Alice Faye or Betty Grable or June Haver. Of the eighty or so films he'd made, only six were Westerns. At the time of *The Restless Gun*, Payne told *TV Guide*, "As Bonner, I ain't a killin' man. I can be a fast draw when the script calls for it, but we don't concentrate on it. People sort of naturally gravitate toward Bonner when they've got problems." Payne concluded, "If there's such a thing as a next-door neighbor in a Western that's Vint Bonner."

On the show, Payne made certain he was the guy in charge—the executive producer, star, and occasional writer and director. Throughout the filmed series that aired during its two season run on Mondays nights 8:00–8:30, a number of future names had early roles, along with Western characters like Dan Blocker (a frequent guest before becoming Hoss Cartwright), and Chuck Connors and Johnny Crawford (though in separate appearances), later to costar in *The Rifleman*.

In 1958, Payne turned down NBC's offer to expand the series (produced by David Dortort, who wrote many of the episodes and then went on to create *Bonanza*) to a one-hour format from thirty minutes. After the seventy-seven episodes of *The Restless Gun*, Payne never starred in another Western—other than two guest shots on *Gunsmoke* and *Cade's County*.

"According to TV," author Gary Grossman pointed out, "the West won with the help of John Payne's *Restless Gun*, Lash LaRue's whip, and Chuck Connors's rifle." But times were a-changing as programmers sought out older audiences. Dick Jones, the star of *Buffalo Bill Jr.*, from Gene Autry's Flying A in the mid-fifties, told the press at the time of a bend in the trail, "Hollywood just stop making the rah-rah shoot-'em-up, good-guys-wear-white-bad-guys-wear-black Westerns. There were a whole bunch of psychological Westerns like *Gunsmoke* and *Maverick*, and people forgot about our Saturday morning shows." But it wasn't over overnight.

The Californians, like *Zorro* and one or two others, arguably only a Western tangentially, had a checkered history. In the beginning, it had a couple of guys, Dion Patrick, a San Francisco store owner, and Jack McGovern, an Irish immigrant hothead, who came West to pan for gold (actors Adam Kennedy and Sean McClory), throwing in their lot to become vigilantes. The network soon decided that the perceivable vigilante glorification was making sponsors nervous and changed direction in the middle of the first season.

NBC threw Kennedy and McClory under the bus, or more aptly, stage-coach, and brought in Richard Coogan to play the new character of Matt Wayne, who bought a local saloon; in the second and last season, he became the town marshal, keeping the rowdy miners and claim jumpers from roughing each other up. Once again composers Harry Warren and Harold Adamson provided the score. The Sons of the Pioneers sang the title song to *The Californians* on their RCA Bluebird album of the time, *Themes of TV's Greatest Westerns*.

In *Wagon Train*, NBC found a mega-hit in one of television's great Western series. This was a Western on a big canvas. Basically it was an anthology drama filled with what actually were name guest star character studies. Major stars (ranging from Ernest Borgnine in the opening episode to Bette Davis to Farley Granger, George Montgomery, Guy Madison, Shelley Winters, Ricardo Montalban, etc.) joined the wagon train along the trail from Missouri to California for a week at a time, playing the title role in the episode named after the character—before moving on. Anchoring it all was Ward Bond as the tough wagon master, Major Seth Adams, along with Robert Horton (for the first few seasons) as frontier scout Flint McCullough, Terry Wilson as assistant wagon master Bill Hawks, and Frank McGrath as grizzled Charlie Wooster, the cook. Bond and Horton reportedly never cottoned to one another. This was revealed in a *Newsweek* piece of the time. Horton was said to have bristled at not being given meatier roles, and later he left the wagons to star in the single-season *A Man Called Shenandoah*.

When Bond, a commanding figure, died while shooting during the 1960–1961 season, veteran actor John McIntire stepped in as wagon master to more than adequately fill his boots, playing Christopher Hale.

After the first five seasons, NBC lost the show to ABC for the next three, and for 1963–1964, expanded it from an hour to ninety minutes (a first for a Western series), then finally back to an hour. There'd be 440 episodes in all.

The genesis of *Wagon Train* was director John Ford's 1950 Western *Wagon Master*, which starred, among other Ford regulars, his old friend Ward Bond

(in a different role). It was because of Bond that Ford was coaxed into making a rare foray into TV, directing a November 1960 *Wagon Train* episode,
"The Colter Craven Story"—and to bring their mutual pal and drinking
buddy John Wayne with him in a just as rare TV acting role. Billed under
the pseudonym Michael Morris, Wayne played Civil War hero General Tecumseh Sherman.

CHAPTER FIVE

From *Wagon Train* and *Bonanza* to *The Virginian* and *The Big Valley*

Who was that *other* "masked man"? As with the Lone Ranger, couldn't people see through his minimal disguise? Whether *Zorro*, a Disney multi-parter starring Guy Williams as the masked do-gooder, belongs in an overview of Westerns might be questioned. Similarly *The Californians* or the later *Yancy Derringer* (set in post–Civil War New Orleans—not on the plains or the frontier or even the wild, wild West) or *The Alaskans* (set, of course, way up north), or those pre– and post–Revolutionary War adventures such as *The Last of the Mohicans* (set on what was the frontier of the time, western New York or Pennsylvania).

Zorro, airing on ABC on Thursdays for several seasons beginning in 1957, might better be referred to as an adventure swashbuckler set in Spanish California in the 1820s. The title character was a creation of Johnston McCulley from the early 1900s. Long before becoming a pop culture figure among the younger set in the fifties and sixties with a hit theme song, Zorro had been portrayed many times on the screen—by, among others, Douglas Fairbanks at the close of the silent era, John Carroll in a popular thirties Republic serial, dashing Tyrone Power in the forties, and Guy Williams, expert swordsman.

Zorro was actually Don Diego de la Vega, foppish son of a Spanish aristocrat, who secretly turns hero by battling tyrannizing dons and helping oppressed locals. His mute buddy was played by Gene Sheldon; his fat, talkative foil, by Henry Calvin; a local señorita by up-and-coming Disney find Annette Funicello. Funicello got a chance to sing a song or two in appearances on the show, but, surprisingly, it was Calvin who had a hit record of

Disney house composers George Bruns and Norman Foster's familiar theme song. Zorro was to return in several later series that had nothing to do with this one.

Among the half-hour syndicated Western series of the day (1957) were *26 Men*, *Boots and Saddles*, *Man without a Gun*, the aforementioned *Last of the Mohicans* (otherwise known as *Hawkeye*), and a Canadian series, *Tomahawk*. Based on historical fact—and seen by many as the equivalent of *Tales of the Texas Rangers*—*26 Men* was a straightforward action show that followed the circa 1900 exploits of Arizona Rangers, limited by law to just twenty-six, who maintained the territorial law in the dying days of the Old West. Former cowboy actor Russell Hayden produced and veteran Tris Coffin (usually, in dozens of B Westerns, he was the nastiest of varmints) starred as Captain Tom Rynning; Kelo Henderson starred as Ranger Clint Travis (others of the twenty-six were seen from time to time). Although rather simplistic in the Western scheme of things, there were about seventy-eight of these half-hour shows.

Boots and Saddles, another formulaic Western, managed thirty-nine filmed episodes and revolved around the officers and men of the Fifth Cavalry at Fort Lowell in Arizona Territory circa 1870. Told from the cavalryman's point of view regarding how they endeavored to live with the Apaches, the series starred Jack Pickard as Captain Shank Adams, Gardner McKay as Lieutenant Dan Kelly, Patrick McVey as Lieutenant Colonel Wesley Hayes, and Michael Hinn as scout Luke Cummings.

Man without a Gun, about a newspaper editor who endeavors to keep the peace in Yellowstone, Dakota, in the 1870s through the power of the press, starred Rex Reason as Adam MacLean along with Mort Mills as the town marshal, Frank Tallman. In the 1957 pilot for the show, Robert Rockwell (Mr. Boynton earlier on *Our Miss Brooks* and before getting the lead in *The Man from Blackhawk*) had the MacLean role.

The Gray Ghost was a 1957 syndicated Civil War Western of sorts, historical fiction based on the exploits of the real-life John Singleton Mosby, a daring Confederate officer with the First Virginia Cavalry who organized a guerrilla unit that staged lightning attacks on the Union troops. Known in Civil War lore as the Gray Ghost, Mosby was played in this syndicated series by Tod Andrews. Mosby was also the subject of several episodes of Disney's *Wonderful World of Color* series in the midsixties "Willie and the Yank" (Jack Ging was Mosby).

Hawkeye and the Last of the Mohicans (syndicated in 1957), from the James Fenimore Cooper classic, had John Hart—once, for a short while, the Lone Ranger—as the fur trader and pioneer in 1750s America, and Lon Chaney as his blood brother Chingachgook, from the last of the Mohicans tribe, teaming up as scouts for the U.S. Cavalry. A later incarnation of *Hawkeye* in 1994 costarred Lee Horsley as Natty Bumppo and Lynda Carter (no, "Wonder Woman" did not play Chingachgook). *Tomahawk*, like the other two Canadian-made shows, was set in the American Northwest of the 1700s. A pair of French Canadian actors starred.

Wanted: Dead or Alive, which made a superstar out of a then relatively unknown Steve McQueen (in his late twenties at the time) kicked off CBS's 1958–1959 season in grand fashion—from a Westerns standpoint. It differed from many shows of its genre by emphasizing action at the expense of character development. In this series, the chase was the story. McQueen played 1870s bounty hunter Josh Randall—a loner distrustful of the establishment—with his trusty sawed-off Winchester carbine he called his "Mare's leg," tracking down wanted men (and women) solely for the reward. "If I have to use it," Josh says of his Winchester, "I want to get the message across." In the initial episode, "The Martin Poster," on September 6, 1958, McQueen went after Michael Landon and Nick Adams, as a pair of murderous outlaw brothers. The series, produced by Vincent Fennelly for Four Star, traced its origins to a pilot episode of *Trackdown* in spring 1958 called "The Bounty Hunter."

At the end of the first episode of *Wanted: Dead or Alive*, the star stepped before the camera just before the closing theme with a sales pitch (not often seen on television)—aimed, it seems, not at the audience but at potential sponsors:

> Hi, my name is Steve McQueen. I hope you liked what you just saw. Kind of a new approach to Westerns. I hope you liked Josh Randall. Oh, he's not a lawman, but he's got a lot of friends who are. And they like him because he respects them and their jobs. Since Josh doesn't wear a badge, he can take the shortest distance between two people. . . . The stories in *Wanted: Dead or Alive* are about the people of the times: their dreams, their problems, their happiness. . . . Any way you slice it, *Wanted: Dead or Alive* is a good show, full of action, drama and adventure. Good entertainment for the whole family—and that's what'll sell any product. . . . See y'all now.

The popular McQueen series filmed ninety-four episodes and made his career—then he moved on to big screen stardom, and never looked back. (McQueen never again made an acting appearance on television.)

Ruggedly handsome Rory Calhoun (a lifelong Los Angeleno) was tapped by Desilu to play wandering ex-gunfighter Bill Longley in CBS's *The Texan*, premiering in September 1958 and running for two seasons (seventy-nine episodes). Despite being portrayed as a charming do-gooder of the Old West, always deferential to the ladies, Longley, a real figure, was one bad dude, a vicious gunslinger. According to the website legendsofamerica.com, Wild Bill Longley, born in 1851 and hanged at age twenty-seven in 1878 after having killed thirty-two men—most, legend has it, either black or Hispanic— "learned how to use a gun before he was a teenager and would soon prove to be one of the fastest draws in Texas with his deadly accurate aim and participation in numerous gunfights." (Longley was portrayed in a 1958 episode of *Tales of Wells Fargo* by Steve McQueen.) The only regular on the series, a fast gun who traveled the Texas frontier in the 1870s helping those in need, Calhoun—age thirty-seven at the time of *The Texan*—also narrated and was one of the producers, along with William T. Orr. Calhoun's Bill Longley, in addition, was the star of a series of comic books of the time (ten cents each!). Amusingly, he even guest starred on the popular Spring Byington sitcom *December Bride* in an episode titled "The Texan, Rory Calhoun" in May 1959. It's unlikely that he was there to help the quite self-sufficient Ms. Byington. The score for *The Texan*, incidentally, was written by William Loose, who was on the staff of Capitol Records' music department.

CBS heavily promoted its other new 1958 Western, *Yancy Derringer*, but it wasn't—a true Western, that is. Jock Mahoney returned here as a stylishly dressed New Orleans riverboat gambler of the 1880s who carried the titular pistol in his hat. His stoic companion (a sidekick of sorts) was Pawnee actor X Brands, who kept a knife in his headband. One of Yancy's female friends, Madame Francine, was played by Frances Bergen (ventriloquist Edgar's wife and actress Candice's mom). The half-hour show lasted one season.

ABC meanwhile brought along *Bronco* (for the network's 7:30–8:00 p.m. slot on Tuesdays for the first two seasons, Mondays for the remaining two— sixty-eight episodes) as a traveling companion for its *Sugarfoot*, and the two generally alternated. The newer show, produced for Warner Bros. by William T. Orr, starred Ty Hardin, as ex-Confederate army captain Bronco Layne, a loner who drifted across the Texas Plains in the 1860s, preferring to avoid trouble and conflict. His sometimes riding buddy was Jack Elam, bringing over his Toothy Thompson character from *Sugarfoot*. The Bronco character had been born, critics have noted, out of the dispute between Warner Bros. and Clint "Cheyenne" Walker, and occasionally turned up on Walker's show during his prolonged absence. ABC ultimately began airing this along with *Sugarfoot* and *Cheyenne* under the umbrella title *Cheyenne*. Among those who crossed paths with Bronco Layne in various episodes were James Coburn as Jesse James, Stephen Joyce as Billy the Kid, Jack Cassidy as Wild Bill Hickok, Jeanne Cooper as Belle Starr, Scott Marlowe as John Wesley Hardin, Efrem Zimbalist Jr. as Edwin Booth, Peter Breck as Theodore Roosevelt, and such up-and-comers as Troy Donahue and Mary Tyler Moore. *Bronco's* title theme was by Jerry Livingston and Mack David, and was sung at first by Hal Hooper and later by arranger Jack Halloran's vocal group; *Sugarfoot's* music was by Ray Heindorf and Paul Francis Webster—interpolating music by Max Steiner from earlier Warner Bros. big-screen Westerns.

Also on ABC's Westerns schedule, airing initially in September 1958, were *The Rifleman* with six-foot-five-and-a-half Chuck Connors and *The Lawman* with six-foot-three John Russell. The Connors show was really a family-oriented Western that ran for five seasons. (Conners once had played basketball with the Boston Celtics and then was a big league baseball player with first the Chicago Cubs and then the Brooklyn Dodgers in the late forties.) It dealt with 1880s New Mexico homesteader Lucas McCain, a widower, and his young son Mark (played by Johnny Crawford, starting out at age twelve) and their small cattle spread. Lucas was a onetime crack shot with a Winchester .44—hence the show's title—who has been teaching Mark life's values, and the show endeavored to keep violence to a minimum. Lucas became known as "the fastest man with a rifle." Like many of the Westerns of the era, *The Rifleman* started life as a CBS episode of *Dick Powell's Zane Grey Theatre* (which would spawn seven cowboy series!).

Among the other regulars on *The Rifleman*—created by Sam Peckinpah— were Paul Fix as Micah Torrence, the town marshal (a rather ineffectual one at that) whom Lucas often seemed to be bailing out; Joan Taylor as Miss Millie Scott, the McClains' "purdy" neighbor gal; Bill Quinn as Sweeney, the bartender at the local saloon; Hope Summers as storekeeper Hattie Denton (for the first two seasons); and later Edgar Buchanan as Dr. Jay Burrage. Patricia Blair was brought in during the middle seasons as hotelkeeper and onetime con artist Lou Mallory. Abby Dalton came aboard at some point as Nancy Moore, who ran the local hotel, and Gloria DeHaven was signed on late in the run as a love interest of sorts for Lucas. Creating a love interest for Lucas and having young Mark beginning to outgrow his cute-young-boy part was the "jumping the shark" moment and didn't help the show's ratings in the last season or so. Composer Herschel Burke Gilbert provided the musical score to the series. After *The Rifleman* left the air in first run in July 1963, it went to syndication heaven as *The Sharpshooter* for decades to come.

In *The Lawman*, a rugged, straightforward, no-nonsense Western, there was big, taciturn, granite-jawed John Russell riding tall in the saddle as Marshal Dan Troop of Laramie. Peter Brown was his young deputy Johnny McKay, who helped him maintain law and order and bring desperadoes, slimy varmints, and horse thieves to justice. Later, Peggie Castle came to town as Lilly Merrill, owner of the Birdcage Saloon, with Dan Sheridan as Jake, the bartender. William T. Orr produced this Warner Bros. series that lasted for 155 episodes and helped anchor ABC's Sunday night schedule until 1962.

The Rough Riders was the fourth new half-hour ABC Western (from the TV syndicator ZIV) that premiered at the beginning of the 1958–1959 season. It had three Civil War veterans, after Appomattox, teaming up to ride the range for peace now and justice later. The Rangers were Kent Taylor as Captain Jim Flagg and Peter Whitney as Sergeant Buck Sinclair, both having fought for the Union, along with Jan Merlin as Lieutenant Colin Kirby, who was an ex-Confederate. Among those whose trails cross theirs were guests like William Conrad, Lon Chaney Jr., Warren Oates, Leonard Nimoy, John Carradine, Dorothy Provine, and Broderick Crawford, who turned up as renegade Western leader William Quantrill.

NBC chose the third of July 1958 to introduce *Buckskin*, about the adventures of a ten-year-old living in his widowed mom's boardinghouse in the 1880s frontier town of Buckskin, Montana. The half-hour show managed to survive until September of the following year and was brought back for network reruns in the summer of 1965. Tommy Nolan was young Jody O'Connell and Sallie Brophy played his mother, Annie. Michael Road played Marshal Tom Sellers.

In October the Peacock Network debuted the half-hour *Bat Masterson*, starring Gene Barry as the legendary real-life lawman. In a frontier setting, Barry would play the character, maybe uncharacteristically, as a dapper and immaculately dressed gambler invariably seen with his derby hat and his gold-tipped cane—which hid a specially designed sword. Naturally he'd also have a gun in the holster strapped to his waist. Masterson was a now-traditional loner on TV—Barry was the only regular cast member. (The real Masterson had been a lawman, an Indian fighter, an army scout, and for a while, a deputy of Wyatt Earp.) Name and soon-to-be-name guests were encountered along the trail every week during the show's three seasons. One happened to be William Conrad, making what appears to have been his first on-screen TV acting role. A veteran of films (usually because of his bulk, the "heavy") and radio, he was a long familiar voice as narrator of countless television dramas and series, and was Matt Dillon on the radio *Gunsmoke* in the fifties. In addition, he even directed a number of *Bat Masterson* episodes.

George Montgomery, another of those taciturn, serviceable leading men from films of the forties who turned to being a cowboy star, played Mayor Matthew Rockford, in the NBC Western *Cimarron City*, which premiered in October 1958 and ran for three seasons. His domain was a boomtown on the rough-hewn Oklahoma frontier of 1890. In addition to narrating the series, he was a cattle baron whose best buds in town were Audrey Totter as Beth Purcell, who ran the local boardinghouse, and John Smith as Lane Temple, the sheriff. Incidentally, Montgomery had the unique distinction while still a relatively major film star of playing, variously, Davy Crockett, Bat Masterson, Pat Garrett, desperadoes Jack McCall and Billy Ringo, James Fenimore Cooper's Hawkeye and Pathfinder, and Raymond Chandler's Philip Marlowe—this all in addition to being Dinah Shore's husband.

Jefferson Drum was an NBC Western set in the lawless gold-mining town of Jubilee during the 1850s. In the titular role, Jeff Richards played an embittered newspaper editor who, following his wife's murder, heads West and decides to take over the town paper after the former publisher's killing. Game show producers Mark Goodson and Bill Todman had, in *Jefferson Drum*, one of their few dramatic series.

From the world of syndicated drama there were several 1958 Westerns. *Union Pacific*, a weekly drama revolving around the building of the railroad across the frontier (at least the last link between Missouri and Wyoming). The show's regulars were Jeff Morrow as operations head Bart McClelland, Judd Pratt as surveyor Bill Kincaid, and Susan Cummings as Georgia, who ran the saloon located, at least for the show, in one of the railroad cars. (There had been a big-screen feature with the same title in the late thirties, starring Joel McCrea, which had nothing to do with this thirty-nine-episode series.)

MacKenzie's Raiders starred Richard Carlson, a colonel with the U.S. Fourth Cavalry, assigned to attempt to end a reign of terror by marauding Mexican renegades and establish law and order using a special detail of undercover agents. The series was set in 1870s Texas and also ran for thirty-nine episodes—based loosely on the exploits of the real Colonel Ranald MacKenzie, who appears to have had a richer, more adventurous life than depicted on television.

Frontier Doctor had veteran screen cowboy Rex Allen doing good as a physician in the Arizona Territory (the fictional town of Rising Springs). This show was nearly classified as a contemporary Western, being set in the early settlement days of the twentieth century.

Sheriff of Cochise was a contemporary Western/crime drama that starred John Bromfield as lawman Frank Morgan—for the first couple of seasons, upholding the law as sheriff in modern-day Cochise County, Arizona; for the last couple, as the federal marshal working in Arizona. (The first thirty-nine episodes were later syndicated as *Man from Cochise*; the last thirty-nine syndicated separately as *U.S. Marshal*.)

And in the realm of "was it or wasn't it a Western" there was *Casey Jones*. We'll err on the side of the Western since it dealt–if only fictiously—with the legendary Cannonball Express engineer for the Midwest and Central Railroad in the last half of the nineteenth century. This half-hour syndicated adventure starred Alan Hale Jr., six or so years before becoming the befuddled skipper on *Gilligan's Island*. Mary Lawrence played Casey's wife Alice, and Bobby Clark their son Casey Jr.

Then came the landmark year of 1959—when there were thirty-one weekly Westerns in prime-time television. If 1939 always is considered the greatest year in feature films, then 1959 was the greatest for the TV Western. The three networks introduced twelve new Western series in the fall of that year—but only two of them lasted for more than three seasons. Leading the (new) parade was CBS's *Rawhide*, premiering January 9, 1959, to the strains of the notable Ned Washington/Dimitri Tiomkin whip-cracking theme sung by Frankie Laine ("Head 'em up! Move 'em out!"), and anchoring the Friday evening schedule. Loosely based on a real-life cattle drover's diary from the 1860s, the series had Eric Fleming as trail boss Gil Favor, a man's man; country singer Sheb Wooley as scout Pete Nolan; Paul Brinegar for comic relief as cantankerous trail cook Wishbone; and, of course, Clint Eastwood as ramrod Rowdy Yates. (By then, twenty-eight-year-old Clint had already done a Western or two on television: an episode of *Maverick* here, of *Death Valley Days* there.) Years later Eastwood recalled to the *Los Angeles Times*, "I was the dumb sidekick, the one who wasn't too swift, the one with a little slack lip." Of the show, Eastwood said, "They were fun years, and they were frustrating, too. I grew to hate exposition and lots of dialogue because on *Rawhide* we had to explain everything in the dialogue." And he concluded, "It was frustrating, too, because I wanted to direct a show or two, but they always found an excuse for me not to. I was pigeonholed as an actor." Who knew?

Rawhide—originally called by creator Charles Marquis Warren "Cattle Drive"—was basically about cattle drives, back and forth across the plains, with people the trio meet up with along the way. In the fall of 1965, for the show's last season (it ended in January 1966), Rowdy Yates takes over as trail boss and organizes his own team to start another drive. *Rawhide* was to have been a September 1958 show, but the network initially had trouble finding a sponsor. The series was an expensive one—sixty minutes at roughly forty thousand dollars per episode. The pilot episode, "Incident West of Lano," was completed in July 1958 with location footage shot near Nogales, Arizona. It turned out to be the eighth episode shown! (Every episode's title through the end of the 1963–1964 season began with the word "Incident."

All told, there would be 217 stories.) As has been pointed out, *Rawhide* was to cattlemen what *Wagon Train* was to pioneers traveling West.

CBS also debuted *Johnny Ringo* and *Hotel de Paree* in 1959. Ringo, played by Don Durant, was an ex-gunfighter turned sheriff, bound to keep law and order in the Arizona town of Veladri during the 1870s, with his deputy, Cal-ley "Kid" Adonas (Mark Goddard). Ringo's lady friend, Lara Thomas, was played by Karen Sharpe. The pilot for this show, created and mostly written by Aaron Spelling, was "The Loner," earlier in the year on *Zane Grey The-atre*. *Hotel de Paree*, premiering one night after *Johnny Ringo* and starring Earl Holliman, followed the exploits of the Sundance Kid, gunfighter turned law enforcer and part owner of the titular hotel in Georgetown, Colorado, with two French women (mother and daughter, played by Jeanette Nolan and Judi Meredith). Sundance maintained flirtations of sorts with both. Also in the cast was veteran performer Strother Martin as the local shopkeeper, Aaron Donager. Various good guys and villains included Theodore Bikel, Sebastian Cabot, Brian Donlevy, Jack Elam, Martin Milner, and Peter Mark Richman. And there even was a comic-book adaptation along the way. Each of these shows lasted just one season.

NBC's big one, premiering in September 1959, was *Bonanza*, the first Western to be televised in color and a truly iconic one. Unbelievably, *Va-riety*'s critic called it, on its premiere, "a long shot—without a fresh twist to distinguish it." It followed the weekly hour-long adventures (individually and collectively) of the Cartwrights on the Ponderosa, a thousand-square-mile timberland ranch outside of Virginia City, Nevada, not long after the Civil War. The four leads in the series had rotating billing in the show's opening from week to week. The admittedly macho, testosterone-driven, all-male cast was headed by Lorne Greene as patriarch Ben Cartwright and his three sons (from different marriages): Pernell Roberts as oldest son Adam, the brainy one; beefy Dan Blocker as Hoss, the middle—rather mountain-ous—one; Michael Landon as often impulsive "Little Joe." Helping them run the spread was Victor Sen Yung as the ever trusty Hop Sing, the cook on the Ponderosa.

The show's memorable theme song, composed by Jay Livingston and Ray Evans (who'd written "Buttons and Bows," "Mona Lisa," and "Que Será Será," among many others), had the unique distinction of being performed once at the end of the first show—with Ben, Adam, Hoss, and Little Joe sad-dling up to *sing* the lyrics—never to be heard again on the series!

Bonanza's protagonists, it must be remembered, were not lawmen, as in *Gunsmoke*, or gunfighters, as in *Tate*, or bounty hunters, as in *Wanted: Dead or Alive*, but typical Westerners—homesteaders—making a living off the land.

Pernell Roberts, a classically trained stage performer who earlier had gained a bit of fame in Shakespearean roles, told the *New York Times* in a 1965 interview, "I feel I am an aristocrat in my field of endeavor. My being part of *Bonanza* is like Isaac Stern sitting in with Lawrence Welk." Around the same time he told the *Washington Post*, "Isn't it just a bit silly for three adult males to get Father's permission in everything they do?" A political activist, Roberts was reported to have chafed at the mostly white complexion of the cast (except of course, Victor Sen Yung), and to have frequently clashed with the show's writers and producer "about the scripts, character development and other things." So he bolted. (When he died in January 2010, it was noted that he was the last of the Cartwrights.)

After Roberts left in 1965 and his character written out, David Canary as Candy, a wandering cowpoke, signed on as a ranch hand—and practically became a family member. The series dealt primarily with the relationships among the principals and with guest stars who moseyed onto the scene. There was virtually no violence in the series—this was not of the shoot-'em-up variety. Another "departure" occurred in May 1972 with the sudden death of Dan Blocker, which may or may not have been a factor in *Bonanza*'s decline the following season. Although only moderately successful for the first two years as a Saturday night NBC entry, *Bonanza* really took off when it moved to Sundays at 9:00 p.m. (for the next eleven years), and between 1964 and 1967 it was the number one show on television.

While the show was a huge success on Sundays—the premiere episode, "A Rose for Lotta," had Yvonne DeCarlo guest starring as nineteenth-century actress Lotta Crabtree, whose carriage breaks down on Ponderosa land and Little Joe fixes it for her—NBC began airing reruns in prime time on Tuesdays under the title *Ponderosa* in summer 1972. *Bonanza* itself moved into that Tuesday time slot in its final half season (1972–1973).

The score for *Bonanza*, other than the familiar Livingston and Evans theme song, was composed by David Rose, a music veteran of radio and films (and once married to Judy Garland). Rose previously had a long association, first on radio and then on television, with Red Skelton (he was music director for Red's entire twenty-year run on TV) before taking on *Bonanza* for its own long run. Jon Burlingame has written that "[Producer David] Dortort not only gave Rose an orchestra of as many as thirty-five musicians, he [Rose] also insisted upon scoring every episode (despite union regulations that, at the time, permitted extensive tracking). The result was one of the richest sounding series of the era, often comparable to the lush sounds of Rose's concert albums." Rose scored the vast majority of the 430 episodes, often orchestrating his own scores. Michael Landon later came to rely on

Rose for *Little House on the Prairie*—204 episodes. Before *Little House* (and its several TV-movie sequels), for Rose there were two more Western series, *The Monroes* in 1966 and *Dundee and the Culhane* the following season. And for Dortort he also wrote the sweeping main theme to *The High Chaparral*. In between, Rose also managed to find time to write a concert piece or two as well as the Grammy-winning pop hit "The Stripper"! He's the rare artist who won Grammys in pop, jazz, and classical music.

Bonanza went on to become the third-longest running Western on television—after *Death Valley Days* and *Gunsmoke*—and an American cultural phenomenon. (Thirty years later the syndicated series *Bonanza: The Next Generation* continued the saga of the Cartwrights with an all-new cast.) Michael Landon's son, later a prominent television director, played the son of his late dad's character here—as he did in a couple of follow-up TV movies: *Bonanza: The Return* (1993) and *Bonanza: Under Attack* (1995). Landon Jr. also cohosted an NBC retrospective special, *Back to Bonanza*, in 1993, with Dan Blocker's son, Dirk.

A new syndicated series called *The Ponderosa*, developed as a *Bonanza* prequel by David Dortort who had created the original series, aired in 2001, premiering on PAX just two days before 9/11. This one, filmed in Australia, returned to the initial grouping of Ben, Adam, Hoss, and Little Joe Cartwright—with a new cast—since three of the four originals had died. This series lasted for twenty episodes, through May 12, 2002.

Scheduled by NBC to follow *Bonanza* in 1959, and premiering the same night, was *The Deputy* starring Henry Fonda in his TV series debut. Three nights after *Bonanza* and *The Deputy* first aired, NBC offered up *Laramie*. *The Deputy*, which would rack up seventy-six episodes, revolved around Marshal Simon Fry and his attempts to maintain the law in Silver City, Arizona, during the 1880s. Fonda as the father figure had a somewhat contentious relationship with Allen Case, as Clay McCord, a young storekeeper and the peace-loving titular character. Fonda may have been given star billing in the series ("That was the Arizona Territory in 1880, and I was its chief marshal," he regularly said over the closing credits), but, apparently, he appeared in only a dozen or so episodes, and in others, he was on-screen only briefly, though he narrated.

Generally, when Fonda wasn't on the scene, the law in Silver City was administered by an older marshal, Herk Lamson, played by veteran actor Wallace Ford, in the first season, and then in the second by Sergeant "Sarge" Tasker, a one-eyed cavalry officer (Read Morgan). After this series, Allen Case would go on to play Frank James in *The Legend of Jesse James* in the midsixties.

Laramie had Slim Sherman and his teenage brother Andy (played by John Smith and Bobby Crawford Jr.) as homesteaders who, with the help of a drifter named Jess Harper (Robert Fuller), operated a swing station ranch and stage depot in 1880s Wyoming Territory. Their dad had been gunned down by land grabbers. Playing Jonesy (for the first season, at least), best friend of the Shermans' late dad, was singer/composer Hoagy Carmichael. Nanette Fabray, Ernest Borgnine, Lloyd Nolan, James Coburn, Edmond O'Brien, Rod Cameron, Brian Keith, and Thomas Mitchell were just some of the guest stars who turned up at or around Slim and Andy Sherman's stage depot. In an overview of the 1960–1961 season, *TV Guide* wrote at the time about the togetherness of the "mature" Westerns that is "a virtue that is spreading throughout the West like prairie fire. In *Laramie* the theme is four hardy fellows against half the people in Wyoming. In *Bonanza* it is a fighting family of Cartwrights against all the unwashed villains west of Jersey City. It is a wholesome idea, we suppose, but it does get kind of preachy." In any event, *Laramie*, with a score by Cyril J. Mockridge, ran for 104 episodes.

Then came NBC's *Riverboat*, with Darren McGavin as the stern-wheeler captain, Grey Holden, plying the Mississippi, Missouri, and Ohio rivers during the 1840s. (So was this, like *Yancy Derringer* and one or two others, truly a Western, or just an "adventure" series set in the nineteenth century?) Holden had won the boat in a poker game. His pilot, Ben Frazer, was played by Burt Reynolds, who left the show after one season—to be replaced, more or less, by Noah Beery Jr., as Bill Blake. Elmer Bernstein wrote the score for the hour-long period drama in what has been noted as a distinctly American idiom. Author Jon Burlingame noted, "The rhythms and colors heard throughout the pilot, and fourteen subsequent Bernstein-scored episodes that first season, presaged the famous score that he would compose the following year for *The Magnificent Seven*."

In his only television series, Joel McCrea acted opposite his son, Jody, in NBC's 1959–1960 Western *Wichita Town*, playing sturdy Marshal Mike Dunbar and his deputy Ben Matheson, respectively, maintaining law and order in 1870s Kansas. *Wichita Town* had no relationship to Joel McCrea's earlier feature film *Wichita*, in which he played Wyatt Earp. (It should be noted that in his screen career, after turning into one of the great cowboy stars from the midforties onward, McCrea also played such legendary figures as Buffalo Bill Cody, Bat Masterson, Sam Houston, and the Virginian.) Music for *Wichita Town* was by Hans J. Salter.

In October 1959, NBC debuted *Law of the Plainsman*, with, following his Cochise role, Syria-born Michael Ansara as Deputy U.S. Marshal Sam Burkhart—who happened to be an Apache Indian. (For whatever reason,

Ansara was typecast on TV as American Indian or other ethnic characters.) Burkhart turned out to be a Harvard-educated lawman—thanks to the patronage of a cavalry captain he had found and nursed back to health after the captain was wounded in an Indian ambush (that's the show's backstory)—and had returned West to New Mexico where he'd spent his youth. There he became a lawman under older marshal Andy Morrison (veteran Western actor Dayton Lummis) and helped uphold the peace in the often hostile territory. The series originated as two episodes of *The Rifleman* titled "The Indian" and "The Raid," earlier that year. Later it became part of a syndicated package along with other TV oaters such as *The Westerners*, hosted by Keenan Wynn. In summer 1962, ABC reran *Law of the Plainsman* episodes in prime time.

NBC also had premiered *Black Saddle* in January 1959, but the following September it moved over to ABC for its fall lineup, which included two other Westerns, *The Rebel* and *The Man from Blackhawk*. Peter Breck starred in *Black Saddle* as Clay Culhane, who decides not to follow the family tradition of being a gunfighter after losing his brothers to a shooter, but to study the law. He travels throughout New Mexico after the Civil War, carrying his law books in his saddlebags, offering possible legal assistance to those who need it. Also starring was Russell Johnson as Marshal Gib Scott, who was somewhat unbelieving that the would-be lawyer had really forsaken his guns. The music for *Black Saddle* was by veteran composer Jerry Goldsmith. "Because [he] was still under contract to CBS at the time," Jon Burlingame observed in *TV's Greatest Hits*, "he penned it under a pseudonym—that of his then brother-in-law J. Michael Hennagin—and never received screen credit for his fast, rhythmically exciting theme for guitars, brass, and percussion."

Nick Adams had the starring role as Johnny Yuma in ABC's half-hour *The Rebel*, sort of an intellectual Western about an embittered ex-Confederate soldier looking for inner peace and self-identity while roaming the West as a loner. This was another of those dramatic series produced by the Goodson-Todman company. Johnny Cash sang the theme song (by composer Richard Markowitz and producer Andrew Fenady), although in the never-aired pilot it was Cash's Sun Records pal Elvis Presley who performed it. NBC reran many of the episodes in prime time in the summer of 1962.

The Man from Blackhawk had Robert Rockwell as Sam Logan, who was an investigator for Chicago's Blackhawk Insurance Company, rather than a lawman or gunslinger. When in a jam, he resorted to his fists rather than a sidearm as he roamed from place to place, looking for all the world like a city slicker with a briefcase, settling claims in the Old West and investigating fraud attempts against his company. *Variety*'s review of the premiere show concluded, "It seems to be a run of the assembly line costume adventure series." The filmed ABC show from Screen Gems that aired Fridays at 8:30 p.m. lasted just one season.

On the syndicated front, there was the 1959–1961 Western, *Shotgun Slade*, which starred Scott Brady. He was a detective on horseback who had a specially designed double-barreled shotgun. One latter-day reviewer labeled this one a nineteenth-century *Peter Gunn*. The show was replete with a cool tough guy; a sultry singer named Monica, played by singer Monica Lewis; a dame that ran the saloon (Marie Windsor); a Mancini-like jazz score by Gerald Fried; and even a title song, "Shotgun Slade of the Two-Barreled Gun," performed by Lewis.

In its review of the initial episode airing in November 1959, *Variety* judged that "Lead Scott Brady [as a gun for hire] is one of those kissing cowboys, preferring women over horses. (He's liable to be read out of the traditional Cowpoke Party for that sin.)" The critic then went on to note that in just thirty minutes, "there was an ambush, a mine explosion, a drag-out fight in a saloon, a hanging, guns firing away, thisaway, thataway. The episode bristled with action, a good deal of which didn't make much sense." The guest star in the premiere episode was, of all people, Ernie Kovacs as a bewhiskered desert rat heavy. *Variety* said, "Kovacs pulled a real surprise. . . . If he ever gives up his cigar and the Nairobi Trio, he might have a future in Dodge City."

Nat Holt, who had done so many Randolph Scott films, produced *Shotgun Slade*. He also was the producer of the earlier *Tales of Wells Fargo* and the later *The Overland Trail* and *The Tall Man*, Westerns all.

Another syndicated show airing for the first time in 1959 was *Pony Express*. Through the years there'd be a number of series (and pilots for prospective ones) about the Pony Express. This was one of the first—a half-hour Western with relatively little known actors like Grant Sullivan, as Brett Clark, troubleshooter in the 1860s for the Central Overland Express Company—better known as the Pony Express—and Bill Cord and Don Dorell as riders Tom Clyde and Donovan (no first name, apparently). Among the better-known (than the lead) guest stars involved in the riders' travels were Burt Reynolds, Claude Akins, Dickie Jones (best remembered for *The Range Rider* and *Buffalo Bill Jr.*), Denver Pyle, Monte Blue, Madlyn Rhue, and others. The series filmed thirty-nine episodes.

NBC debuted *The Overland Trail* in February 1960, but the road ended the following September. It was a one-hour show airing on Sunday nights at 7:00. William Bendix and Doug McClure starred as stagecoach drivers crusty Frederick Thomas Kelly, who fought in the Union army, and, riding shotgun for him, Frank "Flip" Flippen, an adventurous soul who had been raised by

Indians. It's been noted that casting a popular sitcom star (*The Life of Riley*) in a role somewhat alien to the TV viewer—despite the fact that Bendix had a long career in films as a tough bruiser, not just a light comedian—didn't help grab an audience. This series got the jump by several months on ABC's similar *Stagecoach West*, but it didn't last as long—just seventeen episodes.

Tate, another short-lived NBC series that was a summer 1960 replacement for *The Perry Como Show* (at least half of it) followed the exploits of a wandering one-armed gunfighter. His arm, encased in rawhide-stitched black leather, had been shattered during the Civil War, but he was determined to go town to town and sell his services as a fast gun. David McLean had the title role. Later McLean went on to do guest bits on many TV Westerns and then gained fame as the Marlboro Man in a long series of cigarette commercials. Ultimately he died of lung cancer.

Even shorter in its run (just five weeks in summer 1960), was NBC's *Wrangler*, which starred Jason Evers as two-fisted Pitcairn, another footloose cowpoke in the 1880s West, helping those he finds in trouble, while fighting rustlers, hostile Indians, thieving varmints, horse thieves, and others. *Wrangler*, which came out of KTLA, had the distinction of being the first outdoor dramatic series to be shot exclusively on videotape. Reportedly, it was plagued from the start with technical problems, including a remote video crew forced to work under a film director or two unfamiliar with TV, causing what became tales of last-minute panic that are apparently legendary at the station to this day.

The Tall Man and *Outlaws* were NBC's two major Western entries at the start of the 1960–1961 season. *The Tall Man* fictionalized the adventures of Billy the Kid and Pat Garrett. Clu Gulager played the former, Barry Sullivan the latter, friends although on opposite sides of the law. In real life, of course, Deputy Garrett killed Billy in a showdown on July 14, 1881, when outlaw William H. Bonney was just twenty-two—although some Western historians, to this day, maintain it never happened, that Billy lived well into the twentieth century and died in bed.

Outlaws, an hour-long NBC Western airing Thursdays at 7:30 p.m., was set in the town of Stillwater, Oklahoma, during the 1890s. Barton MacLane starred as Marshal Frank Caine and Jock Gaynor played his deputy Heck Martin (both for the first season); Don Collier played fellow deputy Will Forman. The *New York Times* was rather underwhelmed by this show, finding it "molded from the same drab clay as most of the other Westerns of TV," and calling it "a dispensable entry . . . an unnecessary waste of time." The first season showed the action from the viewpoint of the outlaws the marshals were chasing. The second season had the perspective through the eyes of the marshals. Except for Don Collier, the second season featured an entirely new cast, including singer Bruce Yarnell as Deputy Marshal Chalk Breeson; Slim Pickens as Slim, a colorful sidekick; and Judy Lewis (Loretta Young's daughter) as a love interest. The score for the show was one of the few for television by veteran film composer/arranger/orchestrator Hugo Friedhofer, who also later did *The Guns of Will Sonnett* and *Lancer*.

Also on NBC was the short-lived Brian Keith series, *The Westerner*, in which he played Dave Blassingame, who wanders through the Old West—sometimes drunk—looking for causes to champion among exploited pioneers he meets. He carries a .405 Winchester repeating rifle with a telescopic sight and is accompanied by his dog, a rather large mongrel named Brown. The only other regular on the show (September to December 1960) was John Dehner as Burgundy Smith, a spiffily dressed con man he and Brown keep running into. The series was created, produced, and directed by Sam Peckinpah, who would go on to bigger and exceedingly more violent Westerns in feature films. "Too adult," he was said to complain about the show's being cancelled. Peckinpah at this point already had honed his writing skills working on *Trackdown*, *Have Gun—Will Travel*, *Broken Arrow*, *Tombstone Territory*, *The Rifleman*, and at least ten *Gunsmoke* episodes.

Brian Keith's Dave Blassingame was introduced in an episode of *Dick Powell's Zane Grey Theatre* in March 1959. *The Westerner* character later came back in a pilot on *The Dick Powell Theater* in 1963. This time Lee Marvin played Blassingame and Keenan Wynn was Burgundy. Robert Mitchum hosted the pilot, which also featured Rosemary Clooney, in a rare dramatic role. Brian Keith's *Westerner*, it should be noted, had no relationship to a syndicated 1953 pilot with the same title and starring James Craig.

In 1960, ABC offered just one new Western. The hour-long *Stagecoach West* starred Wayne Rogers (later to star in *M*A*S*H* and then go on to become a financial guru on cable television), along with Robert Bray—playing Luke Perry and Simon Kane, drivers for Overland Stage Coach Lines in the eighties. This was kind of a *Wagon Train* in less frontier-like surroundings, with guest stars as assorted passengers along the route from Missouri to California and back. Also along for the ride, more or less as a regular, was Kane's young son David (played by Richard Eyer).

However ABC did have a sitcom that posed as a Western of sorts, a contemporary one, set on a dude ranch in New Mexico. Called *Guestward Ho*, it starred in the unaired Desilu pilot Leif Erickson and Vivian Vance as the couple from the big city who open the dude ranch, which they have bought sight unseen and found to be rather run down. Erickson's and Vance's roles were taken in the one-season series by Mark Miller and

Joanne Dru. J. Carrol Naish was on board as Chief Hawkeye, the comical Indian neighbor who runs the local general store and sells Native American trinkets and is the subject of several individual episodes. One, called "The Honorary Indian," featured Milton Frome and Bella Bruck as Mr. and Mrs. Crazy Horse! The whole affair was based on the book by Patrick Dennis (of *Auntie Mame* fame) and Barbara Hooten—played in the pilot and series by Vance/Dru.

There also was a little-seen syndicated Western during 1960, called *Two Faces West*, with Scottish actor Charles Bateman playing two roles: sometimes hotheaded Marshal Ben January and sometimes his twin brother, Dr. Rick January, who's also what can be described as a trail bum. The town of Gunnison, Colorado, during the 1860s was the setting. Also in the cast were Joyce Meadows as Julie Greer, the local hotel owner; June Blair as Stacy, the saloonkeeper; Francis DeSales as Sheriff Maddox; and Paul Comi as Deputy Johnny Evans. Among the actors who appeared in the series, which lasted for thirty-nine episodes, were then little-known Ryan O'Neal, Dyan Cannon, and Leonard Nimoy.

Additionally, there was *Whiplash*, a 1960–1961 Australian Western, which featured Peter Graves—James Arness's brother, who was star of the 1955–1960 *Fury*—playing Christopher Cobb, the American owner of a stagecoach line that's running on Australia's first stage route. Graves was the only American in the all Aussie cast. The thirty-four-episode series, in which Graves as Cobb did not sport a pistol but relied on a bullwhip when needed, was loosely based on the exploits of real-life Freeman Cobb, who founded Australia's Cobb and Co. Similar in concept was the Aussie series *Five Mile Creek* three decades later.

NBC's *Whispering Smith*, debuting in late spring 1961, may or may not be considered a Western, even though it was set in Denver, Colorado, in the 1870s. Whatever it is, it had an unusual history. Based loosely on the Alan Ladd *Whispering Smith* movie of the late 1940s, it featured World War II–hero–turned–cowboy star Audie Murphy (in his only TV series), along with pop singer Guy Mitchell and actor Sam Buffington. The series was filmed in 1959–1960, when Mitchell had a serious accident on the set. To compound this Buffington died before the series finished filming (he committed suicide). Question remains why the network bothered going ahead with the show that had been in the can for two years—less two of its three leads.

Now as to whether *Whispering Smith* was a true Western or simply a crime drama, one could argue either way: For the record, the show had Audie Murphy as soft-spoken Denver police detective Tom Smith, a lawman who used not only his wits but also his skill with a Colt .45, and it incorporated modern methods of analysis and apprehension in the practice of law enforcement in the West.

Stories, based on Frank H. Spearman's 1907 novel about this pioneer criminologist of the Old West and utilizing actual case histories from the Denver Police Department, follow Tom as he sets out to solve crimes based on the new technology. Mitchell played Detective George Romack, Smith's partner, and Buffington was John Richards, the police chief. (Initially Smith was to have been a railroad detective.) Among the guests in the series were Robert Redford, Forrest Tucker, Clu Gulager, Marie Windsor, Patricia Medina, Alan Hale Jr., and others. The series aired on Monday nights on NBC but only briefly—between May and September 1961. A three-disc DVD set of the complete series (twenty-six episodes) came onto the market in spring 2010, being promoted rather extravagantly as "one of the rarest and most sought after of all television Westerns." Really?!

Gunslinger, created by Charles Marquis Warren, premiered on CBS the second week of February 1961, an hour-long Western as a quick replacement for another show that didn't make it. Tony Young starred as Cord. He's an undercover agent for the U.S. Cavalry who poses as a dangerous gunslinger to apprehend bad guys the army is trying to round up. Preston Foster also starred as his commanding officer, Captain Zachary Wingate, at Fort Scott in New Mexico Territory. The show, which ran on Thursday nights at 10:00, didn't make it beyond May (before it went to repeats). There were only twelve original episodes—and the redoubtable Frankie Laine sang the theme, as he did "Rawhide," also written by Dimitri Tiomkin and Ned Washington!

Like NBC's earlier *Circus Boy*, CBS's *Frontier Circus* (1961–1962) was either a circus drama posing as a Western (because it was set on the 1880s frontier) or a Western posing as a circus drama. This traveling one-ring circus starred Chill Wills as Colonel Casey Thompson, one of the owners, and younger John Derek as Ben Travis, the other owner, who's also the straw boss supervising the workers. Richard Jaeckel played the other requisite hunk on the show, advance man Tony Gentry. In addition to visits from assorted frontier types, the series was basically the interaction and relationships between the circus's workmen and performers. Among the frontier folk were such names as Irene Dunne, Aldo Ray, Elizabeth Montgomery, Brian Keith, Vera Miles, Cloris Leachman, Mickey Rooney, Rip Torn, even Sammy Davis Jr.—a rather unlikely local. The circus folded its proverbial tent after one season.

The first Western to run for ninety minutes was NBC's *The Virginian*, which premiered on September 19, 1962, and anchored Thursday evenings for the network for its entire nine-year run. Adapted from Owen Wister's

1902 book and filmed a number of times through the decades, *The Virginian*, well made and intelligent, followed the exploits of a laconic figure—no other name—through whose eyes the shaping of Wyoming during the 1890s was viewed. It began its TV life as the first episode (thirty minutes) of the 1958 NBC anthology series *Decision*, with James Drury in the lead along with Andrew Duggan, Jeanette Nolan, Steven Joyce, and Robert Burton.

James Drury—a veteran of dozens of Western series episodes at this point, and quite temperamental—portrayed this mysterious cowboy who had the job of foreman of the vast Shiloh Ranch in Medicine Bow, owned by Judge Henry Garth (equally temperamental Lee J. Cobb), his father's old friend. Later in the series, Cobb—who groused about the show in interview after interview that he did the gig solely for "an awful lot of money involved"—left after 120 episodes and was replaced by new Shiloh owners Charles Bickford and John McIntire as Grainger brothers John and Clay. Also starring on the show—and its successor—was then teen heartthrob Doug McClure as the devil-may-care ranch hand Trampas.

And there was a parade of other actors who became semi-regulars for varying lengths of time—Gary Clarke, Pippa Scott, Roberta Shore, Randy Boone, L. Q. Jones, Clu Gulager, Jeanette Nolan, David Hartman, and Tim Matheson. Among the guests who turned up weekly, usually getting off the passing stagecoach, were the likes of Bette Davis, Charles Bronson, James Coburn, George C. Scott, Telly Savalas, and, in one of his earliest roles, Harrison Ford (actually he made two appearances as different characters). *The Virginian* and its successor, *The Men from Shiloh*, all told made up one of the longest-running Westerns in television, after *Gunsmoke* and *Bonanza*.

Drury also starred—then as a somewhat foppish dandy in lace cuffs and shining hunting boots—in the unsold NBC pilot on a short-lived anthology series *Decision*, which aired in summer 1958; with Drury were Robert Barton as Judge Henry and Andrew Duggan as the then ranch foreman Ben Stocker. Years later, when there was a cable remake of Wister's classic Western, Drury rode through as a character known simply as "Rider."

During the 1970–1971 season, *The Virginian* morphed into *The Men from Shiloh* (still running ninety minutes), with James Drury remaining as the title figure; Stewart Granger joining the cast as Colonel Alan MacKenzie, the new owner of the Shiloh Ranch; Doug McClure staying on as Trampas; and Lee Majors joining as fellow ranch hand Roy Tate.

The sweeping, string-drenched title theme and full score for *The Virginian*, filled with multiple themes and musical subtleties, were by Percy Faith. Other composers who scored assorted episodes in the series were David Buttolph, Hans J. Salter, Franz Waxman, and Leonard Rosenman. When *The*

Virginian was revamped as *The Men from Shiloh*, Percy Faith's notable theme music was eliminated, Jon Burlingame observed in his book, "in favor of a new musical signature by Ennio Morricone—his only theme for American series television." (Morricone, of course, found fame scoring many of spaghetti Western–director Sergio Leone's films, and has amassed more than four hundred film credits through the decades, probably more than any other living film composer.) A ten-disc DVD set of the show's first season became available for the first time in 2010.

The Virginian could be said to have been the last great Western series from the boom years of the genre. Except for Fess Parker's *Daniel Boone* (not a true Western) and Barbara Stanwyck's *The Big Valley*, practically all of the ones that followed—at least until *Little House on the Prairie*—ran for only a season or two. The number of new Westerns dropped increasingly from the peak years as audiences' interests began turning elsewhere. It was all, as has been said elsewhere, a case of demographics. And by the midseventies, TV fragmentation was beginning as cable started competing for viewers. HBO officially was launched in November 1972, and Time Life Inc. acquired it several months later. The other major premium pay-cable service, Showtime, initially as part of Viacom, was launched on July 1, 1976, in selected parts of the country at first and then in spring 1978, it went national to compete with HBO and several others. Among the other cable channels were CBS Cable (1981–1982), and NBC's The Entertainment Channel (TEC, 1982–1983)—both of which attracted very limited (upscale) audiences. Both went dark within months of their launch. None of the cable networks developed Western series through the end of the twentieth century.

Meanwhile it remained up to the three original over-the-air networks and one or two off-network syndication groups, like MCA-TV's upstart Operation Primetime, launched in 1976, and Metromedia's Golden Circle (1980), which produced made-for-TV movies (some Westerns).

NBC's other new Western in 1962, after premiering *The Virginian*, was *Empire*, starring rugged Richard Egan as Jim Redigo, foreman of the half-million acre Garrett Ranch on Santa Fe, owned by Anne Seymour as Lucia Garrett, along with her two headstrong children, Connie and Tal, played by Terry Moore and Ryan O'Neal. Charles Bronson was brought in later as tough ranch hand Paul Moreno. And there were the obligatory weekly guest stars. The hour-long *Empire*, the NBC brass apparently decided, wasn't living up to expectations, and after its first season was reworked into the half-hour *Redigo* from September to December 1963. Richard Egan still starred, but with a whole new cast. Meanwhile ABC came along and acquired the initial episodes and reran them in 1964.

Falling, perhaps, into the category of contemporary Westerns were two competing shows that premiered within days of one another at the start of the 1962–1963 season. First up was NBC's *The Wide Country*, with Earl Holliman as rodeo rider Mitch Guthrie and Andrew Prine as his brother Andy. Mitch travels the rodeo circuit seeking the Golden Bucket, the trophy awarded to the world's best broncobuster, and meeting an array of guest stars along the way. Then came ABC's *Stoney Burke*, with Jack Lord (before moving on to greater stardom in *Hawaii Five-O*) in the title role, traveling the same circuit in hopes of winning the same trophy. (Did Holliman's Mitch Guthrie ever meet Lord's Stoney Burke?) During his quest, Stoney becomes entangled in the lives of numerous people and gets into and out of trouble. He is sometimes accompanied by his friends Wes Painter and E. J. Stocker, played by Warren Oates and Bruce Dern (counter-culture buddies before that term was in vogue). Neither *The Wide Country*, which was produced by game show king Ralph Edwards, nor *Stoney Burke*, created and produced by Leslie Stevens, made it to a second season. So basically rodeo shows were out of the network schedules, and there were no other new Westerns that season—none at all from CBS.

Well, not quite none. There was the single-season high-minded CBS series *Great Adventure*, produced by John Houseman and narrated initially by veteran actor Van Heflin and then by Russell Johnson. (Johnson had made his mark as Marshal Gib Scott in the late fifties series *Black Saddle* and later would gain TV immortality as the Professor on *Gilligan's Island*.) *Great Adventure* was a weekly 1963–1964 anthology show on Friday nights that dramatized significant events shaping American history, several dealing with the Old West. Among them were "The Death of Sitting Bull," with Sitting Bull played by Anthony Caruso (Joseph Cotten, Ricardo Montalban, Lloyd Nolan, Claude Akins, and other notables were in that episode); "Wild Bill Hickok—The Man and the Legend" (Lloyd Bridges starred as the title character); "The Testing of Sam Houston" (Robert Culp as Houston, with Victor Jory as Andrew Jackson); "The Pathfinder" (Rip Torn as Lieutenant John Charles Fremont); and assorted others. The theme for the series was written by Richard Rodgers.

ABC introduced its Western *The Dakotas* in January 1963 (it was gone by September). The series followed the exploits of U.S. Marshal Frank Ragan (played by Larry Ward) as he attempts to maintain law and order in the post–Civil War Dakotas. Riding with him are deputies Del Stark, J. D. Smith, and Vance Porter. In those roles were Chad Everett (some years before finding stardom in *Medical Center*), Jack Elam, and Michael Greene. Although Larry Ward had frequent roles on various TV Westerns, this was his only starring one. Produced by William T. Orr, *The Dakotas* was a short-lived spin-off from *Cheyenne*.

As its premiere Western series for the 1963–1964 season, ABC offered *The Travels of Jaimie McPheeters*. It told of the hardships encountered by a wagon train of settlers headed for the California gold rush. The weekly adventures were seen through the eyes of a twelve-year-old youngster in the title role, played by a teenage Kurt Russell. Dan O'Herlihy was the nominal star as Jaimie's dad, Doc Sardius McPheeters. Other regulars were Michael Witney (for a while) as wagon master Buck Coulter, Charles Bronson as Linc Murdock, James Westerfield as John Murrell, and Sandy Kenyon as Shep Baggott, plus Henry T. Coe as Doc's valet. Buck got trampled to death several weeks into the series, and Linc came along to take over the reins for the rest of the journey. This was based on Robert Lewis Taylor's 1958 Pulitzer Prize–winning novel.

NBC's sole new Western series starting in September 1963 was *Temple Houston*, executive produced by Jack Webb. Jeffrey Hunter (hot off starring as Jesus Christ in *King of Kings*) played Temple, attorney son of the legendary Sam Houston, who traveled to circuit courts in the 1880s Southwest, drumming up clients. Traveling with him was Jack Elam as the sidekick of sorts, itinerant marshal, and over-the-hill gunfighter George Taggart, for the twenty-six episodes that the show aired. The real-life Temple Houston, as has been noted, was a contemporary of both Billy the Kid and Bat Masterson, and according to Western lore, was known to have engaged in shooting matches with each of them. The pilot to *Temple Houston*, filmed in March 1963, was released theatrically as *The Man from Galveston*, with the title character's name changed to Timothy Higgins and played by Hunter.

Destry, based on the classic film *Destry Rides Again* (the title of Western author Max Brand's novel), with James Stewart and Marlene Dietrich, premiered on ABC in February 1964. It was a comedy Western about, as the network press release at the time put it, "a tall, easygoing chap who wasn't exactly a coward—just a mite careful. He'd just as soon dive under the gambling table as shoot it out." Square-jawed John Gavin starred as Harrison Destry, son of famed lawman Tom Destry, once a sheriff, who went to prison on trumped-up embezzlement charges. Young Destry wanders about the West in search of the scalawags who had framed his dad—all the while trying to keep out of trouble. *Destry* didn't ride again after the start of ABC's 1964–1965 season. Gavin later—after losing the role of James Bond that Sean Connery was giving up—left acting and became U.S. ambassador to Mexico for a number of years. Although Hollywood initially had scoffed at his getting the diplomatic post, the community came to realize that Gavin was fluent in Spanish, having been a descendant of a family that had been prominent in Spanish California.

Whether NBC's *Daniel Boone* was a true Western can be debated. Fess Parker's big coonskin-cap-wearing role after *Davy Crockett* was as star of this series that lasted for six seasons. Boone was an Easterner who lived in North Carolina, Tennessee, and Kentucky before and during the Revolutionary War, but the stories in the series have him involved with Indians—friendly and hostile—and his various expeditions take him into what was then the frontier, east of the Mississippi. His traveling companion during the first season is a dude named Yadlin (Albert Salmi), and he has an Indian pal, Mingo (Ed Ames of the singing Ames Brothers), who is a college-educated Cherokee. Singer/actor Jimmy Dean became Boone's companion the following season or two, playing Josh Clements. He was followed by Robert Logan as Jerico Jones; then Don Pedro Colley as Gideon, a former slave; then Roosevelt Grier, as runaway slave Gabe Cooper; and then during the final season, by Dallas McKennon as Cincinnatus. Aaron Spelling was one of this series' producers.

ABC moved into the 1965–1966 season full bore, Westerns wise, beginning with *The Legend of Jesse James*—making heroes out of the notorious and murderous Jesse and his brother Frank, as was done in series about Billy the Kid and one or two others. Jesse and Frank, played by Christopher Jones and Allen Case, were depicted as Robin Hoods, rather than Old West desperados, and periodically in the stories, Cole and Bob Younger turned up as did Marshal Sam Corbett. Cult director Don Siegel, who worked frequently on the big screen with Clint Eastwood, was producer of the *Jesse James* series. Siegel also directed at least one episode of the show, titled "Manhunt," which was more or less based on *Jesse James*, the 1939 movie that starred Tyrone Power and Henry Fonda (as brother Frank), as well as the 1957 film *The True Story of Jesse James*, in which Robert Wagner and Jeffrey Hunter played Jesse and Frank.

A Man Called Shenandoah, a second ABC series that season, had Robert Horton playing an amnesiac seeking his identity. He'd been shot and left for dead on the prairie, but was brought into town by a pair of bounty hunters and was nursed back to health by a saloon girl named Katie (Beverly Garland played the part). For the remainder of the single season run, Shenandoah follows the trail to learn who he is while crossing paths with the likes of Warren Oates, Cloris Leachman, Claude Akins, Bruce Dern, Martin Landau, George Kennedy, Leonard Nimoy, and Michael Ansara. Horton also sang the theme vocal, a version of the traditional "Shenandoah."

ABC's major Western that season was *The Big Valley*, an hour-long show starring Barbara Stanwyck as the iron-willed, widowed matriarch at a sprawling cattle ranch—though not as big as the Ponderosa—in the San Joaquin Valley in the late 1870s. The series, called by some through the years "*Bonanza* in petticoats," had silver-haired Stanywck, as Victoria Barkley, running the spread with her grown children: lawyer Jarrod (Richard Long), the levelheaded number-one son; hotheaded Nick (Peter Breck); Heath (Lee Majors, in what appears to be his acting debut), the illegitimate half-breed son of Victoria's dead husband; purdy Audra (Linda Evans, in her star-making role); and teenage Eugene, the fourth son (Charles Briles, who disappeared after season one). Silas, the servant, was played by Napoleon Whiting. *The Big Valley* was an action-filled adventure series—there were murderers, con men, bank robbers, Mexican revolutionaries, schemers, and assorted varmints. And it had name guests popping in and out: Katharine Ross, Charles Bronson, Martin Landau, Ronny Howard, Milton Berle, Robert Walker Jr., Stanwyck's old friend Olivia de Havilland, William Shatner, James Whitmore, Colleen Dewhurst, and more. Stanwyck won an Emmy as Best Actress in a Drama Series the very first year of the show, and nominations the next two. She also happened to be only the second female star (after Gail "Annie Oakley" Davis) to carry a Western drama series. The show itself lasted until 1969 in first run.

Then there was the zany *F Troop*, a comedy Western set post–Civil War at Fort Courage, somewhere west of the Missouri. Heading the ensemble cast were Ken Berry as bumbling Captain Wilton Parmenter (he'd been promoted from private to captain by mistake in the closing days of the war); Forrest Tucker as wily Sergeant Morgan O'Rouke, who had a lucrative side business selling souvenirs from the neighboring Hekawi Indian to tourists; Larry Storch as Corporal Randolph Agarn, who was O'Rourke's chief aide and fellow schemer; pretty Melody Patterson, as a sexy but hard-riding cowgirl nicknamed Wrangler Jane, who has set her sights on the captain; and Frank de Kova as Chief Wild Eagle. There were big names turning up as local Indians, from Edward Everett Horton as ancient Roaring Chicken to Don Rickles as Bald Eagle, and Paul Lynde was a singing mountie. *F Troop* featured a colorful cast of characters in a wild and wacky Western farce that lasted just two seasons on ABC but lives on in syndication, particularly on TVLand.

One of two new Western series on CBS in 1965–1966 was *The Loner*, created by Rod Serling and starring Lloyd Bridges as William Colton, a disillusioned cavalry officer who, after Appomattox, heads West, searching for adventure and a new life. One of the producers was Bruce Lansbury, Angela's brother. Among those who crossed Colton's path were guests like Anne Baxter, Burgess Meredith, Barry Sullivan, Leslie Nielsen, Jack Lord, Dan Duryea, and Beau Bridges, the star's son, then in his twenties. In a not-too-solicitous mood, the critic for the *New York Times* brushed off the show as "the same old gun duel with psychiatric embellishments. Mr. Serling evidently has been among those who have been watching *The Fugitive*." This thinking man's Western was cancelled at the end of the first season, which was said to have made Serling somewhat disgruntled, though he'd have two other memorable series ahead of him.

The other CBS Western that season—and one fondly remembered—was *The Wild Wild West*. Referred to by many as *Maverick* crossbred with *The Man from U.N.C.L.E.*, the lighthearted series costarred Robert Conrad and Ross Martin—their characters had their own private three-car train for ample freedom as they crisscrossed the frontier. Initially veteran cowboy actor Rory Calhoun was announced for the lead but it ultimately went to Conrad, who previously had been one of the *Hawaiian Eye* cast. In this new series he was special agent James West—more than proficient in all forms of self-defense and weaponry—sent to the frontier by President Ulysses S. Grant (played by James Gregory), while Martin was his associate Artemus Gordon, a master of disguises and fancy gadgets. The two battle all sorts of crazed outlaws and nutty scientists and periodically the mountainous and smarmy, Sydney Greenstreet-ish Count Carlos Marco Vincenzo Robespierre Manzeppi (Victor Buono) and their diminutive, sinister archenemy, the dwarf Dr. Miguelito Loveless (Michael Dunn). Loveless often is accompanied by towering Richard Kiel as Voltaire.

The show, produced by Bruce Lansbury, was wildly popular (it had the familiar title format, "The Night of the . . ." as part of every episode), but, at the time of its debut, various PTA (Parent Teacher Association) and educational groups complained to CBS about its sadistic violence. In fact, every one of the colorfully named villains thrilled in conjuring up methods of torture for heroic Jim West. Mere death was too good for him. The network listened and toned down the violence (slightly). In the opener, "The Night of the Inferno," Suzanne Pleshette guest starred as an old flame of Jim's from New Orleans, now working in a local gambling casino. When the show premiered, TV critic Jack Gould wrote in the *New York Times*, "This is the one new Western which has the earmarks of a solid hit. . . . *The Wild Wild West* illustrates the theatrical reward of a little twist well done." Gould also said that the show "is far from epic, just good fun. . . . There's not a psychoneurotic in the concept, just smooth good guys and bad guys that are adequately interesting."

The Wild Wild West suffered a temporary loss when Ross Martin was felled by a minor heart attack. A Friday night staple, it came to an abrupt end after 104 episodes in April 1969, but was brought back in reruns the following summer. Several years later Conrad and Martin were reunited for a two-hour TV-movie sequel, *The Wild Wild West Revisited*, and then another, *More Wild Wild West*, shortly before Martin's death. Both were directed by Burt Kennedy. In 1999, an ill-advised big-screen adaptation of the series was made, with Will Smith and Kevin Kline, but the magic was gone.

Less than two years after *The Rifleman* departed from prime time, Chuck Connors came back with a second Western series, *Branded*. He starred as Jason McCord, disgraced West Point officer dismissed for cowardice (he was dramatically cashiered in the opening credits), roaming the West of the 1880s on his horse Domino, in an attempt to clear his name—to a music score by Dominic Frontiere. This early 1965 NBC Western that ran on Sunday evenings, opposite the second half of Ed Sullivan and preceding *Bonanza*, lasted until September 1966 when the network gave it the boot after forty-eight episodes.

In *Laredo*, Neville Brand as Reese Bennett, Peter Brown as Chad Cooper, and William Smith as Joe Riley are three bickering Texas Rangers that Philip Carey as Captain Edward Parmalee, their stern officer in charge, has to endure at the Laredo ranger post during the 1880s in this hour-long NBC Western series (1965–1967). Robert Wolders was enlisted during the second season as Ranger Erik Hunter, and Claude Akins made periodic appearances as Ranger Cotton Buckmeister. Mixing humor with action, hijinks with hard riding, *Laredo* offered a somewhat different twist to the standard oater, with the three Rangers, while chasing down rustlers and desperados, meeting a gaggle of guest performers, including Burgess Meredith, James Farentino, Julie Harris, Eve Arden, Jack Lord, Peter Graves, and Fernando Lamas.

The *Laredo* pilot aired as a 1965 episode of *The Virginian*, titled "We've Lost a Train," and was released theatrically in 1969 as *Backtrack*. Three episodes of *Laredo*'s first season were also edited into a theatrical feature, *Three Guns for Texas* (1968).

The Road West (NBC, 1966–1967) followed a family of pioneering homesteaders, headed by Barry Sullivan and Kathryn Hays, as they struggle to begin new lives in Lawrence County, Kansas, during the 1860s. With Sullivan and Hays, as Ben and Elizabeth Pride, were Andrew Pine, Brenda Scott, and Kelly Corcoran as their kids; Charles Steel as grandpa Thomas Jefferson Pride; and Glenn Corbett as Elizabeth's brother, who's along primarily for the adventure. George C. Scott turned up in the first two episodes as villainous landowner Jud Barker, who gives the Prides a hard time. Those two episodes were cobbled together and released theatrically in 1969 as *This Savage Land*. The theme for the hour-long series was by Leonard Rosenman.

The Hero, in 1966, was a short-lived NBC sitcom produced by David Susskind's company, Talent Associates, about a faux TV cowboy named Jed Clayton, U.S. marshal, who offscreen (in the Western within a sitcom) is Sam Garret, first-class bumbler. He drives around in a spiffy Cadillac with a longhorn grill and makes himself insufferable to all around him. Richard Mulligan starred—in a character similar to the one he played in the soap sitcom, *Soap*—along with Mariette Hartley as his long-suffering but stabilizing wife.

ABC recycled the Alan Ladd early fifties Western classic *Shane* at the start of the network's 1966–1967 season, with David Carradine as the wandering ex-gunman in Wyoming Territory in the late 1880s. In this ranchers versus cattlemen saga, he signs on as a ranch hand for a homesteading widow (Jill Ireland) and her young son (Chris Shea) and helps them fight evil land grabbers. Despite its pedigree in Western movie lore and the fact that it was produced by Herbert Brodkin, one of the major figures in the early days of live television and its so-called Golden Era, *Shane* was forced by the network brass, and perhaps viewer apathy, to ride off into the sunset on New Year's Eve 1966. This in spite of the efforts of the boy who idolized him to get him to stay around—but there was no "Come back, Shane," the famous final line in the Ladd movie. Carradine would return as another wanderer of the West as Shaolin priest Kwan Chang Caine in *Kung Fu* five years later.

The Monroes, an hour-long series that ABC introduced at the beginning of the 1966–1967 season, was a family Western. The family consisted of five young people whose pioneering parents drowned while fording a treacherous river on their way to Wyoming in the 1870s. Under the guidance of the two older ones (Michael Anderson Jr. and Barbara Hershey), they agree to continue their lost parents' quest and land in a lonely valley their father ten years earlier had laid claim to. They are befriended by a renegade Indian named Dirty Jim (Ron Soble) and are constantly menaced by Major Mopoy (Liam Sullivan), an evil British cattle baron. Veteran cowboy star Ben Johnson also was a regular, playing Sleeve, one of Mopoy's hired hands who, behind his dastardly boss's back, is sympathetic to the Monroe kids. A young James Brolin (twenty-six at the time) had an early recurring role as one of a neighboring rancher's sons. He and everyone else kind of moseyed on in March 1967 after twenty-six episodes. and the show, filmed basically in Grand Teton National Park, went into summer repeats.

Another new Western on the ABC schedule, *The Iron Horse*, premiering in September 1966, had a somewhat longer run. A building-the-railroad-across-the-West series, it starred Dale Robertson as frontier gambler Ben Calhoun, who wins the nearly bankrupt Buffalo Pass and Scalplock Railroad in a high stakes poker game and then has to spend his time and energy on turning the line into a profitable operation. Gary Collins was his buddy Dave Tarrant, the engineer. The girl in the mix, Julie Parsons, was played by Ellen McRae before she became Ellen Burstyn. The genesis of former screen cowboy Robertson's *The Iron Horse* was his *Scalplock*, a movie made for television (the very first Western in this new and rapidly growing genre, about which more later).

Around this time, Universal, which had teamed up with NBC to make TV movies, turned out several that ended up instead as theatrical features. Among them were several Western comedies, for example, *The Ballad of Josie* starring Doris Day; *The Shakiest Gun in the West* with Don Knotts, a remake of Bob Hope's 1948 *The Paleface*; the very funny Dan Blocker movie *Cockeyed Cowboys of Calico County*, which had an all-star cast; and *The Plainsman*, a new version of Cecil B. De Mille's late thirties adventure dealing with Calamity Jane, Wild Bill Hickok, and Buffalo Bill Cody.

The Rounders (ABC, 1966–1967) was a short-lived comedy Western dealing with a couple of not overly bright cowpokes—Ben Jones and Howdy Lewis (Ron Hayes and John Wayne's son Patrick)—hired hands on the ranch owned by Jim Ed Love (veteran Chill Wills). It was based on the feature film of the same title, which starred Glenn Ford and Henry Fonda, and was directed by Burt Kennedy, who on the TV series produced and occasionally directed.

CBS also had a comedy Western that season, *Pistols 'n' Petticoats*—one of the first shows the network regularly broadcast in color. Fading film actress Ann Sheridan had her only starring role on TV as the widowed, gun-toting head of the zany Hanks family homesteading in Wretched, Colorado, in the early 1870s. In fact, everyone in the family, including grandma and grandpa, totes guns. Others in the cast included Gary Vinson as the town's bumbling sheriff, Robert Lowery as the local land baron, and Lon Chaney Jr. and Jay Silverheels (Tonto to the Lone Ranger) as comic Indians Eagle Shadow and Great Bear. One episode, "Shootout at O'Day Corral," spoofed you know what and had Henrietta Hanks and kin getting involved with the murderous Blanton brothers as well as Wyatt Earp and Doc Holliday—but all ends humorously, since this was a Western-oriented sitcom.

Ann Sheridan died of cancer in January 1967 after having completed filming of the entire series, which wasn't renewed.

Then producing partners Danny Thomas and Aaron Spelling served up another comedy Western, *Rango* (ABC, January–September 1967), as a starring vehicle for funnyman Tim Conway as a Texas Ranger working—rather ineptly—out of the Deep Wells Ranger Station in Gopher Gulch. Guy

Marks was fumbling Ranger Rango's cowardly Indian scout, Pink Cloud, and Norman Alden was Rango's exasperated superior commanding officer, who can't get rid of the bumbler because his father (unseen) happens to be the commander in charge. Frankie Laine, of course, sang the series' title song, written by Earle Hagen and Ben Raleigh.

In September 1967, NBC aired a pilot called *Sheriff Who?* which turned the traditional Western upside down: the bad guy always won in the end. Remembered by those who saw it as arguably the funniest TV Western ever, it was created by Garry Marshall and starred John Astin as Evil Roy Slade, the rottenest varmint ever to roam the frontier, killing off every lawman who crosses his path. The idea was to have a different guest star every week playing a new sheriff in town (appropriately called Blood, Texas), gunned down by Slade at the end of each episode. Costar was funnyman Dick Shawn as Crawford Offwhite, the self-styled "fastest interior decorator in the West."

The show, funny as it was, didn't fly, but four or five more attempts through the years were made to, and they were strung together and aired as a TV movie in 1971 titled *Evil Roy Slade*. Pat Buttram was brought in to narrate the film, with Astin in actor's heaven in his ultra-nasty role as Slade and Shawn now being called Marshal Bing Bell. The movie overflowed with name guests, from Mickey Rooney, Dom DeLuise, Edie Adams, and Milton Berle, to Penny Marshall (creator Garry's sister), Pat Morita, and then little-known John Ritter.

ABC premiered three Western series over a period of three nights at the start of the 1967–1968 TV season. The first two lasted only from September to December. First came *The Legend of Custer*, and the title just about tells the whole story. Wayne Maunder made his TV acting debut as Lieutenant General George Armstrong Custer in this rather unsuccessful attempt to tell of the exploits of (arguably) this country's best-known cavalry officer. Custer in real life was a flamboyant career soldier of the post–Civil War era who by the age of twenty-eight had risen to the rank of major general. He was demoted for a while for dereliction of duty, but reinstated (as lieutenant colonel) and put in command of the Seventh Regiment of the U.S. Cavalry, stationed at Fort Hays, Kansas.

Much of the *Custer* series was devoted, primarily, to Custer's personal conflict with Sioux chief Crazy Horse (played by Michael Dante). Other regulars were Slim Pickens as California Joe Miner, a scout; Peter Palmer as Sergeant James Bustard, a former Rebel; Robert F. Simon as Custer's superior, General Alfred Terry; and Grant Woods as Captain Myles Keogh. (In the famous 1941 theatrical film *They Died with Their Boots On*, Errol Flynn had one of his best roles as Custer, Charley Grapewin as California Joe, and Anthony

Quinn as Crazy Horse.) Since the series lasted only seventeen episodes, the famed officer never did make it to the Little Bighorn with his troops.

Also not making it beyond seventeen episodes was ABC's *Hondo*, based on the Louis L'Amour story and the 1953 John Wayne movie. This hour-long Western, produced by Wayne's Batjac Productions and set in Arizona Territory in the late 1860s, had the misfortune of being slotted opposite NBC's *Star Trek* on Friday nights. The series revolved around U.S. Army troubleshooter and former Confederate captain Hondo Lane (played by Ralph Taeger), who, with sidekick Buffalo Baker (Noah Beery Jr.), has continuing run-ins with Apache chief Vittoro (Michael Pate). Pate, an Australian actor—and later writer and producer—who often played Native Americans, was in the John Wayne film in the same role. Also in the TV cast as regulars were Gary Clarke as Hondo's commanding officer, Captain Richards, and Kathe Brown and Buddy Foster, as a widowed settler and her young son. In one episode, "Hondo and the Judas" (November 1967), Ricky Nelson straps on the gun belt and holster to play bad guy Jesse James.

Premiering directly after *Hondo* on ABC was *The Guns of Will Sonnett*. This thirty-minute series produced by Danny Thomas and Aaron Spelling starred old-timer Walter Brennan in the title role as a former Cavalry scout who raises his grandson (played by Dack Rambo) after his own son, the boy's dad (played in a recurring role by Jason Evers), runs off to become a wayward gunfighter. Brennan and Rambo roam for West looking for him—for two seasons (fifty episodes). At the start of each episode, Brennan talk-sings this poem over the opening theme:

> I raised Jim's boy from the cradle
> Until the day he said to me
> I have to go find my father
> I reckoned that's the way it should be
> So we ride, Jim's boy and me.

And each episode ended with Brennan thanking God for leading the way.

CBS's *Dundee and the Culhane* (September–December 1967) was an off-beat Western that very nearly didn't make it beyond pilot stage. Veteran British actor John Mills (in his only American TV series—and before winning the Oscar for *Ryan's Daughter*) starred as an English lawyer who comes to America and rides the trail in the 1870s, along with younger fellow attorney, actor Sean Garrison as a feisty Irish American, nicknamed "the Culhane." Well produced with a different bent, it had as a frequent theme frontier justice for miners. It seems that Dundee worked in a mine as a boy, surviving a cave-in, and he now has a natural affinity for mines. *TV Guide* noted in an interview at the time with CBS programming chief Mike Dann that he had decided to scrap the show before it even premiered, but since the network execs liked the way it played as a pilot, he kept it going for at least half a season—although it never lived up to expectations.

The other new CBS Western series premiering in 1967, the ninety-minute weekly *Cimarron Strip* (not to be confused with *Cimarron City*, the NBC Western of a few years earlier) followed the exploits of Jim Crown, U.S. marshal in the Oklahoma Territory during the 1880s. Stuart Whitman starred, along with Jill Townsend as his lady friend Dulcy Coopersmith, an Easterner who came West to run the local inn for her late father. Randy Boone played Crown's photographer friend Francis Wilde and Percy Herbert was Deputy MacGregor, an itinerant Scot.

The guest star–filled series, the second ninety-minute Western after *The Virginian*, ran on Thursday nights but lasted only one season—although CBS brought it back in reruns during the summer of 1971. Maurice Jarre provided the main theme (at least for the pilot and first episodes). As Jon Burlingame noted, "Jarre's title music, set against a slowly retreating aerial shot of Whitman riding across the prairie, was impressive." CBS music director Morton Stevens brought in several other veteran Western composers to score individual episodes. One was Bernard Herrmann, no less, for a 1968 Jack-the-Ripper-type episode titled "Knife in the Darkness."

With the era of big Western series beginning to wane, NBC weighed in with *The High Chaparral*, which ran on Sunday nights at 10:00 during its first season, moving to Fridays for the rest of its run through 1971—ninety-eight episodes. Something of a copycat to *Bonanza*—also produced by David Dortort—this show had the title spread run by the Cannon family (read the Cartwrights) with Big John Cannon (actor Leif Erickson) as the driven, very ambitious patriarch of the family with a spread to run in Arizona Territory. The other central family of landowners in this series was the Montoyas. Cameron Mitchell costarred as Big John's brother Buck, and Linda Cristal was a Montoya who married Big John. Mark Slade played Blue Cannon, John's son and Victoria Montoya Cannon's stepson. Frank Silvera was her father, Don Sebastian Montoya, during the first three seasons (he died in 1970), and Gilbert Roland played his brother, Don Domingo Montoya, for the final one. NBC would premiere only two more Western series during the 1970s.

ABC's *The Outcasts* might well be the first interracial Western (if you don't count *The Lone Ranger*). Premiering during the 1968–1969 season, it teamed a white ex-slave owner and a former slave as a pair of bounty hunters in the days after the Civil War. Don Murray and Otis Young, as Earl Corey and Jermal David, were the stars of this hour-long, single season series that aired on Monday nights at 8:00.

TV Guide described Here Come the Brides (ABC, 1968–1970) in its fall preview issue at the start of the 1968 season: "The locale is Seattle, circa 1870, a muddy, dreary logging camp, population approximately 150—mostly grubby men plus a few dance hall girls. . . . What the men need are wives." Handsome, stalwart Jason Bolt had his two brothers, Jeremy and Joshua, go back East and get some brides. Joan Blondell was the golden-hearted saloon-keeper. Here Come the Brides was a direct descendant of MGM's memorable musical Seven Brides for Seven Brothers—that itself spawned a CBS series of that title in 1982–1983.

The only other new Western series of the sixties was CBS's hour-long Lancer, which began in 1968. Like The High Chaparral, it used Bonanza's patriarch-landowner-running-a-vast-spread-with-his-sometimes-battling-sons blueprint. Andrew Duggan played old Murdoch Lancer, trying to defend by himself his cattle and sheep ranch in California's San Joaquin Valley in the 1870s. His two sons, by different marriages, are gunslinging, hotheaded Johnny Lancer (James Stacy, whose career would be cut short by a devastating motorcycle accident in which he lost an arm and a leg) and college grad Scott Lancer (Wayne Maunder, who earlier had starred as George Armstrong Custer in his own series). During the second—and last—season, another son is introduced, Chad Lancer, played by John Beck. All came together to help dad manage his vast real estate holdings, along with Paul Brinegar, as vinegary ranch hand Jelly Hoskins (also from season 2). Lancer came to the end of the trail in June 1970, but CBS brought it back in reruns during the summer of 1971.

One might consider NBC's popular Dennis Weaver series, McCloud, a modern-day Western (although it's generally thought of as a cop drama). For seven seasons beginning in September 1970, he played a deputy marshal from Taos, New Mexico, who was plunked down in seventies Manhattan—cowboy hat and drawl included, and sometimes even riding a horse through Times Square—to teach those durn greenhorns from the East a thing or two about "lawing" Western-style. Television was to have no new actual Western series again until 1971—only the ones that had already been introduced in the late sixties and were still running.

CBS got back into TV Westerns, more or less, in September 1971 with actor Glenn Ford's Cade's County. He played Sam Cade—not to be confused, of course, with Sam Spade. Cade is a modern-day sheriff who attempts to maintain law and order in Madrid County, a Southwestern community, with the help of Deputy J. J. Jackson (Edgar Buchanan) and several younger law-men (one of whom was played by Peter Ford, the star's son). This hour-long adventure series/police drama, which aired on Sunday nights, was produced by TV veteran David Gerber.

NBC's one new Western in the 1971–1972 season brought James Garner back in period garb—this period being the "new" West of Nichols, Arizona, in 1914. Here horseless carriages were taking over the unpaved streets that once were trails. Garner brought his charisma to *Nichols*, a character who had no first name (like the later *Columbo* and *Quincy*), returning to his hometown after eighteen years only to discover that his mother has been kicked off of her property by a couple of scoundrels. He drowns his sorrows at the local bar and wakes up to discover he's been appointed sheriff, with his not-so-honest deputy, Mitch, being played by his (Garner's) traditionally shady pal Stuart Margolin—as in all the series they do together. Margot Kid-der played Ruth the barmaid. And so began Nichols's less-than-honorable exploits and get-rich-fast schemes.

The show was officially retitled *James Garner as Nichols* on the eve of its premiere, and *TV Guide*'s Cleveland Amory, reviewing the new series, wrote,

> *Nichols* started out as a terrific idea. The idea was to have three scriptwriters go to work on three possible formats for a show for James Garner. One was to work on a detective show, one a lawyer show, and one a Western. Gee, think of some of the ideas they missed. A doctor show, for example. Or a widower with 17 kids. Anyway, the Western idea won . . . the brain stepchild, appar-ently, of Frank P. Pierson, who decided it would be simply screaming to have a sheriff of a Western town [circa 1914] who was afraid of guns, hated violence, and was fond of homily grits.

In the final episode of the first season, Nichols was—gasp!—gunned down (but was quickly replaced by his twin brother). The series never got a second season.

The lighthearted *Alias Smith and Jones* marked ABC's reentry into West-ern series, also in 1971. Ben Murphy and Peter Deuel played buddies Jed Curry and Hannibal Hayes, amiable outlaws on the mold of Butch Cassidy and the Sundance Kid. The two were released from prison with a provisional amnesty and sent off to roam the Kansas Territory of the 1890s under the names of Thaddeus H. Jones and Joshua Smith to do some good and make up for their former life of crime. This one owed a bit to *Maverick*, and in fact was written by *Maverick*'s Roy Huggins and Jo Swerling Jr., among others, and was created and produced by Glen A. Larson. In recurring roles were Sally Field, Walter Brennan, Burl Ives, Ann Sothern, and Rudy Vallee. The series, which proved popular with younger viewers, was interrupted briefly by real-life drama, when, on December 31, 1971, Peter Deuel died of a self-inflicted gunshot wound. Roger Davis, who had narrated the show and somewhat resembled Deuel, was brought in as his replacement, until the series bit the dust in January 1973, after forty-eight episodes.

Richard Boone's turn-of-the-century Western *Hec Ramsey* kicked off NBC's 1972–1973 schedule. It ran for two seasons. Boone starred as ex-gunfighter turned law enforcer in New Prospect, Oklahoma, circa 1901, using newfangled scientific methods to solve crimes. He somewhat reluctantly reported to the younger, inexperienced Sheriff Oliver Stamp (Rick Lenz). Old Boone pal Harry Morgan narrated the show and costarred as Amos Coogan, the town's ad hoc doctor. The series was produced by Jack Webb's Mark VII Productions. (Morgan, of course, was Webb's *Dragnet* sidekick for a number of years.)

Kung Fu, obviously a new, highly stylized kind of Western, starred David Carradine as a soft-spoken Shaolin priest who wanders the American frontier in the 1870s in search of his missing brother and attempts to live free despite bounty hunters who are seeking him on charges by the Chinese legation in San Francisco that he killed a royal nephew. This series, which aired on ABC from October 1972 to June 1975 (and much later spawned a TV sequel as well as a TV movie "continuation," both with Carradine), might well have been the forerunner of the martial arts craze.

Carradine's Kwai Chang Caine is a disciple of Master Po and Master Kan (Keye Luke and Philip Ahn) and has been taught from childhood to eschew violence—except for the innovative slow-motion fight sequences. There were fifty-nine hour-long episodes, during which Caine crosses paths with John Carradine (David's veteran actor dad), John Saxon, Dean Jagger, Robert Urich, Mako, Andrew Duggan, Chief Dan George, and Harrison Ford. A number of years later, David Carradine, as Caine, not only would star in a new Kung Fu series but also would meet up briefly with Kenny Rogers as Brady Hawkes in the last of the country singer–actor's "Gambler" movies.

"*Gilligan's Island* Out West" was how the syndicated half-hour comedy Western *Dusty's Trail* was described when it first aired in 1973. Bob Denver starred along with Forrest Tucker—the former a Gilligan-type bumbler, the latter an exasperated wagon master. Ivor Francis and Lynn Wood played the Brookhavens, rich socialites (a la the Thurston Howells from *Gilligan's Island*) and Jeannine Riley and Lori Sanders played sassy and sweet girls along for the trip. There were twenty-six episodes, but the show, from *Gilligan* creators Elroy and Sherman Schwartz, was a flop.

In 1974, each of the networks premiered one new Western series. Two of them were short lived. CBS offered the lighthearted *Dirty Sally*, with Jeanette Nolan—in a rare starring role—as a crotchety, hard-drinking collector of prairie junk on her way to gold rush California in the 1880s, and Dack Rambo as a young ex-gunfighter she befriends along the way and comes to regard as the son she never had. Along the trail they meet the likes of John McIntire (Nolan's husband who had starred in *Wagon Train*), Annette O'Toole, Scott Brady, Jackie Coogan, Millie Perkins, and Denver Pyle. (Nolan's Sally Fergus, incidentally, first turned up on several episodes of *Gunsmoke*.) The series ran from January to July before CBS pulled the plug.

ABC's 1974 entry, from February to August, was *The Cowboys*—a half-hour weekly TV adaptation of the 1972 John Wayne movie about a handful of homeless boys who, in the 1870s, go to work on a ranch outside of Dodge City owned by a widow lady (played by Diana Douglas, Kirk's actress first wife and Michael's mom). Wayne, in the film, had been killed off, but several actors, like Robert Carradine and A Martinez, repeated their movie roles as Cimarron and Slim in the series. Jim Davis costarred as Marshal Bill Winter, along with Moses Gunn as Jebediah Nightlinger, the cook. (Actually the Nightlinger character got top billing as the nominal star.)

NBC hit pay dirt in 1974 with *Little House on the Prairie*, less a television Western than a frontier adventure. Arguably, save CBS's *Dr. Quinn, Medicine Woman* and *Deadwood* on cable decades later, this was to be the last great series of the (traditional) Western genre—although many lesser ones would follow over the succeeding years, including a series of films adapted from Janette Oke's faith-based novels about life on the frontier. Based on the books in 1935 by Laura Ingalls Wilder, relating decades-old reminiscences about her family, *Little House* told of a loving family's difficulties surviving on the prairie in the 1870s—in the fictional farming community of Walnut Grove, Minnesota.

The family-friendly series made a major star of Michael Landon, who had gone from playing *Bonanza*'s Little Joe Cartwright to the father, homesteader Charles Ingalls, for the first eight seasons; he also developed into more of an all-around filmmaker, producing and writing many of the episodes, and even directing. Karen Grassle costarred as the mother (also for the first eight seasons), but afterward seems to have disappeared. Melissa Sue Anderson was daughter Mary (at least until 1981), and Melissa Gilbert was daughter Laura, through whose eyes the story was told. (In 2009, Gilbert returned to the *Little House* in a stage musical, playing the mother at this point.)

The show was to be the network's 8:00–9:00 p.m. mainstay, for nine seasons—on Wednesday for the first two and then on Monday. Later there were to be several TV movie sequels to the story in the eighties; in the last one, the producers blew up the *Little House* set in Walnut Grove.

The Barbary Coast, that premiered on ABC at the start of the 1975–1976 season—and was gone by the New Year, may or may not be considered a true Western—as was said of *Yancy Derringer* (set in New Orleans), *Davy Crockett* and *Daniel Boone* (both set primarily east of the Mississippi), *Zorro* (set in Spanish California), the James Fenimore Cooper *Leatherstocking Tales*, and one or two others. Actually, *The Barbary Coast* was an adventure/spy series set in San Francisco in the 1880s, some comparing it in its way to *The Wild Wild West* of a decade earlier. It began life as a ninety-minute made-for-TV movie that first aired on May 4, 1975. Mixing the genres of Western and secret agent drama, the series itself premiered September 8, 1975; the last episode aired January 9, 1976. William Shatner played nineteenth-century government agent Jeff Cable (with a trunkful of disguises) and Doug McClure played his pal Cash Conover, dashing con man and gambler, and owner of the Golden Gate Casino. (In the TV movie, Dennis Cole had that role.) Towering and menacing Richard Kiel played Cash's bouncer, Moose Moran.

CBS's midseason entry was *Sara*, starring Brenda Vaccaro, and NBC's was *The Quest*, featuring Kurt Russell and Tim Matheson; both were short-lived Western series in 1976. The Vaccaro show had her playing Sara Yarnell, a schoolteacher from Philadelphia who finds life all too dull there and journeys west to Independence, Colorado, on the frontier in the 1870s. The Russell and Matheson series—originally a TV movie that aired several months earlier—had the stars playing long-lost brothers, looking for their sister who was separated from them during a Cheyenne Indian attack on their wagon train years earlier. (This was somewhat similar to the premise of John Wayne's *The Searchers*.)

The Life and Times of Grizzly Adams was an hour-long Western that premiered on NBC in February 1977 and ran through July 1978. Set in the West of the late 1800s, it followed the exploits of James "Grizzly" Adams, played by animal-trainer-turned-actor Dan Haggerty. Grizzly is a man falsely accused of a crime who seeks refuge in the wilderness and discovers that life there suits him better than in the city, and with the help of a friend named Mad Jack and an Indian blood brother, Nakuma (Denver Pyle and Don Schanks, respectively), he chooses to live in harmony with nature in a cabin he's built. A four-legged companion who also lives with him is a grizzly bear cub he once had saved. Haggerty earlier had starred with Denver Pyle in a feature film of the same title, as well as a similar one called *The Adventures of Frontier Fremont*. Later he returned as Grizzly Adams in the 1981 theatrical feature *The Legend of the Wild* and then in a TV movie called *The Capture of Grizzly Adams*. Grizzly Adams, it turned out, was a real-life mountain man, though born in Massachusetts in 1812 and living most of his life in the Sierra Madres. An animal lover all of his life, Adams died while on tour with P. T. Barnum, in 1860.

At the start of the 1977–1978 season, NBC premiered *The Oregon Trail*— but the trail ended after just five episodes (the other seven that were filmed apparently never aired). Rod Taylor was the star, leading a group of pioneers from Illinois in a wagon train in the 1840s where land in Oregon is free for the taking. Andrew Stevens played one of his sons. This was an attempt to make a series out of the earlier made-for-TV movie of the same title with Taylor.

A couple of years after wrapping up his two-decade *Gunsmoke* role of Marshal Matt Dillon, James Arness mounted up again, this time as rugged, buckskin-clad mountain scout Zeb Macahan, and rode back to the frontier in early 1977 in ABC's *How the West Was Won.*

In a cover story in *TV Guide*, Arness mused (in 1979), "Zeb Macahan came from an era when men were the law unto themselves. He was a free spirit, made his own times. He was used to taking everything over and not consulting anybody." He continued, "Matt Dillon was the opposite—a guy who not only had to see that the laws were carried out, but lived by them himself. He had to do the right thing. As a consequence, he always had to hold his own personal feelings or desires in restraint."

How the West Was Won, loosely based on the epic all-star theatrical movie of the same name, had an offbeat television history. First there was to be a TV movie called *The Macahans* in early 1975, with Arness, Richard Kiley (as mountain man Zeb's gentleman farmer brother), Eva Marie Saint (Zeb's sister-in-law), Bruce Boxleitner (Zeb's nephew), Fionuala Flanagan (Zeb's sister), and others as assorted members of the Macahan family of Virginia attempting to establish a new life homesteading on the Great Plains during the mid-1860s.

Arness teamed up with much of the *Gunsmoke* production crew, including executive producer John Mantley, producer Jim Byrnes, director Bernard McEveety (and later brother Vincent McEveety), for *The Macahans*, a two-and-one-half-hour movie that emerged as a combination epic Western and soap opera. This served as the pilot to the later hour-long *How the West Was Won* series that aired on Sunday nights from February to August 1978 and then, in a two-hour form, on Mondays from January to May 1979. Richard Kiley, Eva Marie Saint, and Bruce Boxleitner's Macahan characters were killed off before the show resumed in 1979. During the series, which was narrated by William Conrad (ironically, he was Matt Dillon on the radio *Gunsmoke*), an impressive roster of guest stars crossed paths with the Macahans: Lloyd Bridges, Don Murray, William Shatner, Cameron Mitchell, Richard

Basehart, Mel Ferrer, Ricardo Montalban, Brian Keith, Tim Matheson, Vera Miles, Kay Lenz, Slim Pickens, and more. *How the West Was Won* in all had twenty-five episodes.

Similar to *How the West Was Won* was CBS's *The Chisholms*, which aired on Saturdays from January to March 1980. Robert Preston and Rosemary Harris headed a pioneering family traveling by wagon train from Fort Laramie, Wyoming, to California to seek a new life. Other members of the family were played by Ben Murphy, Delta Burke, Glynnis O'Connor, James Van Patten, Brett Cullen, and Victoria Racimo. Mitchell Ryan played wagon master Cooper Hawkins. This series spun off from the twelve-hour miniseries that aired in March–April 1979. The Robert Preston character died off after five episodes, shortly before the series did.

Not long prior to airing *The Chisholms*, CBS revived the *Maverick* series, without—except for a brief appearance in the opening episode—charismatic James Garner. The new, short-lived series *Young Maverick* was an hour-long Wednesday night show airing from November 1979 to January 1980. Charles Frank played the Harvard-educated Ben Maverick, a nephew of Bret and Bart, a dandy who followed the two into the gambling profession. The magic simply wasn't there—two decades after *Maverick*—and despite the fact that Frank costarred with his real-life wife Susan Blanchard (playing Nell McGarrahan, an equally slick operator), *Young Maverick* rode into the sunset after eight episodes. Frank and Blanchard also played the same roles in the September 1979 TV movie *The New Maverick* with James Garner and Jack Kelly.

Bret Maverick, which premiered on NBC in December 1981, was, more or less, a continuation of the original series, with James Garner returning to the role of Bret after nearly twenty years. In this hour-long series that ran on Tuesday nights through August 1982, Bret finally decides to settle down in Sweetwater, Arizona, after winning the Lazy Ace Ranch and the Red Ox Saloon in a poker game, and becomes a solid citizen. Garner was joined here by Stuart Margolin as the crafty Philo Sandine, self-styled Indian scout/con man; Ed Bruce as Tom Guthrie, the former sheriff who is Bret's partner in the saloon; and Darleen Carr as Mary Lou Springer, feisty owner of the local newspaper. Bruce also sang the theme vocal, "Maverick Didn't Come Here to Lose." Jack Kelly even moseyed in for an episode or two as brother Bart Maverick. (In between the two *Maverick* series, Garner had starred in the now-classic lighthearted detective drama *The Rockford Files* along with pal Margolin. They'd also worked together in Garner's pre-Rockford series, *Nichols*.) *Bret Maverick* lasted just one season, but would be rerun by NBC in the summer of 1990.

Taking a brief break from this continuing series of popular Western shows were a couple of fortuitous reunion programs rounding up a posse of TV cowboy stars in different settings. In 1979 ABC aired a stellar special called *When the West Was Fun: A Western Reunion*. Hosted by Glenn Ford in a saloon setting, the program managed to bring together more than fifty-five television cowboys, from Roy Rogers and Dale Evans, to the Lone Ranger and Tonto, to Chuck Connors, Guy Madison, Jack Kelly, Will Hutchins, George Montgomery, Ty Hardin, Ken Curtis, Milburn Stone, John Russell, Rex Allen, Rod Cameron, Iron Eyes Cody, and on and on. Never in the history of television Westerns has there been a roundup of this many cowboy actors.

On a less grand scale, on ABC's *The Fall Guy* (the eighties series in which Lee Majors starred as movie stuntman/modern-day bounty hunter Colt Seavers), there was a 1983 episode titled "Happy Trails." This one gathered together, in one hour, the likes of Roy Rogers and Trigger, Jack Kelly as Bart Maverick, James Drury and Doug McClure as the Virginian and Trampas, Pat Buttram, the Sons of the Pioneers, and others.

Spoofing the Westerns was ABC's single-season, thirty-minute *Best of the West* from the 1981–1982 season. As the network press release pointed out there were "the brave marshal, the villainous saloonkeeper who owns the town, the drunken old sawbones, the incompetent gunslinger, the saloon gal, etc." Joel Higgins starred as Marshal Sam Best, a Civil War vet from Philadelphia who moseyed West in 1865 in the company of his young son and his new wife, Southern belle Elvira. (Sam had met her while burning down her plantation during the war.) They all settle down in Copper Creek, Montana, a town run by nasty Parker Tillman (played by Leonard Frey). Basically, the comedic series revolved around Sam's inept attempt to uphold the laws as town marshal. ABC couldn't find a proper berth for this show and kept moving it to different nights and times before throwing up its programming hands and walking away from it.

The New Adventures of Zorro was a Saturday morning animated series in 1981, recounting the (new) exploits of the masked Robin Hood of Spanish California. During the thirteen-week series, Henry Darrow voiced Zorro. Not long afterward, he played Zorro in CBS's live-action Western sitcom *Zorro and Son*, and later in the eighties, he turned up as Zorro's father in the filmed-in-Spain series *Zorro*, on the Family Channel.

The Indian point of view found a voice in NBC's very short-lived *Born to the Wind* (just three episodes in the summer of 1982 before the plug was pulled). Native American actor Will Sampson starred as Painted Bear. Henry Darrow (a Hispanic from New York), A Martinez (a Latino from Glendale, California), and Dehl Berti (a Pueblo from Pueblo, Colorado) played Low

Wolf, Lost Robe, and One Feather, respectively, in this series. Linda Redfern and Rose Portillo were Painted Bear's squaw Prairie Woman and daughter Star Fire. It was set in 1825 and followed the lives of a tribe of Plains Indians who called themselves "The People." This somewhat obscure Western series initially was to have been called, simply, *The Indians*.

During the 1983–1984 season, NBC would present what were really the last purely Westerns series for the Peacock, the network that gave the genre *The Roy Rogers Show*, *Wagon Train*, *Bat Masterson*, *Bonanza*, and *Little House on the Prairie*. There would be *The Yellow Rose*, a contemporary Western soap opera that resembled *The Big Valley* for a new generation, and the light-hearted *The Rousters*, which told of the fictional exploits of Wyatt Earp III (Chad Everett), a descendant of the famed lawman.

The Yellow Rose in 1983 on NBC was the name of the sprawling two-hundred-thousand-acre ranch that was the setting for this modern-day drama that follows the fortunes of the now dead Wade Champion's widow and offspring as they struggle with money, lust, and power. Cybill Shepherd played the family matriarch, Colleen Champion; David Soul and Edward Albert played her stepsons Roy and Quisto; and Sam Elliott starred as Chance Mackenzie, the newly hired ranch hand who turned out to be Wade's illegitimate son. With the series underperforming, Chuck Connors and Jane Russell were brought in as the spread's former owner Jeb Hollister and his sister Rose Hollister (after whom the ranch was named). The cast also included L. Q. Jones as Sheriff Lee Wallace, and, as ranch employees, Noah Beery Jr., Kerrie Keane, Ken Curtis, and Susan Anspach. The show never made it into season 2, but was rerun by NBC in 1990.

The Rousters, created by Stephen J. Cannell, was a Western solely for the fact that it dealt with the family of the Old West legend. It had Earp working as, among other things, a roustabout for the Sladetown Carnival, together with his would-be bounty-hunter mother and his con-artist brother, Evan.

Gun Shy, which aired on CBS very briefly in spring 1983, was a Western sitcom, adapted from the Disney films *The Apple Dumpling Gang* and *The Apple Dumpling Gang Rides Again*. Barry Van Dyke, Tim Thomerson, and Geoffrey Lewis starred as gambler Russell Donovan and bumbling desperados Theodore Ogilvie and Amos Tucker, respectively (roles played in the feature films by Bill Bixby, Don Knotts, and Tim Conway, respectively). The series, set in Quake City, a small California town, in 1869, follows the exploits of good-natured Donovan and his two wards, won in a poker game, and the two inept gunslingers who are trying to build reputations as outlaws. It was cancelled after six episodes.

There were only a half dozen more *new* Western series during the eighties—four of them on either CBS or ABC. NBC premiered none. CBS reimagined the Zorro legend in *Zorro and Son*, a sitcom of sorts starring Henry Darrow and Paul Regina in the title roles. It was a misstep for the network and lasted only five episodes (April to June 1983).

At the end of the decade, CBS premiered the hour-long *Paradise*, starring Lee Horsley as Ethan Allen Cord, a grizzled professional gunfighter in the frontier mining town of Paradise, Colorado, in the 1890s. There he is forced to take in his dying sister's four young kids, become a peaceable rancher, and adjust to the role of uncle. Actor Dehl Berti, as an Indian medicine man named John Taylor, becomes his best friend (and sidekick of sorts). By the third and final season (it had been gone for half a season and then was brought back), changes were made. The show was retitled *The Guns of Paradise*, Ethan becomes town marshal, and there is a new best friend, a gambler named Dakota. The series also managed to pay homage to bygone Westerns, with appearances by Hugh O'Brian and Gene Barry as Wyatt Earp and Bat Masterson, plus *The Rifleman*'s Chuck Connors and Johnny Crawford—though in different roles. It has been noted that *Paradise* was just the first Western series to be renewed for a second season since the demise of *Gunsmoke*.

On the now defunct Christian Broadcast Network (CBN), there was a thirty-minute series—Canadian made—called *Bordertown* (1984–1986), set in the 1880s, that revolved around the not-always-temperamentally-in-league efforts of U.S. Marshal Jack Craddock (actor Richard Comar) and Corporal Clive Bennett, a Canadian Mountie (John H. Brennan), to keep peace in a growing but lawless town that straddled the U.S.-Canadian border. When not engaged in battling corruption and assorted bad guys, the two lawmen are often competing for the attention of the town's lady physician, Dr. Marie Dumont (Sophie Barjac). When *Bordertown* left the (American) airwaves, so did CBN, to reemerge first as the Family Channel, then FOX Family Channel, and currently ABC Family Channel.

ABC's *Wildside*, which was seen for a few weeks in spring 1985, chronicled the exploits of an elite group of vigilantes, self-appointed members of the Chamber of Commerce of Wildside who take the law into their own hands to preserve peace in a rough-and-tumble county in northern California in the late 1880s. The group is headed by William Smith as shootist Brodie Hollister and his son Sutton (J. Eddie Peck), along with black cardsharp and demolitionist Bannister Sparks (Howard Rollins Jr.). A young Meg Ryan had a role as Cally Oaks, who ran the local newspaper.

On Showtime, the admirable and well-received family series *Tall Tales and Legends*, created by actress Shelley Duvall, offered a number of folk tales dealing with Western figures, imaginatively produced and cast with big names during the 1985–1986 season. For example there were "Annie Oakley," featuring Jamie Lee Curtis as Annie, Brian Dennehy as Buffalo Bill, Cliff De Young as Frank Butler, and Nick Ramus as Sitting Bull; "My Darling Clementine" with Duvall in the lead along with Edward Asner and David Dukes; "Pecos Bill" with Steve Guttenberg in the lead role and Rebecca de Mornay as Slewfoot Sue; "Johnny Appleseed" with a cast that included Martin Short (in the title role), Rob Reiner, Molly Ringwald, Anne Jackson, and Will Sampson; and "Davy Crockett" starring Mac Davis as Davy, with McLean Stevenson as Andrew Jackson.

Outlaws, a brief CBS series during the 1986–1987 season, was a Western of sorts that, thanks to a bolt of lightning, transported four bank-robbing outlaws and the sheriff who was chasing them from 1899 Houston to 1986 Houston. There the five reconcile their differences, more or less, and learn to survive in the new world. They purchase a ranch with their stolen gold coins, now worth a fortune, and go about dispensing their own brand of justice to modern-day outlaws—under the watchful eye of a law woman named Maggie Randall (Christine Belford). Rough and gruff Rod Taylor starred as the sheriff who somehow finds himself pals with the guys he's chasing—and now they're all on the side of the law.

The Young Riders was a 1989–1992 ABC series about the Pony Express. In this somewhat revisionist view of the Old West—in 1869—Anthony Zerbe was the boss, Teaspoon Hunter, overseeing six young riders: Ty Miller as the Kid (as in Billy); Stephen Baldwin as Billy Cody; Josh Brolin as Jimmy Hickok; Travis Fine as Ike McSwain; Gregg Rainwater as Running Buck Cross, half Kiowa Indian; and one girl, Yvonne Suhor, as Lou McCloud—who had disguised her identity to get the job. During the second season, Don Franklin came on board as Noah Dixon, an educated, freeborn black, as did Christopher Pettitet as a teenage Jesse James. Noah was killed in the final episode—to keep the Pony Express all white (rather anti-politically correct).

Producer Jonas McCord, doing promotion for ABC for the series in 1989, told the *Los Angeles Times* pointedly that yesterday's Westerns were not allowed to reveal the cowboy's frailty. "Their pants were always pressed. Now, I show the pain in a hero. I never could have taken Wyatt Earp and shown him hurting because he killed a man." He went on to comment, "The Pony Express riders were 18 and 19, and there was nothing out there for them but killing and terror. It was just like it was for the 18- or 19-year-old dropped from a helicopter into Saigon."

Zorro swashed and buckled once again on television in a new series that was filmed in Spain and aired between 1989 and 1993 on the Family Channel (sixty-seven episodes). *Zorro* starred dashing Canadian actor Duncan Regehr with his father being played initially by Efrem Zimbalist Jr., and then by Henry Darrow, no stranger to the character of Zorro himself, as noted previously.

During the nineties, there were no more than ten Western series—five on CBS, the others either in syndication or on cable, since television by this time had become so fractured.

Craggy old character actors Richard Farnsworth (a onetime cowboy stuntman) and Wilford Brimley (with his distinctive walrus mustache) played crotchety old codgers in CBS's contemporary Western *The Boys of Twilight*, which aired briefly in March–April 1992. They were elderly peace officers— dignified sheriff Cody McPherson and blustery deputy Bill Huntoon—in the scenic mountain town of Twilight, Utah, who were resigned to but didn't cotton to Twilight's explosive growth and the influx of city slickers. The initial title for this series was "Cody and Bill, the Grey Guns."

CBS also aired a contemporary Western sitcom in 1993–1994 called *Harts of the West*, starring Beau Bridges and, occasionally, his dad, Lloyd. Beau is Dave Hart, a laid-back dude who, after suffering a heart attack as a lingerie salesman in Chicago, decides to follow his dream to become a cowboy. He moves his reluctant family—wife, Alison (Harley Jane Kozak), and kids, all named for Dave's Western heroes—daughter L'Amour, and sons Zane Grey Hart and John Wayne "Duke" Hart—to a rundown ranch he has bought sight unseen in Sholo, Nevada, and installs his cantankerous father-in-law, Jake Tyrell (Lloyd Bridges) as foreman. There's also Saginaw Grant as Auggie Velasquez, a Native American who runs the general store; Talia Solo as her granddaughter Cassie on whom Zane has a crush; O-Lan Jones as Rose, waitress at the only restaurant in town; Stephen Root as R. O. Moon, the local sheriff who's been living with Rose; and occasionally Diane Ladd turned up as Alison Hart's mom. The theme song, "In a Laid Back Way," was performed by country star Clint Black. CBS put the show out to pasture after fifteen hour-long episodes.

FOX got into the game with a whimsical, self-mocking Western series called *The Adventures of Brisco County Jr.*, in 1993. The almost campy, hour-long saga, set in 1893, chronicled the exploits of the jut-jawed hero, a Harvard-educated attorney turned bounty hunter, looking for the varmint who gunned down his father, a U.S. marshal. Brisco, it seems, didn't have the fire in his belly to become a lawyer. At Harvard, he majored in English and, as he said in the first episode, "I mostly learned drinking songs and how to unbutton women's unmentionables." (Brisco, it was pointed out by one reviewer, becomes the first Western hero to get a damsel's dress caught in his fly.) Bruce Campbell played the title character and Billy Drago starred as the meaner-than-mean bad guy, John Bly; Brisco had as his pal one James Lonefeather, who called himself Lord Bowler, a black dude (and fellow bounty hunter) with expensive tastes. He was played by the show's other lead, Julius Carry. Occurring characters in this series, divided into cliff-hanging chapters, were John Astin as an eccentric inventor named Professor Albert Wickwire; Christian Clemenson as lawyer Socrates Poole, representing the San Francisco-based firm that hired Brisco, who, to keep Brisco out of his hair, gives him most of his assignments; and Kelly Rutherford as sexy Dixie Cousins, Brisco's sometimes love interest. And then there was Brisco County Jr.'s horse Comet—incredibly intelligent and endlessly resourceful, with a passion for green apples, especially when depressed. "He don't know he's a horse," Brisco told the camera. "He thinks he's human and has to go where I go." The series made it through one season for the upstart network, which since then never has had another Western.

"*The Adventures of Brisco County Jr.* is gratifying nonsense," the *Los Angeles Times* wrote on its premiere, "a low-flaming but often-witty hybrid of *Blazing Saddles*, *Indiana Jones* and Bruce Lee that genially plugs the Western genre right through the heart." The critic summed up, "No, it's not Louis L'Amour."

In the two-hour pilot, Brisco is hired by a group of robber barons (played by such familiar Western TV faces as Robert Fuller, James Drury, Rayford Barnes, and Paul Brinegar) to track down the world's most notorious outlaws. Like the old serials, each half-hour ends with a cliff-hanger.

The Adventures of Brisco County Jr. attained the dubious distinction of being the bloodiest show on the tube in its day, according to a U.S. Senate study of television violence released in fall 1993, and a bill was introduced to require the Federal Communications Commission (FCC) to publish a quarterly report listing the most violent shows on network television and their commercial sponsors, with the study to be a model for how the FCC would conduct its work. It all died down somewhat and things reverted to the status quo, with Brisco relegated to boot hill after just a single season.

CBS was back with another quirky Western in 1994, following a pilot called *The True Story of My Life*, which ran the previous year with Daniel Baldwin in the lead and Luis Avalos as his Mexican sidekick Creencio (Ned was sheriff of his hometown of Plum Creek, Texas, whose previous law enforcer's head now rests in a pickle jar on the bar in a local saloon). The new, whimsical *Ned Blessing: The Story of My Life and Times* premiered (it ran just four episodes) with Brad Johnson as Blessing—an outlaw turned sheriff who is such a crack shot that, he brags, he can crease a man's cheek with a bullet at one hundred yards without killing him. Avalos was back at his side, plus Native American Wes Studi as his enigmatic "crazy Indian pal" One Horse.

An elderly Ned told the story as a notorious bandit, in jail with his memories and waiting to be hanged, about the time in his life when he was a respected sheriff. "Television's Western revival is shooting itself in the foot," critic Howard Rosenberg wrote in the *Los Angeles Times* of this second chance for Ned Blessing. "The difference between *Ned Blessing* and *Brisco County Jr.*," Rosenberg continued, "is the difference between a series that is accidentally humorous and one that aims to amuse, and succeeds. *Ned Blessing* is the former."

The final gasp of the Western series on network television—at least until the present day—came in two long-running CBS shows beginning in 1993. One was the rather traditional though somewhat feminist *Dr. Quinn, Medicine Woman* starring Jane Seymour; the other, the contemporary *Walker, Texas Ranger* with Chuck Norris. The Seymour series, the most notable in the women-on-the-frontier genre, premiered on January 1, 1993. In it Seymour played an independent young woman doctor making a life for herself in the Old West, moving from Boston to Colorado Springs following the death of her father and medical partner. The rough-and-ready town greets her with hostility, at first, and skepticism, but she is befriended by Charlene Cooper (Diane Ladd initially, then Jessica Bowman), who runs the local boarding-house, and she finds love of sort with mountain man Bryon Sully (Joe Lando). Dr. Quinn was a woman ahead of her time, and proved it through the run of the series (final new episode: June 27, 1998).

In the *Walker* series starring bearded, deadpan, not too talkative, martial arts black belt Chuck Norris, his character Cordell "Cord" Walker, a modern-day Ranger working out of the Dallas office, beats up and kickboxes varmints and weekly bad guys into submission from April 1993 through July 2001. Walker's crime-fighting pal is Ranger Jimmy Trivette (Clarence Gilyard), an African American who had grown up in the slums of Baltimore and was hoping for a football career with the Dallas Cowboys until a bum knee sidelined him. Alex Cahill (Sheree J. North) is a country assistant district attorney, Walker's sometimes girlfriend, who frowns on his "persuasive" and only peripherally legal methods. And for a while there was Native American actor Floyd Red Crow Westerman as Uncle Ray Firewalker, who had raised Walker. In a number of episodes, via flashback, Norris even played a Ranger in the Old West—who just happened to look like his contemporary character. *Walker* became CBS's perennial Saturday night adventure show (although having premiered on a Wednesday) following *Dr. Quinn, Medicine Woman* through the nineties.

Lonesome Dove: The Series (1994–1996), set in Dakota Territory during the 1870s, was a syndicated sequel of sorts to Larry McMurtry's memorable miniseries (but not *Return to Lonesome Dove*, with which McMurtry had nothing to do and emphatically disowned). The new series followed the exploits of young Newt Call (Scott Bairstow)—adoptive son to Tommy Lee Jones's character in the original mini—newly arrived in Curtis Wells, Montana, and falling in love with and marrying Hannah Peale (Christianne Hirt), daughter of the local publisher (Paul LeMat) and onetime love of black-clad Confederate officer Captain Francis Clay Mosby (Eric McCormack). Diahann Carroll had the role of Ida Grayson (during the first season), a black settler who takes Call in as a partner to buy the Unity Hotel—the bank probably won't sell to her, she figures, because she is black—and they rename it Lonesome Dove. When it returned for its second (and last) season, the series was heavily revamped and retitled *Lonesome Dove: The Outlaw Years*. Call was now making a living as a bounty hunter, and a whole new supporting cast was brought in. There were forty-three episodes in total.

Legend (1995), a Western with a rather conflicted identity that overdosed on *Wild Wild West* gadgetry and gimmickry, had Richard Dean Anderson as a hard-drinking dime novelist named Ernest Pratt in 1875 San Francisco. He assumes the identity of heroic Nicodemus Legend, his teetotaling literary creation, but is aimless until lured to Sheridan, Colorado, by an eccentric genius, Professor James Bartok (John de Lancie), and prodded into helping those on the frontier who need it—using assorted ahead-of-their-time devices. Among those surrounding him are Mark Adair Rios, as Ramos, Bartok's Mexican assistant; Jarred Paul as Skeeter, a wild-haired bellboy at the local hotel; Robert Donner as Chamberlin Brown, the town mayor and undertaker; and Robert Shelton as Grady, the bartender. *Legend*, which aired from April to August 1995, never found an audience (perhaps because it was on UPN, a relatively little watched network, on which it was the only Western) and was cancelled after just twelve episodes.

The Lazarus Man (January–November 1996) starred Robert Urich as a man who, in the fall of 1865, not long after the Lincoln assassination—a shooting that's woven in and out of the plot—wakes up in a shallow grave in the town of San Sebastian, Texas, with a bad case of amnesia. He is wearing Southern clothing but carrying Northern gold and a Union pistol—and he spends the next twenty-two episodes of the weekly hour-long series, that debuted on cable on TNT, trying to find out his true identity, so he doesn't have to keep referring to himself as Lazarus (he's actually, it's disclosed, one

James Cathcart), after the man that was raised from death by Christ. The series, unfortunately, ran for just one season before being cancelled due to Urich's being diagnosed with cancer.

Dead Man's Gun (a Canadian-made anthology airing on Showtime on cable between 1997 and 1999) focused on a cursed revolver that brings violence to a variety of owners—a different guest star every week—in the American West. The Rod Serling–inspired series (two or three individual related stories told each time) was produced by Henry "the Fonz" Winkler and narrated by Kris Kristofferson. John Ritter starred in the three-part initial episode as the Great McDonacle, described in the publicity for the series as a "a shifty trick-shooter who relies on 'smoke and mirrors' as well as a little buckshot to provide a decent show, but once he gets his hands on the Dead Man's Gun, he realizes he no longer needs any illusions, he's suddenly a crack shot!" When shootists come gunning for him, he has no problem dealing with them, until the Dead Man's Gun has its way! There were forty-four episodes.

CBS gave series Westerns one more network shot with *The Magnificent Seven* (1998–2000), an adaptation of the hit 1960 movie that starred Steve McQueen, Yul Brynner, James Coburn, Charles Bronson, and others—that in turn was inspired by Akiro Kurosawa's *Seven Samurai* years before that. Michael Biehn (in McQueen's part), Eric Close (in Brynner's), Dale Midkiff, and Ron Perlman were four of the magnificent seven in this series that ran for twenty-two episodes.

The Ponderosa (2001–2002) starred Daniel Hugh Kelly as Ben Cartwright along with Matt Carmody (Adam), Drew Powell (Hoss), and Jared Daperis (Little Joe) and was a restart of the old *Bonanza* bonanza. Actually, this was a prequel, according to the publicity, to the venerable fifties series—Ben and sons moving onto some scrub land in the Lake Tahoe area of the late 1840s, hoping to develop a cattle ranch. It was filmed on location—in Australia. (Recall that the original *Bonanza* was later syndicated under the title *Ponderosa*.)

Deadwood, which developed a following when it aired on HBO for a couple of seasons beginning in 2004, was a gritty, violent, profane Western series (anti-Western, some have called it) that was about as far from *Hopalong Cassidy* and *The Roy Rogers Show* as could be imagined. Created and mostly written by David Milch, it also reached cult status and won twenty-eight Emmy nominations in its time. The series starred Timothy Olyphant as the real-life Seth Bullock, a hardware store entrepreneur in Deadwood and U.S. marshal, and Ian McShane as Al Swearengen, ruthless, brutal owner of the Gem Theater, Deadwood's notorious brothel—an Old West mob boss might best describe him. They work their way among other fictional and real Old

West figures—Wild Bill Hickok (played by Keith Carradine), a very foul-mouthed Calamity Jane, Wyatt Earp, Charlie Utter, E. B. Farnum, Sol Star, Jack McCall, prospector George Hearst, and so on—as they chart the growth of lawless Deadwood, South Dakota, from mining camp to town. Powers Boothe also starred as gambler Cy Tolliver (based on the real-life Tom Miller), Swearengen's rival with his much higher-class saloon/whorehouse, the Bella Union. The show had historical truths and fictional elements, as one source put it.

When *Deadwood* reached the end of the trail, so, more or less, did the television Western series as it developed. That show's Timothy Olyphant, however, moseyed on, in spring 2010, to play a courtly though gunslinging modern-day U.S. marshal (working out of rural Kentucky where he was reassigned after a shooting in Miami!) with frontier ways and a cowboy hat, a buckskin jacket, and a pistol in holster strapped to his waist, in *Justice* (originally it was to be titled *Lawman*), "a wonderfully old-fashioned drama bearing the imprimatur of novelist Elmore Leonard," *Variety* noted, reviewing the cable series' premiere. "Olyphant's Raylan Givens is one tough hombre who lives by a credo best articulated by the outlaw Ike Clanton back in *My Darling Clementine*—namely, when you draw a gun, expect to kill somebody." "It's a modern Western," the *Fort Worth Star-Telegram* wrote, "with Olyphant playing a fearless, laconic hero who's quick on the draw, speaking softly but carrying a big gun. He's an anachronism and Olyphant's young Clint Eastwood act would come off a little silly if everything surrounding it weren't so good."

Westerns came into the reality television mix—or as the industry prefers to call it, unscripted programs—with such fare as PBS's six-episode British-made *Frontier House* in 2002 (three contemporary families were placed in an Old West setting to relive the harsh life a real family would have faced back then without modern conveniences) and *Kid Nation* on CBS in 2007, which had a bunch of youngsters establishing their own universe (at Bonanza Creek Ranch in Santa Fe) and reliving what it was like to be a part of the Old West—for at least thirteen weeks.

Animal Planet jumped into the game in mid-2010 with a reality series based on the contemporary exploits of three Montana cattle-ranch owners. Titled *Last American Cowboy*, it was promoted this way: "This epic adventure follows three families of tough, tenacious and headstrong cowboys through freak storms, deadly outbreaks of disease, hungry predators and forest fires that threaten their livelihood. Each ranch will need to rely on family bonds and personal strength to keep this tradition of the American West alive."

CHAPTER SIX

The Made-for-TV
Western Saddles Up

During the midsixties a new genre was finding popularity: the made-for-tele-vision movie, which began as a new dramatic form under the umbrella title Project 120, a collaboration between NBC and Universal Pictures. There would be a series of original two-hour movies, initially, which would be expanded (or contracted) by the other networks. Westerns would be among the dramas (and later, comedies) that would take their place in the movies-made-for-television world, often with fading movie stars. As mentioned earlier, the pilot for Dale Robertson's 1966–1968 series *The Iron Horse* aired as ABC's first two-hour movie, *Scalplock*, in April 1966.

In the 1966–1967 season, three of the movies made for television were Western adventures, each running two hours (less commercial time). First was *The Dangerous Days of Kiowa Jones* (premiering on Christmas Day 1966), with Robert Horton in the title role playing a drifter who is deputized by a dying marshal to deliver two killers to prison, while eluding a pair of bounty hunters who want his charges. Diane Baker, Sal Mineo, and Gary Merrill were in the cast. This actually was a pilot for a prospective series that never materialized.

Next was *Return of the Gunfighter* starring Robert Taylor as an aging gun-fighter who teams up with a wounded saddle tramp (Chad Everett) to help a Mexican girl avenge the death of her parents, murdered for their land. This solid Western was from a tale by genre writer/director Burt Kennedy and Robert Bruckner.

And then there was *Winchester .73*, a TV remake of the 1950 James Stewart Western with Tom Tryon (in Stewart's role) and John Saxon (the

Stephen McNally part) as brothers—one a law officer, the other an ex-con—vying for possession of the famed repeating rifle of the title. Of interest here was that Dan Duryea was in both versions—theatrical and television. In the original he played a sadistic bad guy who made things tough for Stewart; in the remake, he was the good guy cousin of the two brothers. Shelley Winters's saloon girl role in the original was revamped somewhat for Joan Blondell in the TV remake.

Henry Fonda made his TV movie debut during the 1967–1968 season in *Stranger on the Run*, directed by Don Siegel. Fonda played a drifter who finds himself wrongly accused of murder by a hostile sheriff (Dan Duryea) and chased into the desert with a horse, some supplies, a one-hour start, and a deadly posse on his heels. The female costar in this was Anne Baxter (also her TV movie debut) as a gun-toting broad who befriends the Fonda character.

During the following TV season, Dan Blocker (Hoss Cartwright from *Bonanza*) had a rare starring role on *Something for a Lonely Man*, as a gentle frontier blacksmith who finds the love of a good woman (Susan Clark)—a mail-order bride—and a book of Ralph Waldo Emerson's essays.

In December 1969, Lloyd Bridges starred in *The Silent Gun* (produced by Bruce Lansbury, Angela's brother), an offbeat Western about a gunfighter who totes an unloaded pistol in his holster after nearly shooting an innocent child. Being made sheriff of a lawless frontier town, he rides into frays on the strength of his reputation as a fast gun. This was written by Clyde Ware, who had done dozens of scripts for such Western series as *Rawhide*, *Gunsmoke*, *The Road West*, *The Guns of Will Sonnett*, and *The High Chaparral*.

Danny Thomas and Aaron Spelling offered up a ninety-minute comedy Western—and probably prospective pilot to a new series—in 1969's *The Over-the-Hill Gang* with a stellar cast of Western veterans, including Walter Brennan, Pat O'Brien, Edgar Buchanan, Chill Wills, Andy Devine, and Jack Elam, along with Gypsy Rose Lee, Ricky Nelson (in his TV movie debut), and his wife, Kris Harmon Nelson. O'Brien played a retired Texas Ranger who, with three aged pals, played by Brennan, Wills, and Buchanan, tries to clean up a town run by a crooked mayor (Edward Andrews), a drunken judge (Devine), and a trigger-happy sheriff (Jack Elam). Rose's turn—at sixty-eight—as an aging saloon gal named Cassie marked her final acting appearance (she died not long afterward). Walter Brennan, at the time having had an unexpected hit album or two as a "singer," performed a Western ditty called "Texas Rangers." Hugo Friedhofer scored the film.

The Over-the-Hill Gang Rides Again (1970) was another (unsuccessful) Thomas-Spelling attempt to get a series going, with old-time comrades in arms Brennan, Buchanan, Wills, and Devine (now one of the boys) joining forces to sober up an old buddy, Fred Astaire as the Baltimore Kid, a down-and-out drunk, and restore his reputation. This was Astaire's TV movie debut—and the only Western he ever did. Once again, Brennan sang ("Come All You Texas Rangers")—although Astaire didn't! The music to this film was by David Raksin, "the venerable feature film composer," Jon Burlingame pointed out in his book, "whose score for *Laura* is one of the most memorable film scores ever written, and whose theme is one of the most recorded tunes in history."

Cutter's Trail, which premiered on CBS in early 1970, was a formula Western about a U.S. marshal (played by square-jawed John Gavin, the actor who later became ambassador to Mexico), finding his town nearly destroyed by Mexican bandits during his absence and vowing to track them down with the help of a Mexican mother and her young son (Marisa Pavan and Manuel Padilla Jr.).

The Intruders (1970, though filmed in 1967), featured Don Murray as, according to NBC's press release at the time, "a local marshal, having lost both his nerve and his skill with a pistol, who is put to the test when the James/Younger gang rides into town." Future star Harrison Ford had a small role in this one.

The Young Country (1970) was a lighthearted Western with Walter Brennan as a cantankerous sheriff keeping an eye on a resourceful young gambler named Stephen Foster Moody (Roger Davis) who's searching for the owner of a mysterious fortune, with the help of con-artist pal Honest John Smith (Peter Deuel). This movie, it turns out, was the pilot to *Alias Smith and Jones*, and, ironically, after Deuel took his own life in real life in the middle of *Alias Smith and Jones*, Davis replaced him. This film, that also starred Joan Hackett and Wally Cox, was written, produced, and directed by Roy Huggins, the guy behind *Maverick* as well as *The Fugitive*.

Wild Women (1970) was a boisterous if innocuous Western from Aaron Spelling, adapted from Vincent Forte's *The Trailmakers*, in which Hugh O'Brian leads a group of army engineers in the 1840s who recruit five female convicts to pose as their spouses on a secret government mission to run guns and help free Texas from Mexican control. Anne Francis, Marie Windsor, Marilyn Maxwell, Sherry Jackson, and Cynthia Hull had the collective title role.

Sam Hill: Who Killed Mr. Foster? (1971) starred Ernest Borgnine as an alcoholic drifter who finds himself offered the small town sheriff's job—if he can find the killers of a visiting preacher. This was a creation of Richard Levinson and William Link (later to be renowned for TV's *Mannix*, *Mc-Cloud*, *Columbo*, and *Murder She Wrote*).

The Trackers (1971), starring Ernest Borgnine and Sammy Davis Jr., was a questionably racist Western. Produced by Aaron Spelling as a ninety-minute TV movie/pilot, it told of tracker Sam Paxton, a marshal hired by a wealthy rancher to search for a bandit gang that killed his son and kidnapped his daughter. The lawman's deputy and protégé happens to be a black man named Ezekial Smith, a former frontier scout, but the color of the guy's skin seems to upset those who are rooting for the girl's return. Davis, incidentally an incredible all-around talent and a whiz at twirling guns and fast draw (as part of his act), was no stranger to Western series. He'd guest starred on *Dick Powell's Zane Grey Theatre* (Sammy's TV acting debut in 1959); *Lawman*; *Frontier Circus*; *The Wild Wild West*; and *The Rifleman*.

The Devil and Miss Sarah (1971), a different kind of sagebrush saga, a horror Western, teamed the guy who once played the Virginian with the guy who once played Bat Masterson—James Drury versus Gene Barry. The former starred as a notorious outlaw named Rankin, possessed of satanic powers; the latter a homesteader who's escorting him to prison as a favor to the town marshal—until he finds out the bad guy is trying to possess his wife.

Yuma (1971) starred big Clint Walker—hoping to hit pay dirt again after *Cheyenne*—as a marshal who sets out, with the help of his aging deputy (Edgar Buchanan), to clean up a lawless frontier town filled with brawling cattlemen, crooked officials, and various bad guys out to discredit him. This was a failed Aaron Spelling pilot.

Powderkeg (1971) played out as a lighthearted adventure in the pre–World War I West with Rod Taylor and Dennis Cole playing a pair of trouble-shooters hired to retrieve a hijacked train. They continued their roles and battled early twentieth-century crime in the short-lived late 1971 CBS series *Bearcats!* The movie pilot was produced, written, and directed by Douglas Heyes.

Lock, Stock and Barrel (1971) was an amiable ninety-minute Western about a young frontier couple who elope (Tim Matheson and Belinda J. Montgomery), are pursued by the girl's displeased father and brothers, are joined by an escaped convict (Claude Akins), and become involved with a phony preacher (Burgess Meredith). It was a failed pilot.

Black Noon (1971) turned out to be an occult Western about a circuit-riding minister and his wife (Roy Thinnes and Lyn Loring), who are caught up in a web of witchcraft involving a mute beauty (Yvette Mimieux) and a satanical gunfighter (Ray Milland).

The Bravos (1972) featured George Peppard, playing the rugged commander of a beleaguered frontier cavalry post, who tries to stop an Indian war and find his kidnapped son (played by Vincent Van Patten). Pernell Roberts, Adam Cartwright in *Bonanza*, costarred along with Belinda J. Montgomery and L. Q. Jones on this, another failed pilot.

The Daughters of Joshua Cabe (1972) starred Buddy Ebsen as a fur trapper who schemes to keep his land holdings in the wake of a new homesteading law by recruiting a prostitute, a thief, and a pickpocket to pose as his purdy daughters, Charity, Mae, and Ada. The amusing ninety-minute Western pilot was from the house of Spelling/Goldberg—and when it didn't sell, they tried it again and again, first (in 1975) with *The Daughters of Joshua Cabe Return*, this time with veteran dancer Dan Dailey, and then with *The New Daughters of Joshua Cabe* the following year, starring *Wagon Train*'s craggy-faced John McIntire. Joshua kept changing, and so did his daughters, and so did Joshua's pal Bitterroot.

Female Artillery (1973) was about an outlaw named Deke Chambers (Dennis Weaver) who joins up with a wagon train of pioneer women, headed by Ida Lupino as Martha Lindstrom and Nina Foch as Amelia Craig, and secretly hides some stolen loot with them. However his old gang (headed by Albert Salmi) shows up and wants their money—and the traveling ladies. This lighthearted ninety-minute sagebrush saga provided a Western change of pace for veteran actress Lupino, who had become one of the partners in Four Star Television and one of the very few female film directors post–World War II, alternating her time between directing episodes of Western series like *Have Gun—Will Travel* (she did at least seven of them), *Hotel de Paree*, *The Virginian*, and others, and acting on *Zane Grey Theatre*, *Bonanza*, *Death Valley Days*, and *The Wild Wild West*.

Honky Tonk (1974) was a ninety-minute television movie that hoped to create new interest in the early forties Western feature that starred Clark Gable and Lana Turner (and only loosely based on it). This one starred Richard Crenna and Margot Kidder, as Old West gambler/con man Candy Johnson and his partner, Lucy Cotton, daughter of a judge (Will Geer). Stella Stevens portrayed saloon gal Gold Dust, played in the original by Claire Trevor. It was a pilot that never made it to series.

The Hanged Man (1974), from Bing Crosby Productions, was about an ex-gunslinger (Steve Forrest) who survives his own hanging and turns into a mystical avenger fighting for justice in the Old West. His first adventure in this obvious pilot had him coming to the aide of a young widow who is attempting to keep her silver mine from the clutches of an unscrupulous land baron (Cameron Mitchell).

This Is the West That Was (1974) was a somewhat lighthearted Roy Huggins–produced look at the Wild Bill Hickok legend, having him fighting off the bad guys and avoiding (if only half-heartedly) the advances of Calamity Jane. Ben Murphy and Kim Darby starred, along with Matt Clark as Buffalo Bill Cody. Jane Alexander, Anthony Franciosa, and Stuart Margolin also were in the cast.

Sidekicks (1974) was a Western spoof based on the 1971 feature *Skin Game*, with Lou Gossett re-creating the role he played in the film and Larry Hagman stepping into James Garner's boots. (Garner's company, Cherokee Productions, produced this one but Garner himself was elsewhere occupied.) This lark, a pilot to a prospective series that never materialized, had a couple of hapless post–Civil War con men, one black, one white (passing themselves off as slave and master), on the sagebrush trail trying to collect a fifteen thousand dollar bounty on an outlaw's head. It's universally agreed that Hagman, with all of his "J. R. Ewing charm," isn't Garner, and Garner was apparently what was needed. Also in the cast of this ninety-minute pilot were Blythe Danner as the feisty daughter of local sheriff Harry Morgan, plus a posse of veteran actors steeped in sagebrush sagas. *Sidekicks* was produced and directed by Old West aficionado Burt Kennedy, who knew his way around Westerns, lighthearted and otherwise.

Mrs. Sundance (1974) starred Elizabeth Montgomery, not outta place as Etta Place. Etta, the schoolteacher "widow" of the Sundance Kid here is on the run with a price on her head, when she hears rumors that her lover may still be alive. Montgomery's real-life lover, Robert Foxworth, played her traveling companion, one step ahead of Pinkerton man Charlie Stringo (L. Q. Jones). This incidentally was Montgomery's first role after wrapping up *Bewitched*, and it set her on the path to becoming the most popular female actress in television in a string of movies—in which she never again played comedy.

Shootout in a One-Dog Town (1974) starred Richard Crenna as a small-town banker in a frontier community pitted against a vicious gang who'll stop at nothing to steal the two hundred thousand dollars in his vault. Noted animators Joseph Barbera and William Hanna were the atypical producers of the lean "High Noon"–type Western, directed by genre veteran Burt Kennedy.

The Godchild (1974), a TV movie remake of John Ford's *Three Godfathers* from the forties, starred Jack Palance in John Wayne's big-screen role, along with Jack Warden and Keith Carradine. They played Union prisoners fleeing across the desert to escape both their Confederate pursuers and rampaging Apaches. Along the way, they come across a dying woman and her infant child and promise her that they will take care of the child and get it to safety, despite not knowing anything whatsoever about babies. This oft-filmed Western tale originally came from Peter B. Kyne's *Saturday Evening Post* story.

Nevada Smith (1975) continued a somewhat convoluted lineage, going back to Harold Robbins's 1961 best seller *The Carpetbaggers*. The book then became a feature film in 1964—the number one moneymaker of that year—starring George Peppard (as a Howard Hughes type), along with aging actor Alan Ladd as a cowboy character named Nevada Smith, a former Western sharpshooter turned actor (it was Ladd's last role). The *Nevada Smith* character, a half-breed gunslinger (Ladd as a half-breed?), then was the basis for a Steve McQueen movie prequel of that title in 1966, and that film was the inspiration for this two-hour NBC movie that the network thought it might spin off into a series, with Cliff Potts in the title role and *Bonanza*'s Lorne Greene as his mentor Jonas Cord (the Peppard character originally). *Nevada Smith* failed to make the cut as a series pilot.

Nakia, set in the contemporary West, had Robert Forster as a Native American lawman, Nakia Parker, and Arthur Kennedy as his boss, Sam Jericho, battling unscrupulous housing developers in modern day New Mexico. This spawned a short-lived 1974 ABC series.

The Last Day (1975) starring Richard Widmark, dramatized how the Dalton gang met its end while trying to rob two banks at the same time in Coffeyville, Kansas, October 5, 1892. This trim Western produced by veteran A. C. Lyles, had Widmark as a fictional retired gunman forced to strap on his gun belt once more when the Daltons (played by Robert Conrad, Richard Jaeckel, and Tim Matheson) come to town with blazing guns.

I Will Fight No More Forever (1975) was a TV movie reenactment of the story of Chief Joseph of the Nez Percé Indians, who lived in the Wallowa Valley of Idaho and Oregon. In 1877, President Ulysses S. Grant opened the valley to white settlement, and the Nez Percé and their leader were given thirty days in which to move to the Lapwai Reservation. The government sent the one-armed soldier-chief General Oliver Otis Howard (played by James Whitmore) to enforce the order and clear all Nez Percé out. Chief Joseph was played by actor Ned Romero, who has made a career more or less of playing Native Americans—although he has only a trace of Indian blood (he's of Spanish and French background and hails from New Orleans).

One of General Howard's officers, Captain C. E. S. Wood (Howard's real-life aide-de-camp), was played by Sam Elliott, who, in the contemporary era of the movie Westerns, had become, arguably, the very personification of the American cowboy, with his deep, gravelly voice; his piercing eyes; his thick, droopy mustache; and his John Wayne–style bandana—even more so than Clint Eastwood, who has gone on to other pursuits. (Wood, a West Pointer, was born in 1852 and died in 1944.) Elliott was to be the star of eleven made-for-TV Westerns through the end of the 1990s, a number of them from the stories of Louis L'Amour.

Bridger (1976) featured James Wainwright in the fictional exploits of the real-life Jim Bridger, an explorer, scout, and tracker who was known as the Daniel Boone of the Rockies, ordered by President Andrew Jackson to blaze a trail from Wyoming to California in just forty days. Dan Blocker's actor son Dirk played Bridger's sidekick, Joe Meck, and Ben Murphy rode onto the scene as Kit Carson. Sally Field was on board as Bridger's (fictional) love interest.

Banjo Hackett: Roaming Free (1976) starred former football star Don Meredith in an amiable Western (pilot) about an itinerant horse trader who travels the frontier in the 1880s with his orphaned nine-year-old nephew looking for the boy's prized Arabian mare that had been snatched by ruthless bounty hunters—one of whom is played by Chuck Connors. There were lots of familiar names in this one: Gloria De Haven, Anne Francis, Jan Murray, Dan O'Herlihy, Slim Pickens, and others.

James A. Michener's "Dynasty" (1976) was the saga of the Blackwoods, a pioneer family—husband, wife, and brother-in-law—torn by jealousy, deception, and rivalry in love and business as they seek their fortune on the Ohio frontier. The clan had Harris Yulin, Sarah Miles, and Stacy Keach in the leads, with Harrison Ford and Amy Irving among the younger family members. Produced by Britisher David Frost, for his Paradine Productions, the story, originally entitled "The Americans" and covering a thirty-five-year period starting in the 1820s, looked to be a trial run for Michener's subsequent American epic *Centennial*. (Amusingly, the cover of the DVD of *Dynasty* has Harrison Ford—in cowboy hat—with top billing, then Sarah Miles, Amy Irving, and Stacy Keach, all above the title; no mention at all of the nominal star Harris Yulin.)

Several of Michener's historical fiction best sellers—those dealing with the American West or the frontier—were produced for television, as were those, of course, of Western writers ranging from Owen Wister and Zane Grey to Mark Twain and O. Henry to Max Brand and the more contemporary Charles Marquis Warren (credited as creator of *Gunsmoke*) and Louis L'Amour. Not included in this bunch was John Jakes—who wrote historical fiction not about the West but about the American Revolution (the Kent Chronicles trilogy) and the Civil War (the North and South trilogy), all six filmed as individual miniseries.

Young Pioneers and *Young Pioneers' Christmas* (both 1976) were two movies, each a pilot, aimed at the youth audience with Linda Purl and Roger

Kern as a pair of frontier newlyweds seeking to tame the Dakota wilderness in the 1870s, along with their friend, played by Robert Hays. The movies were based on books by Rose Wilder Lane (who had died eight years earlier at the age of eighty-one). She'd been a journalist, novelist, and the founding mother of the American Libertarian Party and happened to be the daughter of Laura Ingalls Wilder of *Little House on the Prairie* fame. ABC decided to go ahead early in spring with a brief series that didn't make it beyond three episodes.

Wanted: The Sundance Woman (1976) had Katharine Ross returning to the role of Etta Place that she began in *Butch Cassidy and the Sundance Kid*, despite Elizabeth Montgomery's TV interpretation a couple of years before. Originally this was to have been called *Mrs. Sundance Rides Again*, and it had her being chased all over the West by a Pinkerton man Charlie Stringo, here played by Steve Forrest, and even becoming a gunrunner for Pancho Villa (Hector Elizondo).

The Invasion of Johnson County, written and produced by Roy Huggins, was a fictionalized version of the real-life tale of Johnson County. Bill Bixby starred as a greenhorn from Boston who goes West and becomes involved with a Wyoming cowpoke (Bo Hopkins) who's out to block dastardly John Hillerman's private army's land-grab scheme against local ranchers.

Charlie Cobb: A Nice Night for a Hanging (1977) was another Western created by Richard Levinson and William Link. Clu Gulager, in the title role, is a private eye in the Old West, hired by a wealthy rancher (Ralph Bellamy) to find his long-lost daughter. There's a new wife involved here, the rancher's shady top hand (Christopher Connelly), and a crooked sheriff (Pernell Roberts). All in all, another NBC pilot that failed to fly.

True Grit: A Further Adventure (1978) was a TV movie inspired by (if not a remake of) the John Wayne classic Western for which he won his Best Actor Oscar. Warren Oates saddled up and took Duke's role of tough, grizzled, hard-drinking, one-eyed U.S. marshal Rooster Cogburn—in this two-hour proposed series pilot—agreeing to shepherd an orphaned teenage girl from Arkansas to her relatives in California. (Oates just previously had assumed the Bogart role as Charlie Alnutt in a TV movie of *The African Queen*.)

Donner Pass: The Road to Survival (1978) was a Classics Illustrated version of American history and the fight waged by a pioneer, the real-life James Reed (played by Robert Fuller, late of *Wagon Train* as its last scout) to save the lives of his family and others in a wagon train. They themselves are trapped in deep mountain snows of the Sierra Nevada in the late 1840s and facing starvation that leads them to (unspecified) cannibalism.

Standing Tall (1978) was a better-than-average twentieth-century West-ern set in the Depression thirties and starred Robert Forster as Luke Shasta, a small-time half-breed cattle rancher struggling to eke out an existence. He finds himself subjected to a terror campaign—which he fights with his Indian pal Lonny Moon (Will Sampson)—after refusing to sell out to a ruthless land baron (played by L. Q. Jones). Also in the film were Chuck Connors, Linda Evans, and Buck Taylor.

Thaddeus Rose and Eddie (1978) had Johnny Cash starring with Bo Hop-kins in a modern-day Western as a couple of cowpokes, small-town ranchers on the Texas panhandle, who've done their share of boozing, brawling, and womanizing—with Diane Ladd and June Carter Cash. This was the first of several TV movies in which the Cashes costarred (in one she played his mother!). The pair also had starred together several years earlier in an *NET Playhouse* (later PBS) drama called *Trail of Tears*, dealing with American history (with Pat Hingle as George Washington, Jack Palance as Andrew Johnson). Johnny Cash portrayed John Ross, chief of the Cherokee Nation in the late 1830s and often referred to as the Moses of his people.

Go West, Young Girl (1978) had perky Karen Valentine playing a naïve, foolhardy, Nellie Bly–type reporter from back East heading thataway to the West in search of allegedly dead Billy the Kid (played by Richard Jaeckel), in the company of Billy's rugged sister, a cavalry officer's wife. Sis, it seems, doesn't believe her rogue brother really was a showdown casualty. The *TV Guide* ad copy for this not-to-be-taken-seriously tale—a failed two-hour pilot—read, "They've Taken Off Their Petticoats and Strapped On Their Guns!"

Around the same time, there was another "green" gals-out-West pilot, *Lacy and the Mississippi Queen*, with Kathleen Lloyd as a coolheaded cowgirl who teams up with Debra Feuer as her gun-toting half-sister, both ranchers moonlighting as detectives for the Union Pacific Railroad, to track down a pair of train robbers who are suspects in their father's shooting.

Kate Bliss and the Ticker Tape Kid, another comedy Western pilot from Aaron Spelling and directed by Burt Kennedy, costarred Suzanne Pleshette with Dandy Don Meredith and a bevy of names (Harry Morgan, Tony Ran-dall, Burgess Meredith, Harry Carey Jr., Don "Red" Barry, Buck Taylor, Gene Evans). Pleshette played a turn-of-the-century lady investigator who goes to the wide-open spaces to capture a gang of outlaws led by a charming Robin Hood of the plains. Randall was a stuffy English land baron who's cheating dispossessed ranchers of their property.

Mr. Horn (1979), a sprawling two-part, four-hour Western saga, was based on the legend of frontier folk hero Tom Horn (David Carradine) and his role in the track-down of Geronimo in the 1880s with fabled Indian scout Al Sieber (Richard Widmark), his mentor and pal. It also dramatized Horn's later days as a Pinkerton detective and the way he was used by both sides in turn-of-the-century cattle wars, leading to his tragic death. Around the same time, Steve McQueen made a theatrical film about Horn—with a somewhat different bent.

The Last Ride of the Dalton Gang (1979); the title just about tells it all. Starring were Cliff Potts, Randy Quaid, and Larry Wilcox as Dalton brothers Bob, Grat, and Em, respectively, plus Sharon Farrell as Flo Quick, known in Western lore as "Bob Dalton's bandit bride"; Dale Robertson as Judge Isaac Parker, remembered as "the Hanging Judge of the American West"; and Jack Palance as the Daltons' arch enemy, railway detective Will Smith. As a conceit, the film, produced and directed by Dan Curtis, was framed by then elderly Em Dalton, who survived and was living in Hollywood well into the 1930s.

The Legend of the Golden Gun (1979) was all about a handsome, dazzlingly blond cowboy (Jeffrey Osterhage) in post–Civil War Kansas, who with his pal, a Bible-quoting former slave (Carl Franklin), sets out to kill infamous Confederate guerrilla leader William Quantrill (Robert Davi) after being presented with a golden gun from a legendary sharpshooter (Hal Holbrook). This Western evokes the personas of greats of the Old West, including General Custer, Sitting Bull, and Buffalo Bill. "Imagine *Star Wars* as a Western," the network publicity pointed out. This apparently was an NBC pilot that never got to series.

The Wild Wild West Revisited (1979), followed in 1980 by *More Wild Wild West*, reunited Robert Conrad and Ross Martin as James West and Artemus Gordon, and even brought along little person Michael Dunn as Dr. Miguelito Loveless. In the first, the intrepid team of Old West government intelligence agents are brought out of retirement after ten years to hunt down a cunning new adversary, the son of their former archenemy, who is suspected of cloning imposters to be substituted for the crowned heads of Europe and perhaps even the president of the United States (Grover Cleveland, played by Wilford Brimley).

In the second, West and Gordon are up against the evil Albert Paradine II, a mad professor played by Jonathan Winters. Paradine, it turns out, had bumped off four sets of twin brothers. Also in the cast was Victor Buono, this time playing Dr. Henry Messenger (a spoof of Henry Kissinger), President Benjamin Harrison's secretary of state. Also along for the adventure in both films was Harry Morgan playing Robert T. "Skinny" Malone, who supplies West and Gordon with all the fancy gadgets—which they never seem to use. Burt Kennedy directed both films.

The Sacketts, the first of a number of TV Westerns from author Louis L'Amour, aired in 1979. It starred Sam Elliott and Tom Selleck along with Jeffrey Osterhage and was based on L'Amour's first two Sackett novels, beginning with 1959's *The Daybreakers*. The book chronicled the story of three Sackett brothers, Tell, Orin, and Tyrell, moving west to escape the feuding and poverty of the Tennessee mountains. They join one of the first cattle drives to Kansas, seek their fortunes on the southern plains, and finally settle in Mora, New Mexico. As they explore the landscape of the West, they learn the cost of friendship and love, and the value of education. (This was from a website devoted to the Sacketts' fortieth anniversary.) Also in the two-part, four-hour saga was a cast of Western performers as long as your arm: Glenn Ford, Ben Johnson, Gilbert Roland, Ruth Roman, Jack Elam, Slim Pickens, Pat Buttram, Buck Taylor, L. Q. Jones, Gene Evans, and on and on.

In the follow-up of sorts, *The Shadow Riders* (1982), Elliott, Selleck, and Osterhage were the Traven brothers, the two older ones having fought on opposite sides in the Civil War (the younger one having been abducted by a raging band of renegades). Ben Johnson was their uncle Jack, Harry Carey Jr. and Jane Greer were their pa and ma, and Elliott's girlfriend and soon-to-be wife, Katharine Ross, was his screen girlfriend—who had also been taken with the youngest brother.

Wild Times (1980), a purely fictional Western with Sam Elliott as the real-life Hugh Cardiff, dime-novel hero turned sharp-shooting saddle tramp, Indian fighter, buffalo hunter, and Wild West show impresario. Dennis Hopper costarred as Doc Holliday, L. Q. Jones as Wild Bill Hickok, Ben Johnson as Doc Bogardus (a combination of two real-life rival sharpshooters), Bruce Boxleitner as Vern Tyree, lots of other veteran Western actors, and Pat Hingle, as Bob Halburton, the enterprising journalist who made Cardiff a household name around the turn of the century.

Belle Starr (1980) returned Elizabeth Montgomery to the Old West in this dramatization, with contemporary feminist overtones, of the last few months in the life of the notorious bandit queen, from the time she was burned out of her ranch in Texas, where she was living with her Indian husband and her son by Jim Reed and daughter by Cole Younger (Cliff Potts), to her being gunned down in an ambush on 1889. All the usual Western suspects are here: Frank and Jesse James, the Daltons, the Younger Brothers, and so on. This version hewed pretty much to the semi-fictional lines of the forties film about Belle Starr with Gene Tierney.

Kenny Rogers as the Gambler (1980) had the country star turned actor finding gold through a hit song, playing amiable Brady Hawkes, who knows when to hold 'em and when to fold 'em. Bruce Boxleitner was Billy Montana, the good-looking farm boy who idolizes him, and Linda Evans (in the second movie and beyond) was Kate Muldoon, the gun-toting bounty hunting saloon performer. The film was the highest rated TV movie of the year and spawned a sequel three years later that ran twice as long.

There'd be two other sequels following, the last of which in 1991 (*The Luck of the Draw*) had Brady Hawkes crossing paths with nearly a dozen TV Western greats who happened to come from many different years as he embarks on a cross-country adventure that ends in a big card game with Teddy Roosevelt (Claude Akins) and Diamond Jim Brady (Dion Anderson) in San Francisco.

During his travels Brady bumps into Gene Barry as Bat Masterson, Jack Kelly as Bart Maverick, Hugh O'Brian as Wyatt Earp, Chuck Connors and Johnny Crawford as Lucas and Mark McCain, David Carradine as Caine, Brian Keith as Dave Blassingame, Clint Walker as Cheyenne Bodie, and others. Country singer Reba McEntire made her TV movie debut as Burgundy Jones, a feisty ex-madam. That most of the Western stars came from different times over a forty-year period—and included a humorous encounter with Mickey Rooney as a D. W. Griffith–type moviemaker (he's billed as D.W.) from the early years of the twentieth century—never concerned the writers of this cowboy star-packed Kenny Rogers Western.

California Gold Rush (1981) was a cobbling together of two classic Bret Harte stories, "The Luck of Roaring Camp" and "The Outcasts of Poker Flat" by the Classics Illustrated folk. Robert Hays played author Harte (and narrated), who, in this plot, goes west in the 1850s in search of adventure. (The real Bret Harte, born in Albany, New York, went to California sometime before the Civil War and became, variously, a miner, a teacher, a journalist, an author of pioneering life there—and he was a pal of sorts of Charles Dickens.) John Dehner was Captain John Sutter, Victor Mohica wandered in as Joaquin Murieta—both were legendary figures during the gold rush days in California—and Ken Curtis played a frontier character called Kentuck.

The Legend of Walks Far Woman (1982) featured Raquel Welch as a real-life 19th-century Blackfoot Indian woman determined to avenge her husband's death at the hands of the white man. Welch, in her TV movie debut, aged to about 102, shortly before Walks Far herself died in 1953. Actually, it was filmed in 1979 as a three-hour movie, adapted by novelist Evan Hunter from Colin Stuart's 1976 book, and sat on the shelf for several years. When finally shown, it was shorn to about 150 minutes, with the final reel lopped off and the last scene or two patched on. Other than Bradford Dillman as a white trader who became Walks Far's lover, virtually the entire cast was comprised of Native Americans or Mexican Americans. (Raquel is of Bolivian/

Irish American descent and in her later, post-sex-symbol career specialized in playing strong Hispanic women.)

The Wild Women of Chastity Gulch (1982) was a comedy Western from Aaron Spelling that united a Missouri mining town's barroom belles and their self-righteous sisters to fight off a ragtag band of renegade soldiers after their own men have marched off to war. Representing the shady ladies were Joan Collins as the town madam, Phyllis Davis, and Morgan Brittany. The virtuous ones included Priscilla Barnes, Pamela Bellwood, and Jeanette Nolan. Howard Duff was the leader of the marauders; Donny Osmond, his son; and Lee Horsley, a Confederate doctor riding with them. Susan Kellerman represented the law on Chastity Gulch.

I Married Wyatt Earp (1983) starred Marie Osmond as Old West singer/dancer Josephine Marcus, a middle-class Jewish girl from San Francisco who was seeking a nineteenth-century show biz career. Bruce Boxleitner was a rather charming Earp, the guy she ended up falling for when she happened to run into him at age nineteen in Tombstone and was with him for the next forty-seven years. No official record of their marriage exists, however. This film is based on Marcus's published memoirs. A number of the notable Westerners of the time—from Doc Holliday to Ike and Billy Clanton to the other Earps (Morgan; Virgil; Wyatt's common law wife, Mattie; Virg's wife, Allie; and Morgan's wife, Louisa)—all were part of the proceedings. John Bennett Perry costarred as Sheriff John Behan, Earp's rival for Josephine's attentions.

Cowboy (1983) is a contemporary Western with James Brolin as tenderfoot rancher Ward McNally, a disillusioned schoolteacher who returns from the big city to fulfill a boyhood dream. Ted Danson played a crippled ex-rodeo performer who tries to teach him the ropes and help him run the spread. Annie Potts was the local café owner; Randy Quaid, the local land baron; Michael Pataki, the nasty sheriff; and George DiCenzo, the crooked banker—the last three conspiring to grab McNally's land.

Ghost Dancing (1983), another contemporary Western, was an original drama by Phil Penningwroth. It starred Dorothy McGuire as a feisty, widowed desert farmer in Utah who takes on the water company by dynamiting the city-owned reservoir to spotlight her cause: the depletion of the valley's water to feed the city's aqueduct system. Bill Erwin was her dear old Paiute Indian friend; Victoria Racimo, his adopted daughter whom McGuire had educated as a lawyer; Richard Farnsworth, the sympathetic sheriff, a longtime family friend; and Bo Hopkins, the water department's chief engineer reluctant to fight the widow.

Calamity Jane (1984) featured Jane Alexander in this exploration of the myths surrounding the colorful Western heroine and both the legendary Wild

Bill Hickok (Frederic Forrest), with whom she had an unorthodox courtship, and the flamboyant Buffalo Bill Cody (Ken Kercheval), between the 1870s and the turn of the century. Although sharing a title, this film has nothing to do with the way the character was romanticized in the 1954 Doris Day musical that, itself, was restaged for television in 1963 with Carol Burnett.

The Cowboy and the Ballerina (1984) was about, not especially surprisingly, just what the title indicated—amiable plot but kind of wafer thin. Lee Majors was an ex–world championship rodeo rider, and Leslie Wing played a defecting Russian ballerina. Decades earlier, producer Sam Goldwyn wanted to pair up two of his stars, Gary Cooper and Merle Oberon, and ordered up a script that came across his desk as *The Cowboy and the Lady*, devised by a battery of writers. Goldwyn was said to have asked, "What's it about?" A similar question could have been asked on this one. It's about ninety-eight minutes (plus commercials).

Wild Horses (1985) gave singer Kenny Rogers a chance to get out of his Brady Hawkes "Gambler" duds and into a contemporary Western as an ex–rodeo champion itching to get back in the saddle again and being given the chance after losing his frustrating factory job. He leaves his wife and kids to their middle-class life to pursue his dream. Veteran Western actors Ben Johnson and Richard Farnsworth, both former rodeo riders and movie stuntmen, are reunited for this film, joining an acting (and singing) Kenny on his wild horse roundup.

Down the Long Hills (1986) was a Disney family adventure, adapted from one of the myriad of Louis L'Amour best-selling Western novels, telling of the struggles of a teenage boy and a young girl to make their way with their red stallion through the Utah wilderness. They'd escaped a wagon train massacre, while keeping a step or two ahead of a deadly grizzly bear and a pair of murderous horse thieves who want their stallion. Bruce Boxleitner played the boy's widowed father; Jack Elam, his mountain man buddy; and Bo Hopkins and Michael Wren were the villains.

Houston: The Legend of Texas (1986) starred Sam Elliott in the title role, along with Michael Beck as Jim Bowie, William Russ as William Travis, Richard Yniguez as General Santa Anna, G. D. Spradlin as President Andrew Jackson, and dozens of others. This three-hour CBS drama recounted the exploits of frontier war hero, politician, and statesman Sam Houston from 1829 to 1863. (Katharine Ross, Mrs. Sam Elliott, had an uncredited role at the Alamo.) This was first of two television movies during the 1986–1987 season to deal with the siege at the Alamo.

Thompson's Last Run (1986), another contemporary Western, had Robert Mitchum as a bank robber being pursued—after busting out of jail—by an aging lawman (Wilford Brimley) who had been a longtime pal. Mitchum at the time was nearly seventy, and Brimley, who (like Walter Brennan) always looked decades older, was in his early fifties.

The Last Days of Frank and Jesse James (1986) starred Johnny Cash and Kris Kristofferson as Frank and Jesse along with Willie Nelson as Rebel general Jo Shelby and June Carter Cash (playing husband Johnny's and Kris's mother!), at the head of a lengthy cast. Filming of the now familiar legend retold was done not in the West but in and around Nashville—probably so that Cash, Kristofferson, and Nelson could remain close to their recording studios.

Stagecoach (1986), featuring Willie Nelson, Johnny Cash, Kris Kristofferson, and Waylon Jennings—the self-proclaimed outlaws themselves, the Rat Pack of the country music world—was, of course, the remake more or less (actually the second one) of John Ford's towering classic of 1939 that made a star of John Wayne. Kristofferson here had the Duke's role of Ringo, Nelson was Doc Holliday (Thomas Mitchell's original part), Cash played Marshal Curly Wilcox (George Bancroft's part in Ford's film), and Jennings had the role of Hatfield (played in the earlier movie by John Carradine). Also in the very large cast—a disparate group of passengers setting out across the Arizona badlands for Lordsburg—were Elizabeth Ashley as Dallas, the starring role that Claire Trevor had originally; Mary Crosby (daughter of Bing, who had the Mitchell role in the earlier remake twenty years before) as the pregnant Lucy Mallory; and John Schneider, Anthony Newley, Tony Franciosa, and June Carter Cash.

The Gunfighters (1987), a Canadian-made Western with at least one American (George Kennedy), followed the adventures of a pair of brothers and their cousin out to avenge the loss of their Kansas ranch to a land baron and his henchmen, circa 1881. "*The Gunfighters*," *Variety*'s critic found, "sure aims low. With acting ranging from careless to indifferent, telefilm sets the Western back even farther into the sunset."

Desperado (1987) was the first of four TV movies with poker-faced Alex MacArthur as an enigmatic saddle tramp named Duell McCall, a loner with a long coat and a fast gun who roves the frontier fighting evil and here faces down corrupt powers-that-be in a company-controlled mining town. It was written by novelist Elmore Leonard and used as its title theme the classic Eagles song of the same name. Robert Vaughn was the weak-willed town sheriff in this one; Gladys Knight (without the Pips) was Mona Lisa, the town madam; and Pernell Roberts played the slimy marshal.

Independence (1987) told of Sam Hatch (John Bennett Perry), a dedicated frontier sheriff in the 1880s who, after his first family is wiped out by marauding renegades, gets a chance for revenge years later when the same tattered gang threatens his new family and the town (Independence) he single-handedly tamed. This was a busted pilot for NBC from Sunn Classics Productions, the outfit behind the earlier Classics Illustrated series of TV movies.

Louis L'Amour's "The Quick and the Dead" (1987) was one of the first cable Westerns to air on HBO. Sam Elliott played an enigmatic gunslinger named Con Vallian who gets involved with a family of homesteaders (Kate Capshaw and Tom Conti) newly arrived in 1976 Wyoming Territory and—as almost by tradition in horse operas—beset by bad guys and renegade Indians.

The Alamo: Thirteen Days to Glory (1987) starred James Arness as Jim Bowie, Brian Keith as Davy Crockett, Alec Baldwin as Colonel William Travis, and Raul Julia as General Santa Anna, fighting the battle of the Alamo once again in this adaptation of Lon Tinkle's 1958 book. *Variety*, for one, was far from bowled over with this three-hour film, finding it "a bloodless, sweatless, nattily costumed hygienic recounting of one of history's most gallant and gory stands . . . frittered away with stock characters and trivial pursuits." The review ended with three words: "Courage demands more." It was shot in Brackettville, Texas, at the same location used for the John Wayne Alamo movie. Seventy-two-year-old Lorne Greene's special appearance in a single scene as forty-three-year-old Sam Houston was his acting swan song; he died shortly afterward.

Gunsmoke: Return to Dodge (1987) had James Arness saddling up once again as Matt Dillon—a dozen years after the landmark two-decade series came to the end of the trail. Amanda Blake returned as Kitty Russell and Dub Taylor as his old deputy Newly O'Brien. This time Dillon's on the trail of a nasty varmint named Will Mannon (Steve Forrest), newly released from a frontier prison and looking to take vengeance on Dillon who had him sent there in the first place. This revival movie was popular enough to warrant CBS's ordering up four sequels that aired between 1990 and 1994 with basically a whole new "posse" (Amanda Blake had died in 1989).

Red River (1988), about an epic cattle drive and the tempestuous relationship between the no-nonsense boss of the drive and his hotheaded son, had James Arness, Bruce Boxleitner, and Gregory Harrison in the roles played four decades earlier on the screen classic by Arness's mentor John Wayne, Montgomery Clift, and John Ireland, respectively. This version was gimmicked up by the "special appearance" casting of several TV cowboys: Ty Hardin (*Bronco*), Robert Horton (*Wagon Train*), John Lupton (*Broken Arrow*), and Guy Madison (*Wild Bill Hickok*). *Red River* is based on Western writer Borden Chase's 1946 serial novel *The Chisholm Trail*.

The Tracker (1988) found Kris Kristofferson back in the saddle as Nobel Adams, a onetime frontier tracker, Indian fighter, and scout who is now a retired rancher in Arizona, at odds with his only son, the graduate of a law school back East where he wants to practice. Dad, however, wants him to stay and take over the spread. Circumstances team the two up together to track a ruthless killer, Red Jack Stillwell (played by Scott Wilson), a wild-eyed Mormon seeking vengeance against not only the Indian but also anyone not Mormon, across the deserts of the Southwest, and they learn to be father and son again. This fictional Western that aired on HBO also was known as *Dead or Alive*.

Stranger on My Land (1988) was a contemporary Western starring Tommy Lee Jones as a Vietnam vet fighting the military, who want to appropriate his land out West for an air force base. He's helped in his cause—almost at gunpoint—by Ben Johnson as his older brother. Edward Hume wrote the story and the teleplay, appropriating Western themes that had been worked over countless times, as in a Jimmy Stewart movie or two—"The Windmill" episode of the *General Electric Theatre* in the fifties, for one.

Longarm (1988) emerged as a whimsical Western, set in New Mexico in the late 1870s about a chiseled, Dudley Do-Right–type U.S. marshal, Custis Long, and his adventures with pretty women, colorful outlaws, and fractious horses. Rene Auberjonois turned up briefly as real-life Governor Lew Wallace, busy writing *Ben-Hur* and suggesting the somewhat dim-witted lawman take some hints from it. Based on the Longarm character from the books by Tabor Evans, the film, actually a ninety-minute pilot to a prospective—and unrealized—series, starred John T. Terlesky.

Gore Vidal's Billy the Kid (1989) was writer Vidal's third go through the years at the Billy the Kid legend. In the fifties, he'd written a television play dealing with the gunman, who was played by Paul Newman. Then he reworked it for a big screen version, also with Newman. Val Kilmer had the title role in this TV movie Vidal reimagining. Duncan Regehr (who'd played Zorro on television) had the part of Pat Garrett, and Wilford Brimley was Governor Lew Wallace.

Pair of Aces (1990) reteamed Willie Nelson and Kris Kristofferson in this contemporary Western as, respectively, Billy Roy Barker, a resourceful con man and safecracker, and Captain "Rip" Mitchell, an upstanding Texas Ranger, reluctantly thrown together while the latter tries solving a serial murder case with the latter's colleague, played by Rip Torn. This was a prospective series pilot to have been called "Rip" (for Kristofferson's character), also the original title of this film. The following year, there was a sequel, *Another Pair of Aces: Three of a Kind*, with Torn's character now the object of a Texas Ranger manhunt after he is accused of murdering a recently released convict, and the other two vowing to clear him. All three actors, incidentally, also appeared together in the film *Songwriter*. This sequel, *Variety* felt, emerged as "the natural descendant of the classic Western. . . . It's a fun, involving entertainment, a well-crafted derivative of that good ol' Texas mythology."

The Rose and the Jackal (1990) starred Christopher Reeve as Union detective Allan Pinkerton, who in this fanciful Western drama/historical fiction, falls in love with an aristocratic Southern belle caught spying for the Confederacy. Pinkerton was a Scotsman who was the head of the Secret Service during the Civil War. Among the sources for this period piece was Margaret Leech's *Reveille in Washington*.

Montana (1990) costarred Gena Rowlands and Richard Crenna (as a grizzled Walter Brennan type here) playing two spirited old soldiers of the prairie, Bess and Hoyce Guthrie, both stubborn as mules. In this contemporary, made-for-cable tale by Larry McMurtry about friction on a family ranch in the Northwest, times are changing: father and son are eager to sell the spread to a power company; mother and daughter want to save the land and preserve their traditional way of life.

Son of the Morning Star (1991) was a sprawling two-part, four-hour pseudo-biography dealing with George Armstrong Custer, the bloody Plains Indian Wars, and the Battle of the Little Bighorn. Gary Cole swaggered as Custer and Rosanna Arquette was his wife, Libby. Among those in the lengthy cast were Dean Stockwell as General Sheridan, and Native American actors Rodney A. Grant and Floyd Red Crow Westerman as Crazy Horse and Sitting Bull, respectively. This adaptation of Evan S. Connell's 1984 best seller—the title refers to the name bestowed on the flamboyant Custer by his Indian scouts—was by Melissa Mathison (who wrote *E.T. the Extra-Terrestrial*, among others).

Louis L'Amour's Conagher (1991) had Sam Elliott—in his fourth L'Amour Western—playing a hardworking cowpoke named Conn Conagher. He becomes involved with a widow lady (his real-life wife, Katharine Ross) struggling to stay alive while raising her two children alone on a remote homestead, as they fight the elements, Indians, outlaws, and loneliness.

Blood River (1991), written by cult figure John Carpenter (of *Hallowe'en* fame), was a spare "buddy" Western, the buddies being young Rick Schroder as a directionless young drifter named Jimmy who's taken off for the mountains after gunning down a rancher's son he thinks killed his parents for their land, and curmudgeonly but wise Wilford Brimley as an old trapper and mountain man, who becomes Jimmy's traveling companion and protector. But the old codger really turns out to be a U.S. marshal.

Into the Badlands (1991) spun three separate stories of the Old West involving the supernatural adventures of a bounty hunter named Barston "played with malevolent gusto" (as *Variety*'s critic pointed out) by Bruce Dern. With Dern as the link, the three individual tales—set not in South Dakota but in Texas—featured the likes of Helen Hunt, Mariel Hemingway, Dylan McDermott, and Lisa Pelican. "*Into the Badlands* doesn't spare the bloodletting and violence," *Variety* found. "It's a remarkably tough work."

Sarah, Plain and Tall (1991) plus sequels in 1993 and 1999, were from Patricia MacLachlan's books, with Glenn Close as Sarah Wheaton, a spinster from Maine, and Christopher Walken as Jacob Whiting, a widowed Midwestern farmer with two small kids, who advertises for a new bride. The initial movie (Emmy winner as Outstanding Movie or Miniseries, with nominations going to both leads) aired as a Hallmark Hall of Fame presentation, and its huge popularity made two follow-up movies with the same pair an inevitability. Thus we later got *Sarah, Plain and Tall: Skylark* in 1993 and *Sarah, Plain and Tall: Winter's End* in 1999.

Four Eyes and Six Guns (1992), a quirky cable-TV Western, followed a nerdy greenhorn optometrist from New York (Judge Reinhold) to the wide-open spaces to open a storefront in Tombstone. There he becomes an unlikely gunslinger while intent on fitting a drunken, increasingly nearsighted Wyatt Earp (Fred Ward) with a pair of glasses.

Lakota Moon (1992) was a Western about, and basically starring, Native Americans, that seems never to have aired. Historical fiction written by John Wilder, who developed and produced *Centennial* and *Return to Lonesome Dove*, among many others, it depicted the life of a small Indian tribe, in a time shortly before the white men became a threat. The main focus of the story is on the young brave Skywalker (Zahn McClarnon, of Native American descent), who woos pretty Morning Sun (Tailihn Forest Flower) but can't seem to convince her father, Rolling Thunder (Gordon Tootootsis), of his worth. An attack by a rival tribe on their camp gives Skywalker hopes for an opportunity to impress the older man. Barbara Carrera (Latina from Nicaragua), Rodney A. Grant, Richard Tyson (Caucasian), and August Schellenberg were among the other leading players. It was directed by Christopher Cain, father of prolific young actor (and former NCAA football star) Dean Cain.

Geronimo (1993) was the first production in Ted Turner and Jane Fonda's ambitious series of periodic films exploring U.S. history from the indigenous people's point of view and apart from Hollywood's traditional distortion, cast primarily with Native American actors, including three playing the famed Apache chief at different ages. This version should not be confused with Walter Hill's theatrical *Geronimo: An American Legend*, which premiered concurrently.

The Broken Chain (1993), with Graham Greene and Wes Studi, was the second in Ted Turner's series of films focusing on Native American cultures from the American Revolution to contemporary times. This one deals with two young Mohawk braves who are forced to choose sides when the Revolutionary War divides their loyalties and breaks the chain of peace binding Iroquois Confederacy member nations for the common defense. One young warrior (Eric Schweig) ends up the adopted son of an influential English trader (Pierce Brosnan), but after receiving a formal education, later returns to his people.

Broken Chain was followed by *Lakota Woman: Siege at Wounded Knee* (1994, from the autobiography of Mary Crow Dog), with Irene Bedard, Tantoo Cardinal, and Floyd Red Dog Westerman; *Tecumseh: The Last Warrior* (1995, from the novel *Panther in the Sky* by James Alexander Thom, one of the leading writers of Westerns and historical fiction on the contemporary scene); and *Crazy Horse* (1996) with actor Michael Greyeyes in the lead role and August Schellenberg as Sitting Bull. The *Tecumseh* film, which told of the Shawnee chief who tried to unite all of the Indian nations in the nineteenth century, had, in the title part, Jesse Borrago, not a Native American but of Mexican descent.

Rio Diablo was a 1993 Western on CBS that moved Kenny Rogers away somewhat from his "Gambler" persona and made him grizzled, rather shady Old West bounty hunter Quinton Leech. It starred him with fellow country singers Travis Tritt as upstanding-turned-vengeful farmer Ben Tabor, and Naomi Judd as saloon proprietor Flora Mae Pepper (Tritt and Judd were making their acting debuts here), along with Stacy Keach as a rival bounty hunter. Rogers, whose production company made this film, even managed to perform a song or two, though this was hardly a musical. This was more of a Sergio Leone–style Western than a John Ford one.

Sodbusters (1994), a Canadian-made Western spoof, written and directed by SCTV alumnus Eugene Levy, starred Kris Kristofferson as an itinerant cowpoke named Destiny who ambles into the frontier town of Marble Hat, Colorado, and finds its good citizens, homesteaders all, under the thumb of a greedy powerbroker named Slade Cantrell (John Vernon). Grizzled Destiny, as *TV Guide* wrote, "doesn't take kindly to his reception in the local tavern at the hands of Cantrell's ruffians." He's soon recruited by the locals, among whom is one Gunther Schteuppin, to help them fight off Cantrell and his land-grabbing scalawags. *Sodbusters* was a takeoff on nearly every oater from *Shane* to *Blazing Saddles*.

Wyatt Earp: Return to Tombstone (1994) with Hugh O'Brian came about, presumably, because CBS had such success bringing back Matt Dillon in

Gunsmoke. Less a TV movie than a special, it combined colorized footage from the fifties ABC television series *The Life and Legend of Wyatt Earp* with new scenes shot in Tombstone, and showed the return of the legendary former marshal to his old stomping grounds. He visited old friends, taught bad guys some manners, and revealed secrets about his early life. Bruce Boxleitner costarred as Sam, sheriff of Cochise County, and old-timer Paul Brinegar was back as Jim "Dog" Kelly, Earp's mayor friend from Dodge. This was to be Hugh O'Brian's swan song role, literally riding off into the sunset.

An aged Wyatt Earp, during his last days working in Hollywood in the twenties doing consultant gigs in Western films, was portrayed by Leo Gordon in an episode ("The Hollywood Follies") of George Lucas's fanciful *Young Indiana Jones Chronicles* in the midnineties. Because of his varied career as outlaw and lawman—and movie consultant about outlaws and lawmen—and for the length of his life, Wyatt Earp might well be the most often portrayed real-life legend of the Old West.

Frank and Jesse (1995), another take on the James brothers—here played by Rob Lowe and Bill Paxton—was a standard Western saga recounting the exploits of the two Jameses and the Younger brothers as they rob banks, trains, and stagecoaches while dodging Alan Pinkerton, who would go on to law enforcement for the railroads and the newly established Secret Service. Country singer Randy Travis not only portrayed Cole Younger but also wrote and performed the song "The Way He Is." This film, a direct-to-video Western written and directed by Robert Boris, was not well received.

Buffalo Girls (1995) was a rip-roaring two-part saga adapted from Larry McMurtry's best-selling 1990 novel about tough-talking and straight-shooting Calamity Jane and other legends of the Old West. The film earned eleven Emmy nominations, including Outstanding Miniseries; Anjelica Huston as Best Actress for her Calamity Jane; and Sam Elliott as Best Supporting Actor for his Wild Bill Hickok. Peter Coyote played Buffalo Bill Cody and Reba McEntire was Annie Oakley—years before starring on Broadway in *Annie Get Your Gun.* Others in the film were Melanie Griffith, Jack Palance, Gabriel Byrne, and Russell Means (as Sitting Bull).

Desperate Trail (1995) was a gritty Western dealing with a vengeful lawman's relentless pursuit of an escaped murderess, who has hooked up with a frontier dandy. Sam Elliott played the marshal; Linda Fiorentino, the woman; Craig Sheffer, her lover. This was first-time director and cowriter P. J. Pesce's violent homage to Sam Peckinpah.

The Avenging Angel (1995) was best described as a revisionist Western about a (fictional) freelance bodyguard, Miles Utley (played by Tom Berenger), hired to protect a Mormon prophet from a gang of would-be assassins in nineteenth-century Utah. According to legend, the Mormons of the time used to hire what might be considered "hit squads" to find and take care of those who were bodily threats to their church leaders. These people were called Danites or Avenging Angels, many groomed from childhood for the "profession." In this dramatized version of real-life events, Charlton Heston, in another of his larger-than-life portrayals of historical figures, starred as Brigham Young and James Coburn was Porter Rockwell, a fanatical lawman in the Utah Territory, who was nicknamed Old Port and labeled "the Destroying Angel of Mormondom." This film was based on Gary Stewart's nonfiction 1983 novel.

Black Fox (1995), based on the 1994 novel by Matt Braun, nominally starred Christopher Reeve as plantation owner Alan Johnson—shortly before Reeve's debilitating accident. The title character, though, was his "blood brother" (black actor Tony Todd), the former slave who was Johnson's childhood friend. The two ultimately settle in West Texas in the 1960s as ranchers, and their presence effects peace between homesteaders and two Indian tribes, the Comanches and the Kiowas, that had joined forces under rebellious Running Dog (Raoul Trujillo)—although it took two TV movie sequels that year to do it.

James A. Michener's Texas (1995), a sprawling two-part, four-hour adaptation of the noted author of historical fiction's 1987 novel, melded real-life legends like Sam Houston, Davy Crockett, Jim Bowie, Stephen Austin, and Santa Anna (Stacy Keach, John Schneider, David Keith, Patrick Duffy, and Lloyd Battista, respectively) with a seemingly endless roster of fictional characters played by the likes of Maria Conchita Alonso, Benjamin Bratt, Rick Schroder, and country singer Randy Travis. The whole shebang was produced by Aaron Spelling and John Wilder. Under the headline "Texas, All of It, According to Michener," *New York Times* TV critic John J. O'Connor considered, "[It] aims for Lone Star State dimensions. As Charlton Heston, the narrator, sonorously puts it at the very beginning, talking about Texicans, as they were called then, 'This is the story of their fight for freedom. This is the story of Texas.' Well, sort of, wrapped in the devices of fiction."

The Good Old Boys (1995), directed by and starring Tommy Lee Jones, who also adapted the story from the 1978 book by Western novelist Elmer Kelton, was an amiable chronicle of overlapping eras in which a roving cowpoke, Hewey Calloway, finds himself caught between the end of the Old West and the beginning of the twentieth century. Hewey is torn between the life he loves on the shrinking frontier and the schoolmarm, Spring Renfro (old pal Sissy Spacek), who makes him think of settling down. Wilford Brimley, Sam Shepard, Terry Kinney, and Frances McDormand costarred, along with a young Matt Damon (twenty-five at the time).

Ruby Jean and Joe (1996) was a contemporary Western with Rebekah Johnson and Tom Selleck in the title roles (which is which can be surmised). Selleck played a fading rodeo rider who picks up the young female hitchhiker, and even though he is constantly being corrected by her, their budding, if somewhat unlikely, friendship grows, and their conversations on the road put both in a position to deal with their lives. Like dozens of other small- and big-screen Westerns through the years, *Ruby Jean and Joe* was written by James Lee Barrett.

Riders of the Purple Sage (1996), with Ed Harris and Amy Madigan, was a new version, produced by husband and wife Harris and Madigan, of the Zane Grey classic, written in 1912 and considered one of the seminal works of Western fiction. This gritty sagebrush saga of frontier justice is often seen as a parable of individual freedom in which a frontier woman struggling to hold on to her ranch must turn for help to a mysterious drifter when the people she has trusted betray her.

The Cherokee Kid (1996) was a rather wacky, offbeat Western about a klutzy black cowboy wannabe named Isaiah Turner (Sinbad) who decides to call himself the Cherokee Kid and goes gunning for a coldhearted land-grabber, Cyrus B. Bloomington (James Coburn), whom the Kid remembers seeing kill his family many years earlier. With the aid of the self-styled "best mountain man in Texas," grizzled Otter Bob (Burt Reynolds), a onetime gunslinger turned drunk, the Kid trains till he is good enough to take on Bloomington. But Bloomington has an ace up his sleeve—a gunfighter named the Undertaker (Gregory Hines)—to stop the Kid. The Undertaker, however, turns out to be the Kid's estranged brother.

Last Stand at Saber River (1997), from Elmore Leonard's late fifties book, starred Tom Selleck as Paul Cable, an embittered Confederate soldier who returns from the war to reclaim his Arizona homestead from Rebel pioneers who sympathize with the Union war effort. Desperate to rebuild the life he once knew, Cable ultimately joins forces with Vern Kidston (Keith Carradine), his Union adversary, to make a last stand for the one thing worth fighting for—his family. David Carradine also stars as Vern's not-so-solicitous brother.

The Cisco Kid (1997) came back to television in this lighthearted new adventure with Jimmy Smits playing the dashing Mexican do-gooder, wrongs-righter, and woman-charmer and Cheech Marin playing his bumptious sidekick. In this incarnation, set against the French occupation of Mexico in 1867, the heroes foil double-dealing gunrunners, greedy government officials, and French imperialists. The famous Cisco Kid theme from the early fifties TV series, updated by the rock group War, is performed by Cheech Marin, the Pancho of the 1990s.

Buffalo Soldiers (1997) dramatized the story of the all-black (most former slaves) U.S. Tenth Cavalry that protected the Western territories in post–Civil War times. Danny Glover and Tim Busfield were among the leads, playing First Sergeant Washington Wyatt and his white superior Major Robert Carr in the brutal, sometimes racist fact-based drama.

True Women (1997) was a feminist Western from Texas writer Janice Woods Windle's popular 1994 book based on the lives of several of her ancestors. It spanned five decades, from the Texas Revolution through Reconstruction and beyond, with Dana Delany as Sara Ashby McClure; Annabeth Gish as Euphemia Ashby King, one of the leaders in the battle for women's suffrage in the mid-nineteenth century (after having made a stand against Mexican General Santa Anna); and Angelina Jolie as Georgia Lawshe Woods. John Schneider popped up in the role of Sam Houston.

Ebenezer (1997) put Jack Palance in somewhat alien turf as a Western Scrooge, land baron and gunman, in this reimagining of Dickens's *A Christmas Carol*. Rick Schroder costarred as a tenderfoot who, along with the ghosts of Christmases past, present, and future, helps Scrooge see the error of his ways—or, as W. C. Fields once facetiously noted in his famous one-line review of the Dickens tale, "the story of a good guy who goes bad."

Two for Texas (1998), a frontier adventure, based on James Lee Burke's epic novel, was set in 1836 during the time of Sam Houston (played here by Tom Skerritt) and the siege of the Alamo. The tale had a pair of escapees from a Louisiana penal colony (Kris Kristofferson and Scott Bairstow) who join Houston's Texas Volunteer Army to lose themselves in a crowd, but find themselves on the firing line of Santa Anna's troops. Peter Coyote played Jim Bowie.

The Cowboy and the Movie Star (1998) was a lighthearted contemporary Western all about, well, a cowboy and a movie star. Perry King played Clint Brannan, a down-on-his-luck cowpoke who, with his dog Scratch, goes on his last cattle drive. They find Sean Livingston (Sean Young), a film starlet who is stranded after she, while making a movie in the middle of nowhere, swerves her car to avoid hitting a cow, drives off a deserted road, and ends up in a ditch.

You Know My Name (1998) starred Sam Elliott as real-life cowboy Bill Tilghman, who once rode with Wyatt Earp and Bat Masterson and by the early 1920s had gone Hollywood, had become a movie director/producer, and now wants to put on the screen a more realistic view of the Old West's cowboys and outlaws. But funds have dried up for his project, and he turns to taking a job as sheriff in the farming community of Cromwell, Oklahoma, which needs cleaning up—and that means going after a corrupt federal agent named Wiley Lynn (Arliss Howard), who has had the old sheriff killed and is throwing his weight around. Elliott not only starred but also co-executive produced this semi-modern-day Western, where, as Bill Tilghman, he seeks to bring Old West morality values to present-day crime.

Outlaw Justice (1999), an homage to Sergio Leone's fabled spaghetti Westerns, starred Willie Nelson and Kris Kristofferson as grizzled gunslingers, hunting down the killers of former crony Tobey Naylor (Waylon Jennings), with the help of the latter's greenhorn son (played by Chad Willett). Singer Travis Tritt played a sheriff on their trail. Tobey is gunned down before the opening credits but "narrates" though his diary. This was later retitled *The Long Kill* for DVD release.

Purgatory (1999) was a really offbeat Western—a morality play of sorts—in which a band of desperadoes led by Eric Roberts and Randy Quaid descend upon a strange frontier town called Refuge and find that the ghostly inhabitants are not what they seem to be at first. Sam Shepard played the deceptively laconic sheriff with his own code of law in this drama with echoes of Serling's *Twilight Zone*.

The Virginian (2000) had taciturn Bill Pullman in this new film version of Owen Wister's early twentieth-century Western classic. Diane Lane, John Savage, and Dennis Weaver also starred, along with Canadian actor Colm Feore as Trampas. James Drury, star of *The Virginian* in the early sixties, turned up in a cameo of sorts as the Rider. In addition to starring, Pullman produced and directed.

High Noon (2000), nearly fifty years after establishing itself as one of the great Western classics on the American screen, was remade with stalwart Tom Skerritt in the Gary Cooper role of lawman Will Kane, seeking help from the townsfolk who have turned their collective backs on him and hoping that his new bride (then, Grace Kelly; here, Susanna Thompson) would not forsake him on this their wedding day. Reed Diamond played his cowardly deputy Harvey Pell (Lloyd Bridges in the original). Dennis Weaver played Kane's friend (the old Lon Chaney role), who chooses not to help, and Maria Conchita Alonso was Kane's onetime lover (the Katy Jurado part). That there had been an ill-advised *High Noon II* TV movie in 1980 with Lee Majors was best forgotten, despite it having had a script by the estimable Elmore Leonard.

The Ballad of Lucy Whipple (2001), a relatively gentle frontier saga set in the late 1840s about a spirited widow and her three children from the East during the California gold rush, starred Glenn Close and Jena Malone. In this dramatization of Karen Cushman's 1996 novel for young people, Close, now running a boardinghouse for local miners, has to contend mainly with her headstrong twelve-year-old (Malone in the title role), who is not happy with having to be uprooted but ultimately comes around to thinking—in the style of contemporary pseudo-rebellious teen-oriented flicks—that California ain't so bad. Rock star Meat Loaf played a storytelling blacksmith.

Louis L'Amour's Crossfire Trail (2001) had Tom Selleck—doing his Gary Cooper best—as Rafe Covington, a steadfast cowpoke. With a couple of sidekicks, he vows to fulfill a promise to a dying friend to look after the latter's widow (Virginia Madsen) and his Wyoming homestead, both being coveted by a conniving landowner (villainous Mark Harmon) and his hired guns. This one's from L'Amour's 1954 Western novel.

Skinwalkers (2002), *Coyote Waits* (2003), and *A Thief of Time* (2004) were three contemporary Westerns from novels by author Tony Hillerman about two Navajo lawmen, Joe Leaphorn and Jim Chee (Wes Studi and Adam Beach), patrolling, solving crimes, and maintaining the peace on their reservation. The entire cast was comprised of Native American actors. Robert Redford was the producer of these three Navajo Tribal police films that premiered on PBS's *Mystery!* (Hillerman, until his death in 2008, wrote eighteen books about the Navajos, many in his Leaphorn/Chee series.) "When my own Jim Chee of the Navajo Tribal Police unravels a mystery because he understands the ways of his people, when he reads the signs in the sandy bottom of a reservation arroyo, he is walking in the tracks Bony made 50 years ago," Hillerman said in a 1988 interview. Bony was Napoleon Bonaparte, not the legendary figure of history, but half-European, half-aboriginal Australian hero, a detective-inspector created by one of Hillerman's idols, Australian author Arthur W. Upfield.

King of Texas (2002) starred Patrick Stewart in this Old West adaptation of Shakespeare's *King Lear* set in the late 1800s, playing egomaniacal, self-made ranch tycoon John Lear who divides his holdings among his three daughters (played by Marcia Gay Harden, Lauren Holly, and Julie Cox) but finds that once they have his property, they reject him.

Johnson County War (2002) was a sprawling two-part, four-hour traditional Western set in 1891 Wyoming, pitting three homesteading brothers, led by Tom Berenger, against old-time cattle barons who call themselves the Cheyenne Social Club—with Burt Reynolds signing on as the club's hired gun. Larry McMurtry wrote the teleplay, based on Frederick Manfred's 1957 book *Riders of Judgment*.

Monte Walsh (2003), a remake of the 1970 Lee Marvin/Jack Palance movie, starred Tom Selleck in the title role and Keith Carradine as Chet Rollins, longtime cowhands, working whatever ranch work comes their way, but "nothing they can't do from a horse." Their lives are divided between months on the range and the occasional trip into town. Monte has a long-term relationship with prostitute Martine Bernard, (Isabella Rossellini; Jeanne Moreau in the original) while Chet has fallen under the spell of the widow who owns the hardware store. Camaraderie and competition with the other cowboys fill their days, until one of the hands, Shorty Austin (George Eades), loses his job and gets involved in rustling and killing.

The Last Cowboy (2003) was about a modern-day rancher named John William Cooper (ruddy Lance Hendriksen) trying to keep his spread running in hard times with the help of his friend and foreman, when his estranged, headstrong daughter returns for her grandfather's funeral. As in virtually all family dramas of this type (this one being a feel-good *Hallmark Hall of Fame* presentation), they clash over how to run the place before coming to a last reel rapprochement.

The Lone Ranger (2003) offered a revisionist look at the well-loved Western legend—and it was embarrassing and widely scorned. Chad Michael Murray had the title role and Nathaniel Arcand (at least a Native American actor played the part) was Tonto.

The Legend of Butch and Sundance (2004) was a new, rather lame take on the outlaw duo that had been portrayed, one might argue, definitively by Paul Newman and Robert Redford. This two-hour version, made for NBC but never appearing on its schedule, starred youthful David Clayton Rogers and Ryan Browning in the title roles and Rachelle LeFevre as Etta Place, along with Blake Gibbons as Durango, the relentless Pinkerton man who's chasing them.

Laura Ingalls' "Little House on the Prairie" (2005) was a three-part movie based on the writings of Laura Ingalls Wilder (published in 1935) and her pioneer family's trek across the Kansas Territory at the end of the nineteenth century. According to the network publicity, it is "in no way based on the television show of the 1970s [but] marks a return to the autobiographical books written by Ms. Wilder." The mini was executive produced, though, by Ed Friendly, who served the same function on the popular Michael Landon–led series of the seventies and eighties. Cameron Bancroft played Pa Ingalls in this version, Erin Cottrell was Ma, and relatively unknown Kyle Chavarria and Danielle Chuchran were daughters Laura and Mary.

In 2000, there had been another TV movie related to the subject: *Beyond the Prairie: The True Story of Laura Ingalls Wilder*. It was a portrait of the life of the author of the *Little House* book series, blossoming into adulthood (as played by Meredith Monroe) in the Dakota Territory in the late 1880s, as recalled by the mature Laura Ingalls Wilder in 1944 (played by Tess Harper). The Waltons' erstwhile John-Boy, Richard Thomas in full beard, portrayed her pioneering father (inspiration for Michael Landon's character). And there was a later sequel to this one, *Beyond the Prairie II: The True Story of Laura Ingalls Wilder Continues*.

Desolation Canyon (2006) was a fairly traditional Western tale with Stacy Keach as an aging gunslinger who teams up with an old pal, Patrick Duffy, now a local sheriff, to hunt down the former's outlaw son—now riding with a notorious gang—who has kidnapped the old man's grandson from his estranged wife.

Broken Trail (2006) starred Robert Duvall and Thomas Hayden Church, respectively, as flinty drover Prentice "Print" Ritter and his estranged nephew Tom Harte, who, in 1898, while driving wild horses from Montana to Texas, become the reluctant guardians of five abused and abandoned Chinese girls. The Western, adapted by Alan Geoffrion from his novel, won the Emmy as Outstanding Miniseries (though it ran only two episodes), Duvall as Best Actor, and Church as Best Supporting Actor. This was the very first original movie on AMC. Critic Alessandra Stanley judged in the *New York Times* that "*Broken Trail*, which has Mr. Duvall once again in the role of a crusty, worn-out cowboy, here called Print Ritter, is much more in the debt of *Lonesome Dove*, probably a little too much, since it too cannot live up to that legendary epic. . . . *Broken Trail* is not as well written or compelling as *Lonesome Dove*, but Mr. Duvall brings an earthy believability to even the most plodding lines."

Bury My Heart at Wounded Knee (2007), based on the 1970 best seller by Dee Brown (he died in 2002), chronicled the displacement of the American Indian as the United States expanded west. Academy Award–winner Anna Paquin starred as real-life Elaine Goodale, a schoolteacher who worked to improve life for the Indians on the reservation; Native American actor Adam Beach played Charles Westman, a Dartmouth-educated Sioux doctor (whom Goodale married); and Aiden Quinn was U.S. Senator Henry Dawes, one of the architects of the government policy on Indian affairs. August Schellenberg portrayed Sitting Bull, Colm Feore was General William Tecumseh Sherman, and Fred Thompson (around the time he was preparing a real-life presidential run against Barack Obama, Hillary Clinton, et al.) turned up as President Ulysses S. Grant.

A Gunfighter's Pledge (2008) had an ex-lawman (Luke Perry) on the trail of an escaped prisoner (C. Thomas Howell) who's killed the former's wife and son, and faces him down in a gunfight, during which an innocent bystander is shot. As penance, the onetime sheriff agrees to help the dead rancher's wife fend off a land baron's attempt to steal her property for its valuable water rights.

Prairie Fever (2008) was about a boozed-up sheriff (Kevin Sorbo), seeking a road to redemption and agreeing to escort a band of outcasts—three troubled women, all suffering from "prairie fever"—back to civilization in this period Western with the traditional good guys and varmints.

Aces 'n' Eights (2008) was a decidedly traditional Western, whose cast of characters included elderly rancher Thurmond Prescott (Ernest Borgnine, then age ninety-one and still tall in the saddle) who's had his land for thirty years and aims to keep it, with the help of his ranch hand Luke Rivers (Casper Van Dien). In the past, Luke made his livelihood with a gun. Bruce Boxleitner played an outlaw named D. C. Cracker, one of the hired guns of the wealthy railroad man who's got an eye on Borgnine's property. The show's title is gambler speak for "a dead man's hand."

Angel and the Badman (2009) turned out to be a rather flat made-for-cable adaptation of the John Wayne film of the forties about a gunslinger named Quirt Evans (here played by Lou Diamond Phillips), who is found injured and taken care of by a Quaker girl (Debra Unger in the role originally played by Gail Russell) and her violence-free family. Luke Perry played one of Quirt's outlaw pals, Laredo (Bruce Cabot in the older film). A great deal of the publicity for the new movie was on Brendan Wayne, the Duke's grandson, who had a small role. (Ignored almost universally, incidentally, was the fact that in the years in between the two versions came the Harrison Ford movie *Witness*, which bore a strong resemblance plot-wise to the Wayne film and won the Oscar for Best Original Screenplay.)

The Gambler, the Girl, and the Gunslinger (2009) was, as the title not-so-subtly hinted, a Western—lighthearted at that—romantic triangle. The Gambler is charming con man Shea McCall (Dean Cain) and the Gunslinger is B. J. Stoker (James Tupper). Each has won ownership of half of the Thundering Ranch in the small town of Brazos; neither, though, wants anything to do with the other, and they make plans for a shootout, when a Mexican invasion falls into their laps, forcing them to work together. Purdy widow Liz Calhoun (Allison Hossack) owns the spread neighboring Thunder Ranch—and is the middle part of the film's title.

High Plains Invaders (2009) falls into a new mini-genre, the alien Western—somewhat in the mold of the sagebrush serials that were segments of NBC's failed *Cliff Hangers!* of three decades earlier. James Marsters was featured as a scurvy Old West outlaw, Sam Denville, about to be hanged when giant, vicious alien bugs land outside of town to gorge themselves in the uranium deposits nearby. Sam is "recruited" to team up with a fast-talking, fast-shooting female bounty hunter who's in the local jail with him to stamp out these nasty creatures.

CHAPTER SEVEN

The Great Western Miniseries

Among the expansive multipart Western-themed dramas, there was the granddaddy in 1978 and 1979, *Centennial*, an adaptation of James A. Michener's sprawling (fictional) history of America from the pre-Revolutionary days through frontier times to 1970s Colorado. This epic, with an impressive cast of nearly eighty stars, aired, rather spasmodically, on NBC and ran for more than twenty-nine hours over many months (a longer time span in fact than most series of the day) in two- and three-hour segments. Later, it was slightly refashioned and reconfigured time-wise and aired on HBO in order over many nights.

Narrated by David Janssen, the *Centennial* epic begins with the meeting in the initial chapter titled "Only the Rocks Live Forever" of a French Canadian fur trapper named Pasquinel (Robert Conrad) and a fugitive Scotsman, Alexander McKeag (Richard Chamberlain), who strike up a partnership in the late 1750s. The two befriend an Arapaho leader, Lame Beaver (ubiquitous TV "Indian," Syrian-born Michael Ansara), whose lovely daughter Clay Basket (Nicaraguan-born Barbara Carrera) becomes Pasquinel's squaw. The three men forge an uneasy alliance with warlike Pawnees on the frontier.

Variety wrote of the opening "chapter," "It's an adventure story (Michener in a genial intro to the telefilm describes it as 'the great adventure of the American West'), filmed beautifully and convincingly." The trade paper's critic went on to say, "[Creator/writer John] Wilder, with the Indians using sign language and limited vocabularies when talking with whites, has them speak eloquently in English among themselves, an effective device indeed."

Through the succeeding years, Pasquinel and McKeag are reunited through intermarriage of their respective families—the second chapter spans the years between 1809 and 1830, the following one takes place on a wagon train West from St. Louis in 1845, the fourth leads up to the Civil War, and so on until we get to the late twentieth century.

At this final point, series narrator David Janssen turns up as one of the leading citizens of 1970s Centennial, Colorado, with the assorted descendants of Pasquinel and McKeag—telling his story to visiting history professor Andy Griffith. Truly a massive television undertaking in its day—not long after the equally epic *Roots*, which, of course, was not a Western—*Centennial* remains a landmark in the medium, and the longest miniseries in television history. The massive Michener source novel was executive produced by John Wilder, who also wrote a number of the television chapters. (If Michener's *Centennial* can be classified in its way as historical fiction, then the History Channel's six-part documentary *America: The Story of Us* decades later told a factual parallel tale spanning this country's progress from pre-Revolutionary days through the Internet era.)

Next, 1978's *The Awakening Land* had Elizabeth Montgomery and the struggles of the character she played, frontierswoman Sayward Luckett Wheeler, in Ohio during the late eighteenth century and early nineteenth century. Hal Holbrook was her husband, "the Solitary"; Jane Seymour was her sister, Genny. The drama's authenticity came in part from the distinctive speech patterns and dialects adapted for the actors by former dancer Marge Champion. This lusty pioneer saga—a frontier soap opera—was the recipient of a number of Emmy nominations (including, at the time, a tenth for Montgomery). *The Awakening Land* was based on the trilogy by Conrad Richter in this three-part, seven-hour movie, with each chapter being given its own title.

The Mystic Warrior told an epic tale about a proud band of Sioux Indians and the efforts of one brave (actor Robert Beltran, of Mexican–Native American ancestry—he refers to himself as Latindio) to save his people from destruction through the use of mysterious powers handed down by ancestors. Originally planned as a nine-hour miniseries entitled *Hanta Yo* (the title of the book by Ruth Beebe Hill on which the movie was based) to be aired in 1980, it instead was televised in 1984 as a five-hour miniseries renamed *The Mystic Warrior*. It had a mostly all Native American cast. "[The film] had and missed its opportunity to enlighten the American public about the lifestyle and plight of the American Indian," *Variety*'s critic wrote. "*Mystic Warrior* was, for all intents and purposes, just another cowboys-and-Indians picture (sans cowboys) and it wasn't even as engaging as some."

Dream West (1986) was a sweeping adventure, adapted by Evan Hunter from David Nevin's historical 1983 best seller, about explorer, politician, and—some say—opportunist John Charles Fremont (Richard Chamberlain, at the time dubbed the king of the miniseries) and his vision of a Western extension of the United States during the mid-1800s. The three-part miniseries epic teamed Chamberlain once again with Alice Krige (they costarred in *Wallenberg: A Hero's Story* earlier), playing the free-spirited daughter of a U.S. senator who decides to share her life with the dreamer Fremont and to chronicle his adventures. Rip Torn was Kit Carson, Fremont's longtime trail companion and most trusted friend; Ben Johnson portrayed legendary trapper and explorer Jim Bridger; Jerry Orbach played John Sutter, the prosperous settler who claimed California for himself; Fritz Weaver was the powerful senator Thomas Hart Benton, Fremont's disapproving father-in-law; and F. Murray Abraham turned up as Abraham Lincoln.

And then came Larry McMurtry's sweeping *Lonesome Dove* in 1989, followed by its prequels and sequels—and a series. The *New York Times* wrote, "Railroads forever changed the Wild West, and *Lonesome Dove*, the 1989 miniseries based on Larry McMurty's best-selling novel and that starred Robert Duvall and Tommy Lee Jones, forever changed the television Western; every cowboy drama since has been held up against *Lonesome Dove* and fallen a little short."

Lonesome Dove followed the exploits of two grizzled, old, retired Texas Rangers pals as they drive a herd from Montana from their Hat Creek Cattle Company and Livery Emporium—known as the Outfit—in the small dusty Texas border town of Lonesome Dove. There's easygoing, philosophical Captain Augustus "Gus" McCrae (Robert Duvall), a widowed rambler who, unfortunately, never got around to marrying Clara Allen, the love of his life (played by Anjelica Huston). Just the opposite is taskmaster Woodrow Call (Tommy Lee Jones), a workaholic, who refuses to acknowledge his bastard teenage son, greenhorn Newt Dobbs (Rick Schroder), by the only woman he ever loved, Maggie, a prostitute who has died. McCrae and Call were memorably played by Duvall and Jones. Joshua Deets (Danny Glover), a black tracker and scout, and not-too-bright Outfit wrangler and blacksmith Pea Eye Parker (Timothy Scott) are two guys who worked with McCrae and Call during their Ranger days. Robert Urich is opportunistic Jake Spoon, another former colleague turned bad guy, who now is on the run after having gunned down someone back in Arkansas—and that someone happens to have been the brother of the local sheriff in Lonesome Dove, July Johnson (Chris Cooper).

Added to this mix of characters, whom McCrae and Call encounter on their frontier drive that brings Gus and Clara together again somewhere in

Nebraska, are—among many others—another Lonesome Dove whore, heart-of-gold Lorena Wood (Diane Lane), who wants to move on and finds in Spoon her ticket out of town when he reluctantly agrees to take her to San Francisco; Frederic Forrest (like Urich, cast rather against type) as Blue Duck, a renegade half-breed who used to ride with Rangers McCrae and Call; Glenne Headley, July Johnson's coldhearted, pregnant wife, who, shortly after he leaves to track Jake Spoon, departs town in search of an old flame; and Barry Corbin as Roscoe Brown, July's incompetent deputy who prefers to stay far away from any gunplay. The whole adventure comes to a bittersweet close with Gus dying before trail's end and Call moving on after burying his saddle pal.

Lonesome Dove earned eighteen Emmy nominations, but lost out on the award as Outstanding Miniseries that year to War and Remembrance. Aussie director Simon Wincer, however, won the Emmy. Other nominations went to both lead actors, director, writer, composer, editor, and production designer.

On the strength and undeniable success of Lonesome Dove was spawned Return to Lonesome Dove in 1993 with Jon Voight as Woodrow Call, returning to the trail after having just buried his old saddle pal Gus McCrae near Lonesome Dove and preparing to return to his ranch in Montana. Rick Schroder was back as Newt Dobbs and Barbara Hershey signed on as Clara Allen. A behind-the-scenes controversy ensued. It seems that Larry McMurtry did not write this one (John Wilder, cocreator of the estimable Centennial, did). Accusations flew that McMurtry's characters were being ripped off. He not only emphasized publicly that he had nothing to do with Return but he completely disowned the project, as well. Instead he went ahead with a filming of a Lonesome Dove sequel, The Streets of Laredo, in 1995. (A side note: This was the title McMurtry had proposed for the early seventies film The Last Picture Show, a contemporary Western, which put him on the map in the first place.)

The Streets of Laredo starred James Garner as Woodrow Call—ironically, he was one of the actors who turned down the role that ultimately went to Tommy Lee Jones in the original—here, after Gus McCrae's death, tracking a Mexican bandit who is preying on the railroad. Sissy Spacek and Sam Shepard took the roles of Lorena Wood and Pea Eye Parker, originally played by Diane Lane and Timothy Scott. Randy Quaid turned up as real-life outlaw John Wesley Hardin and Ned Beatty played Judge Roy Bean. Chronologically in McMurtry's oeuvre, this novel, which came out in 1993, was the last in his original Lonesome Dove series, although it was published second.

Dead Man's Walk (1996), a Lonesome Dove prequel, involves Gus McCrae and Woodrow Call—here David Arquette and Jonny Lee Miller—in their earliest adventures, technically making this one the first in the series (although published third—in 1995). In *Dead Man's Walk*, McCrae and Call are just joining up with the Texas Rangers on a trek (fictional) that McMurtry based somewhat loosely on the historical 1841 Santa Fe Expedition. Early on McCrae and Call find themselves stalked by Buffalo Hump, the Comanche war chief (Eric Schweig), before embarking on the expedition to capture and annex Santa Fe for Texas (later New Mexico), led by soldier-of-fortune Caleb Cobb (F. Murray Abraham), and are forced to march the Jornada del Muerto—or "Dead Man's Walk." The cast also included Keith Carradine, Brian Dennehy, Edward James Olmos, Jennifer Garner, Harry Dean Stanton, and Tim Blake Nelson.

Comanche Moon (2008), Larry McMurtry's Western, was the last of his Lonesome Dove quartet (excluding *Return to Lonesome Dove*, which was not written by him). This, according to network publicity, was a bridge between *Dead Man's Walk* and *Lonesome Dove*, with Texas Rangers Gus McCrae and Woodrow Call (here played by Steve Zahn and Karl Urban) in their middle years. Under the leadership of Captain Irish Scull (top-billed Val Kilmer), accompanied by Kickapoo tracker Famous Shoes (David Midthunder), they're on the trail of celebrated Comanche horse thief Kicking Wolf (Jonathan Joss) who's boldly stolen Scull's steed to give to vicious Mexican bandito Ahumando (Sal Lopez). Also involved in the proceedings are Buffalo Hump, the Comanche chief (Wes Studi) who leads his nation on the warpath, and his half-Mexican son Blue Duck (Adam Beach), who later gains notoriety as the leader of a gang of bandits. Both reappear in *Lonesome Dove*.

Ken Burns's *The West*, an eight-part twelve-and-a-half-hour documentary that aired on PBS in 1996, was directed by Stephen Ives and narrated by Peter Coyote, with more than four dozen name actors reading the words. It traced the history of the vast territory that has always embodied open spaces, new beginnings, and unlimited possibility. "*The West* ranges far and wide, telling a story that begins in prehistory and ends in 1914"; so indicated the publicity from Ken Burns's Florentine Films. "It describes the Indian tribes that occupied the land, and their transformation into warrior societies with the arrival of new technology: the horse. It includes the stories of Indian warriors, homesteaders, mountain men, adventures, missionaries, Mormons, displaced slaves, conquistadors and gold-panners." TV critic Caryn James talked about it in the *New York Times* as an epic documentary about how the American frontier was settled and how its myths took shape, calling it "fiercely and brilliantly rooted in fact."

The sweeping *Into the West* in 2005 earned fourteen Emmy nominations, including Outstanding Miniseries. Executive produced by Steven Spielberg, it had more than 250 speaking parts and told the story from two sides—the white settlers and the Native Americans—mainly through the third-person narration of Jacob Wheeler (Matthew Settle) and Loved by the Buffalo (Joseph M. Marshall III). The epic drama spanned the period of expansion of the United States in the American West, from 1825 to 1890. Virtually every Native American actor who was a member of the Screen Actors Guild (and even Canadian Indians) had a part, and when that roster ran out, there were darkened politically incorrect Caucasians playing Indians. Most critics, however, found that *Into the West* left something to be desired, no matter Emmy nominations or its intentions.

CHAPTER EIGHT

Western Pilots

Through the years, the generally unspoken rule at the networks was that virtually everything in drama and sitcoms amounted to a television pilot—an idea, a concept, performances by an actor or an ensemble cast that possibly could be spun off from one proven hit to maybe a new one, and a new one after that. A doubling of the producers' bets.

"A television pilot is a sample episode of a proposed weekly series," media historian and TV producer Lee Goldberg wrote in the introduction of his *Unsold Television Pilots*. "An unsold pilot is much, much more. It's fresh faces and old favorites lining up for a one-night stand with the viewing public. It's producers, writers, directors, and network executives scrambling to keep up with the changing trends in American taste. It's the betting stub you're left with after your horse has lost the race."

Of course, many, many pilots that aired found enthusiastic audience response and succeeded into popular series—dramas, comedies, Westerns. Here are some through the years in the Western genre that had one shot on the network (or in syndication) and others that were produced but never aired, possibly because the programmers got cold feet. They hedged their bet, more or less.

In the early days on the tube, for instance, a program with, say, the very popular onetime movie cowboy Wild Bill Elliott appeared to be a terrific idea for attracting the kiddy audience—the Saturday matinee crowd that relished the Old West shoot-'em-ups. So Wild Bill got a shot in the early evening with *The Marshal of Trail City* (1950) with Dub Taylor as his obligatory sidekick

Cannonball. Being billed as U.S. Marshal Wild Bill Elliott, the venerable cowboy star played a peace-loving lawman who has to deal with trail drovers and local varmints. (Wild Bill apparently never again did television.)

Hey, let's do something with Dale Evans, hands down the best-known cow gal in recent movie history. So in 1950 she made a thirty-minute pilot titled *Dale Evans: Queen of the West*—as she was billed in all of those forties Westerns with hubby and riding partner Roy Rogers. This was before Evans and Rogers took to the happy trails together on their immensely popular television series. The pilot, on the other hand, went unsold and never aired—although it's available in a DVD package called *Roy Rogers & Dale Evans Present the Television Collection: Pilots and Rarities.*

Hey, Red Ryder was a bonanza in theatrical B Westerns, in comic books of the day, on radio. Let's try to market him as a television star. Good enough for the Lone Ranger. So producers did—twice. First in 1953 there was an unsold pilot for a *Red Ryder* series starring Jim Bannon, who, with his young Indian chum, Little Beaver, had ridden the big screen range as the popular character several times in 1949. But it didn't take. Three years later, the character was remounted on his horse Thunder for another go, this time with Allan "Rocky" Lane. Rocky had played Red Ryder in B Westerns in the midforties, so he'd be a natural. Wrong. The second pilot didn't take either. (Rocky ultimately went off to conclude his long movie cowboy career as the voice of TV's *Mister Ed*, the talking horse.) It's strange that producers didn't consider using Wild Bill Elliott, who had been the most famous Red Ryder of the screen, before Bannon and Lane. Or perhaps they *did* consider.

Skip ahead twenty or so years. Jane Fonda and Lee Marvin had great success with a 1965 big-screen Western spoof called *Cat Ballou*. Perhaps, producers surmised, it could be retooled successfully into a television series. So there were two pilots made with different casts at different times that aired on successive nights on NBC in September 1971. The first starred Lesley Ann Warren as the alternately prim and feisty Cat, schoolteacher turned outlaw, and cowboy veteran Jack Elam as the ornery, generally drunk ex-gunman Kid Sheleen. And for good measure Tom Nardini was back from the original movie as their all-knowing Indian pal Jackson Two-Bears. The next night it was Jo Ann Harris and Forrest Tucker. Neither show got beyond a single airing.

How about trying prospective series on real-life Western legends, like Calamity Jane and Belle Starr and Doc Holliday? After all, Wyatt Earp and Bat Masterson and Wild Bill Hickok had very successful (fictional) runs on the tube. Thus we had the Calamity Janes of Joan Blondell in "The Pussyfootin' Rocks," a 1952 pilot from *Schlitz Playhouse of Stars*; of Elaine Rooney (a onetime wife of Mickey) in a 1957 pilot for John Wayne's Batjac Productions; of Jane Alexander and Anjelica Huston and Kim Darby in assorted made-for-TV movies; of profane Robin Weigert in *Deadwood*.

Singing cowboys were popular on the screen in the heyday of the B Western—Gene Autry, Roy Rogers, Tex Ritter, Ken Maynard, Dick Foran, Ken Curtis, Monte Hale. Why not on television? So there were several pilots about singing cowboys. Some examples:

- *Riders of the Purple Sage*, with Foy Willing and his popular group, who were part of Gene Autry's ranch wranglers in his movies, performing songs about cowboys and the West. This was an unsold pilot from 1956.
- *Curley Bradley—The Singing Marshal*, a fifteen-minute show from 1955 (unsold), with Curley, best known for playing the Tom Mix character on radio in the forties, vocalizing for the young 'uns.

In the fifties, a significant number of episodes of dramatic and Western anthologies—*Schlitz Playhouse of Stars, Dick Powell's Zane Grey Theatre, Ford Television Theatre, Four Star Playhouse, Wagon Train, Death Valley Days*—served as pilots for prospective network shows.

Here's an assortment of—but by no means all—Western pilots on television through the years. Those that began life as series episodes are so noted in parentheses.

The Westerner (1953), a syndicated pilot, starred James Craig as a frontier town sheriff who is bushwhacked by a gang of outlaws and is forced to escort over the border two scummy brothers who have knocked over an express office.

Johnny Moccasin (unaired, 1955) featured Jody McCrea in the title role, a stripped-to-the-waist, pinto-riding paleface with long blond hair and a single enormous feather in his headband, who was raised by an Indian tribe and is caught between them and angry white settlers. (This "lost Western" unsold pilot is included, with several others, in a six-DVD set, *The Classic TV Western Collection*, that features forty series episodes.)

Arroyo (NBC, 1955; *Screen Directors Playhouse*) starred normally light comic Jack Carson as a self-appointed judge trying to uphold law and order in the town of Arroyo, New Mexico. Carson is Judge Lamar Kendall and cowboy veteran Bob Steele is the local deputy.

Cavalry Patrol (CBS, 1955) was written, produced, and directed by Western fiction writer Charles Marquis Warren. Dewey Martin is Lieutenant Johnny Reardon, with a ragtag group, "ex-mutineers, deserters, confederate prisoners," as the opening narration described them, manning a fort in Arizona Territory in 1868.

The Trailblazer (unaired, 1955) was a series based on the life of frontiersman John Charles Fremont (played by Steve Cochran) and his exploits in the untamed wilderness with trail scout Kit Carson (James Gavin). Unaired, this had the alternate titles of *Adventures of Fremont* and *Fremont the Trailblazer* (it's available on DVD). Fremont was portrayed a number of times in assorted situations—most notably by Richard Chamberlain in the miniseries *Dream West* and by Jeffrey Hunter in *Destiny, West*.

Elfego Baca (ABC, 1957; *Telephone Time*) starred Mexican character actor Manuel Rojas as the legendary—some to this day say infamous—outlaw/lawyer who held sway in and around Albuquerque in the mid-1880s (he died in 1945). This should not be confused with Disney's more fanciful series *Nine Lives of Elfego Baca*.

Ballad for a Bad Man (CBS, 1958; *Westinghouse Desilu Playhouse*) featured Steve Forrest as Chris Hody, bounty hunter pursuing an outlaw in the Old West and getting involved with a traveling musical show run by Jane Russell as Lili Travers and Jack Haley as Barnaby Tibbs.

Doc Holliday (CBS, 1958) had Dewey Martin portraying the famously consumptive doctor/gunfighter. The pilot, written by Aaron Spelling, originally aired on the *Zane Grey Theatre* as "Man of Fear," and had Doc helping rid a town of a corrupt sheriff who'd been terrorizing the place.

The Frontier World of Doc Holliday (ABC, 1959), a pilot, starred a pre-*Batman* Adam West in an episode initially airing on the series *Cheyenne* as "Birth of a Legend." West said to *TV Guide* at the time, "I played him as an alcoholic with a consumptive cough. This isn't too attractive when you kiss your horse, and the horse dies. I don't think ABC, Warners, or Madison Avenue appreciated it at the time. And probably rightly so."

A handful of proposed series (1958–1959) with Western themes were chronicled in Lee Goldberg's *Unsold Television Pilots*. None of these apparently got off the drawing board: *Lady Law* had Barbara Stanwyck playing a female sheriff who inherits a stagecoach line; *The Story of a Star*, with Joel McCrea hosting an anthology featuring stories about frontier sheriffs; *Western Musketeers*, in which a government investigator travels with a pair of singing cowboys (Carl Smith, Webb Pierce, and Marty Robbins were scheduled to star, but it's unclear which of the three were the two singing cowboys because, in real life, all three were); *Rawhide Riley* with veteran action star Richard Arlen, in the guise of a frontier barber in Tucson, Arizona, as the narrator of this prospective anthology series; and *The Young Sheriff*, a vehicle for popular Grand Ole Opry star Faron Young (whose nickname in the world of country music was the Singing Sheriff).

The Quiet Man, an unsold 1959 pilot that had nothing to do with the John Ford/John Wayne Irish-themed classic, starred Jack Lord as, what was described as, a Western hero who is a man of few words, who years before had been sent for a Harvard education and has returned to the homestead dedicated to living by his wits and not his gun—at which he had proven quite adept. But when his dad and his fiancée are murdered, he seeks revenge with his gun. Prolific Western novelist Frank Gruber created this one.

The Elizabeth McQueeny Story, a vehicle for Bette Davis in 1959, was just one of a number of episodes of NBC's *Wagon Train* that served as prospective series pilots (in truth, just about every one of them did, since each dealt with a different guest star in a different situation). Davis, who might well have been the biggest name guest star in the venerable Western show, played the den mother of an all-female dance troupe traveling through the Old West.

They Went Thataway, a comedy Western pilot that aired on CBS in summer 1960, told the story of Black Ace Burton (avuncular James Westerfield), a man striving to earn the title "Meanest Man in the West."

Code of Jonathan West (1960; *General Electric Theater*) gave Fess Parker a prospective show in the years between *Davy Crockett* and *Daniel Boone*, as a traveling preacher roaming the post–Civil War West as a do-gooder.

The Reno Brothers (1960), a spin-off by producer Aaron Spelling from the *Johnny Ringo* series, followed the exploits of a pair of young lawmen brothers ("co-sheriffs," they described themselves) dedicated to keeping the peace in a small Texas town. The brothers were Mike and Chris, played by Jim Beck and Ben Cooper.

Mountain Man (1960) was a half-hour pilot for Peter Palmer (late of *Li'l Abner* fame), who played Critter Calhoun, the proprietor of a fur station in the Rockies circa 1840. Jack Weston and Harry Shannon were two of his pals, Stringer and Hoss.

The Man from Everywhere (1961) had Burt Reynolds as a roving cowpoke named Branch Taylor, picking up odd jobs wherever he can in this pilot that originated on *Zane Grey Theatre*. Although Reynolds's *The Man from Everywhere* went nowhere, he much later turned up as the star of a sports-themed TV movie called *The Man from Left Field*.

The Jayhawkers (1961), from producer Roy Huggins (of *Maverick* fame), had Jack Betts and Jock Gaynor as two roaming cowpokes from Kansas exploring the West. Costarring were three better-known actors, Dan Dailey, Ann Blyth, and Eddie Foy III.

Outpost, which aired as the episode "Charge!" on *The Outlaws* series, was an hour-long pilot on NBC following three bickering cavalry scouts, a la Kipling's *Gunga Din* and *Soldiers Three*. Claude Akins, Jay Lanin, and Chris King starred, yelling "Charge!" every time they bolted into action. Frank De Kova (a white character actor from New York who made a virtual career of playing Indians on television and mobsters in the movies) was their Native American pal, Chief White Tongue.

Sam Hill was a 1962 Western pilot that aired as an episode of *Bonanza* and was directed by Robert Altman. Claude Akins starred in the title role as a strong but kindhearted blacksmith who rambled around the Old West. Another Western pilot nine years later that used *Sam Hill* in its title but was totally unrelated was from Richard Levinson and William Link, *Columbo* creators. It aired as a made-for-television movie starring Ernest Borgnine.

Night Rider (1962) was an unsold pilot for a Johnny Cash series in which he costarred with several other country singers: Merle Travis, Johnny Western, and B-Western star Eddie Dean, along with Dickie (*Buffalo Bill Jr.*) Jones. It apparently was to have been a low-budget anthology series with Cash as a somewhat sullen gunslinger named Johnny Laredo.

Medicine Man, an unaired ABC pilot, was created by and starred Ernie Kovacs and Buster Keaton, as a con man and his silent Indian partner, respectively. Completed just a week before Kovacs's death in an auto accident, it was never shown.

Adam McKenzie, a 1962 NBC spin-off from *Wagon Train*, starred Michael Ansara—not playing a Native American for a change—in the title role of a doctor in the Old West. In the pilot, he goes to the aid of a Mexican girl accused of being a witch.

Which Way Did They Go? (ABC, 1962; *The Rifleman*) followed widowed farmer Neb Jackson (Peter Whitney), who heads West with his three young sons and stumbles on a small frontier town in need of a sheriff—only once he takes the job, he finds it ain't easy.

The Dog Troop (1964; *Wagon Train*) had Ron Hayes as Lieutenant Duncan McIvor leading a group of frontier soldiers who try to maintain order in the badlands.

Diamond Jim Brady (1965) was an unsold pilot starring Dale Robertson—in his "down time" between playing Jim Hardie for a long time in *Tales of Wells Fargo* and Ben Calhoun later in *The Iron Horse*. This prospective series took a fictional look at the real-life Diamond Jim, making him a ramrod for the railroad in Colorado of the mid-1870s. He actually did work for the railroads while in his early twenties.

Bend of the River (1965) was not a remake of the 1952 James Stewart movie of that name but an episode of *Wagon Train* (the final one). It starred Rory Calhoun as Jarbo Pierce, who leads a frontier family attempting to establish their homestead. Universal Pictures, which owned the title to the Stewart film and also produced the TV series (under its Revue TV subsidiary), apparently usurped the title for an episode with a vaguely similar plot.

This Gun for Hire, on NBC in 1966, had Jack Lord playing Jab Harlan, a tough gunslinger in the Old West. Lola Albright, as an about-to-be-hanged man's wife, hires Harlan to free her husband, wrongly convicted of bank robbery. He actually was framed by no-good Neville Brand who has hightailed to Texas—with Harlan in pursuit. This aired as "Above the Law," an episode of *Laredo*.

Roaring Camp, from Bing Crosby Productions in 1966, was a pilot that aired on ABC following the adventures of a U.S. marshal (Richard Bradford) in a Colorado gold rush town run by a widow (Katherine Justice) and a gunslinger (Jim McMullan).

The Kowboys (1970) came from the imagination of rock impresario Don Kirshner, the creator of the Monkees and the Archies, pop music sensations of the day. The Kowboys are a singing group of four guys and a girl, roaming the Wild West in the late nineteenth century and trying to save a town from the evil rancher bent on destroying it. Enie Pintoff produced and directed—but Kirshner and Pintoff struck out with this NBC pilot.

Prudence and the Chief (ABC, 1970) put musical comedy star Sally Ann Howes into a lighthearted Western about a widowed teacher/missionary who packs her two kids and her mother onto a wagon train and heads West to start a school in uncivilized Cheyenne territory. It isn't long before she's clashing with an Indian chief named Snow Eagle (Manhattan paleface Rick Jason in Indian makeup)—with whom, if this pilot made it, she probably would have developed a love/hate relationship. This came from Jean Holloway, who had created *The Ghost and Mrs. Muir*, which, with that series just ending, she might well have reworked into this Western plot.

McMasters of Sweetwater, an unsold syndicated pilot from 1974, was a Western drama that starred Jack Cassidy as a Boston schoolteacher named Marion McMasters, who confronts the difficulty of frontier life when coming to teach in Sweetwater, Arizona. A single dad with two young kids, he receives a cold reception from the townsfolk—who were expecting a "schoolmarm," not a "schoolmaster."

Black Bart, the year following *Sidekicks*, gave Lou Gossett another go at a Western spoof after the no-go of *Sidekicks*. This 1975 pilot on CBS was based on *Blazing Saddles* and told once again the adventures of a black sheriff and his fast-drawing sidekick (played by Steve Landesberg, comparable more or less to the Gene Wilder role in the feature), fighting corruption and bigotry in the Old West. *Blazing Saddles* had been written by Mel Brooks together with Andrew Bergman, Norman Steinberg, Richard Pryor, and Alan Uger, but only Bergman was involved in the TV follow-up.

Hearts of the West, based on the theatrical film with Jeff Bridges, was an unsold NBC pilot that aired in 1977. Charles Frank took over the Bridges role as a would-be Western screenwriter in Hollywood of the thirties who works as an extra in cowboy serials. Also in the cast were Lonny Chapman as a cowboy has-been reduced to being an extra, Allen Miller as the cheap producer, and Allan Case as the preening cowboy star, Lyle Montana. Larry Gelbart wrote the script.

The Buffalo Soldiers (1979) was to be an NBC series following the exploits of the U.S. Army's 10th Cavalry, a mostly black regiment patrolling the 1860s West, led by a white officer (John Beck as Colonel Frank O'Connor). Stan Shaw also starred, as the highest ranking noncommissioned officer.

The Pony Express, a 1980 NBC pilot that had Carroll O'Connor as executive producer, was about a couple of teenage riders (John Hammond and Harry Crosby, Bing's son, as Jed Beechum and Albie Foreman) for the Pony Express during the 1860s. Victor French played their boss. A similar theme was the basis of the later ABC series *The Young Riders*.

The Cherokee Trail (CBS, 1981) was from a Louis L'Amour sagebrush tale—he received "created by" credit (the novel wasn't published until 1982). Cindy Pickett played widow Mary Breydon, who, with daughter Peggy (Tina Yothers), operated a stagecoach way station in the Colorado wilderness in 1864 with the help of grizzled hired hand Ridge Kenton (Richard Farnsworth), a mysterious gunman named Temple Boone (David Hayward), an Irish cook, and an orphan boy. "I deliberately chose a woman from a cultured background," L'Amour told the press when promoting this venture, "so that she would be facing many situations that are foreign to her. She had to adapt, and that was so typical of the West. The early Westerners all came from somewhere else and they all had to adapt."

This family-oriented pilot came from Walt Disney Productions and the producers were the same team that did L'Amour's *Sacketts* miniseries. Although *The Cherokee Trail* didn't get picked up in the United States, it became an Australian series that ran for three years Down Under, according to Louis L'Amour's website.

Actually, *The Cherokee Trail* became *Five Mile Creek*, featuring, in its final season, a teenage Nicole Kidman. *Five Mile Creek* is an anomaly—an Australian Western series seen on the Disney Channel in the beginning in 1983.

Set in the mid-late 1800s, it told of a group of Americans and Australians managing to run a coach line business, the Australian Express, and the titular way station, while trying to make ends meet in the Outback.

Maggie Scott (Louise Caire Clark, an American from New Orleans) and her daughter, Hannah (Priscilla Weems), travel from San Francisco to Australia to meet up with her (Maggie's) husband, Adam (Jonathan Frakes), who is out looking for gold. Con Madigan (Jay Kerr), a charming Texan who is traveling on the same ship, also comes to Australia to start a coach line with Jack Taylor (Rod Mullinar), a man who'll jump at anything before thinking first. Their journeys all lead them to Five Mile Creek, owned by Eddie Wallace (James Healey) and his no-nonsense sister, Kate (Liz Burch). Eddie disappears, leaving Kate to run the place by herself with Irish handyman Paddy Malone (Michael Caton). But with the aid of the new coach line and with Maggie's help, Kate manages to keep the way station in shape.

Fort Smith, a Western that went into development for AMC in late 2007 but, as of the publication date of this book, still has not seen the light of day, was described as "a drama about Isaiah Parker, who polices the five points—comprised of five different Indian tribes—with his posse in the lawless post–Civil War West."

CHAPTER NINE

Cartoon Westerns

The best-known animated shows aired primarily on Saturday mornings and had Western settings. *Adventures of Pow Wow the Indian Boy*, an animated series of (initially) fifteen-minute moralistic stories with a Western bent based on Indian folklore, was produced and directed by Sam Singer. It dates back early 1949, when it was a local Sunday morning program on the NBC outlet in New York. The series, produced by Temple-Toons in the midfifties, was shown as 52 five-minute black-and-white films on *Captain Kangaroo* on CBS and later went into syndication. Pow Wow's adventures involved an assortment of pals, like Ruffy Rabbit, Percy Pelican, Vagabond Mouse, and others, and of course a wise medicine man, who gave young Pow Wow sage counsel.

Like *The Adventures of Pow Wow*, *The Adventures of Lariat Sam* aired as an animated segment of *Captain Kangaroo* between 1962 and 1965, the difference being that Lariat Sam was created by the Captain himself, Bob Keeshan. There were thirteen episodes, each containing 3 five-minute chapters. Lariat Sam was an idealistic cartoon hero who never carried a gun—just a lasso. His sidekick was Tippytoes the Wonder Horse, who wore a derby and spouted poetry. (Both Sam and Tippytoes were voiced by Dayton Allen.) Their nemeses were Badlands Meaney and cohort J. Skulking Bushwhack.

Dayton Allen, who voiced Oky Doky years before as well as Phineas T. Bluster on *Howdy Doody*, also was Deputy Dawg in the late fifties and into the early seventies, a hangdog hound who was a simpleminded Mississippi lawman with a distinct drawl. Originally a Terrytoons cartoon character, he was the star of sight-gag-laden Western adventures that generally were seven minutes long, produced by CBS as *The Deputy Dawg Show*, and were packaged four at a time and shown as a half-hour program in syndication. Deputy Dawg remains part of American pop culture, as does, in his way, Dayton Allen, who was the voice over the years of dozens of memorable cartoon characters.

Equally as popular as Deputy Dawg around the same time was Quick Draw McGraw, the star of a cartoon series that ran in syndication beginning in 1959. *The Quick Draw McGraw Show* was the third cartoon television production created by William Hanna and Joseph Barbera, who were responsible for *Huckleberry Hound* and *Ruff & Ready*. Quick Draw was a well-intentioned but somewhat dim cartoon horse/lawman whose sidekick was a Mexican burro named Baba Looey (after Desi Arnaz's trademark song) who spoke Spanglish. The show was sponsored by Kellogg's, which put Quick Draw on the package of one or another of its cereals. Voice actor Daws Butler performed Quick Draw, Baba Looey, and others. Butler also would be the voice of Yogi Bear and (for a while) Barney Rubble on *The Flintstones*.

The 1959 syndicated Western cartoon series *Bucky and Pepito* is often cited by TV aficionados as the worst animated series ever on the tube. Created and produced by Sam Singer (who also was responsible for *Adventures of Pow Wow the Indian Boy* of a decade before) for his Samsing Productions, *Bucky and Pepito*, voiced by Dallas McKinnon (not his fault, to be sure), actually managed to set TV animation back to the early crude days. Cartoon historian Harry McCracken was quoted as saying the pair "set a standard for awfulness that no contemporary TV cartoon has managed to surpass. They were great at what they did, which was being bad."

The series (today's PC police would be appalled) revolved around a young, white, Anglo Southwestern-style boy who lived on a ranch. He didn't dress like a cowboy, but like a kid dressing up like a cowboy. He hung around with the younger Pepito, who was pure Mexican stereotype—from the huge sombrero that covered his eyes to the slow, lazy ways, so prominent a part of his character that they were mentioned in the show's theme song.

Wally Western was not only the title of this syndicated show in 1962 but also the name of its animated host who worked with a cartoon assistant. It featured reedited Western films of Ken Maynard, Hoot Gibson, Tex Ritter, and Bob Steele in cliff-hanger installments.

The Lone Ranger (CBS, 1966–1968) rode again as a Saturday morning cartoon series. Michael Rye (aka Rye Billsbury, who'd played "Jack Armstrong, the All-American Boy" on radio) voiced the famed masked man, and radio veteran Shepard Menken, his faithful Kimosabe. Marvin Miller was the opening title narrator. The arch-villain in this animated series was a dwarf named Tiny Tom, voiced by Dick Beals. Among the other guest voices were Agnes Moorehead and Paul Winchell. The show, which lasted for thirty episodes (the last one was on March 9, 1968), was split into three separate segments, with the middle one being a solo Tonto animated adventure.

The New Adventures of the Lone Ranger was another CBS animated series a decade later. This morphed into *The Tarzan/Lone Ranger/Zorro Adventure Hour*, animated shorts of three great—but totally diverse—action characters, produced by Norm Prescott and Lou Scheimer's Filmation and premiering on CBS September 12, 1981. William Conrad narrated and, using the pseudonym J. Darnoc, voiced the Lone Ranger. Ivan Naranjo voiced Tonto, and with the other two cartoon series with which it shared an overall title, the show took on a realistic educational tone not associated with earlier incarnations.

Go Go Gophers (CBS, 1968–1969) featured cartoon figures Ruffled Feathers and Running Board as a pair of Indian-resembling gophers, trying to safeguard their domain from Kit Coyote, an army colonel determined to rid the West of gophers. Voiced by Sandy Becker, George S. Irving, and Kenny Delmar, respectively, the animated series ran for twenty-four episodes.

Riders in the Sky (CBS, 1991–1992) was a Saturday morning children's series featuring not only the popular Nashville musical group of that name but also a multimedia mix of live-action, animation, Claymation, and puppetry. This *Pee-Wee Herman's Playhouse* knockoff with misshapen, garishly painted sets—that only lasted for a handful of episodes—featured cowboy characters living and goofing around on the Harmony Ranch and welcoming such "names" as Ray Sharkey and Julia Sweeney (later of *Saturday Night Live*) as Spongehead and Tunga Tujunga. Riders in the Sky, a contemporary country Western group that claimed as its inspirations the Sons of the Pioneers and the Riders of the Purple Sage from Roy Rogers/Gene Autry days, was comprised of Ranger Doug, Woody Paull, Too Slim, and "Cowpolka accordion king" Joey Miskulin. The show's regulars included Chris Barbers as Butch, Patrick Bristow as Sourdough, Stan Kirsch as Axl, and Deanne Oliver as Miss N'Formation, among others. The show was created and produced by Alan Sacks.

The Wild West C.O.W. Boys of Moo Mesa (1992–1993) was a CBS cartoon series (twenty-six episodes) set in the 1800s. A mysterious comet has hit the U.S. Southwest, transforming the local cattle and animals into their own version of the Old West called Moo Mesa, complete with several lawmen dealing with bizarre outlaws. Among the voices were Jim Cummings as Dakota Duke, Jeff Bennett as Cowlarado Kid, and Pat Fraley as Marshal Moo Montana.

Legend of Calamity Jane (WB, 1997–1998) did the Jane tale as a rather stylized Saturday morning cartoon, with the voices of Barbara Scaff, Frank Welker (as pal Joe Presto), and Clancy Brown (as Wild Bill Hickok). Apparently only three episodes (of thirteen filmed) of this French-produced series aired on the WB before the show was quietly pulled from the schedule (too violent for the kiddy audience).

CHAPTER TEN

Western Documentaries

Beyond the dozens of Western series and television movies through the decades, there have been various television documentaries depicting the Old West with and without actors reenacting events. Dramatizations put contemporary figures into juxtaposition with costumed figures of the time in somewhat simplistic—though today remembered fondly perhaps as nostalgic—form in the fifties on *You Are There* and *DuPont Cavalcade of America*.

One of the premier documentary series of the fifties, NBC's Sunday afternoon *Wide Wide World*, a ninety-minute show developed by Sylvester "Pat" Weaver and hosted by Dave Garroway, spent one complete program in June 1958 examining "The Western," tracing its evolution with a lineup of more than two dozen cowboy stars ranging from Broncho Billy Anderson, William S. Hart, and Tom Mix (in archival film footage) to James Arness, Gene Autry, Gary Cooper, James Garner, Clayton Moore, all the way to John Wayne—some there live, some on film and tape. A live segment of the show originated from Autry's Melody Ranch in Newall, California.

In the fifties through the seventies, NBC aired its memorable, though very periodic, *Project Twenty* (or *Project XX*) anthology drama series, including one or two dealing with the American West. The series, produced by Don Hyatt and scored by Robert Russell Bennett, included, among others, an acclaimed hour-long look at "The Real West" in March 1961, hosted by Gary Cooper, just before he died. "Well, we brought law and order to the territory; built railroads, homes, towns and I guess you might call it civilization," Cooper famously said at the show's closing, "but by damn, wouldn't it be fun to tear it down and start all over again!" Some time later, Walter Brennan turned up on *Project Twenty* as narrator of "End of the Trail," talking about Indian history. Of "The Real West," in addition to calling it "exceptional," critic Jack Gould wrote in the *New York Times* that it was "a fascinatingly authentic look at the West" that "was at its best in deflating the myth makers of the West and possibly the illusions of some young TV viewers."

CBS, in the early seventies, had a series of periodic hour-long specials under the umbrella title *Appointment with Destiny*, and in late February 1972, offered up—*You Are There*–style—"Showdown at the O.K. Corral," narrated by Lorne Greene. A cast of unfamiliar faces played Wyatt Earp, Doc Holliday, and the Clantons. Leslie Raddatz wrote in a "background" piece on the show in *TV Guide*, "Whatever the legends and conflicting evidence, when the smoke cleared that October afternoon, Tom and Frank McLaury and nineteen-year-old Billy Clanton were dead, Virgil and Morgan Earp seriously wounded. *The [Tombstone] Epitaph* editorialized: 'The feeling among the best class of our citizens is that the Marshal was entirely justified in his efforts to disarm these men, and that, being fired upon, they had to defend themselves, which they did most bravely.'"

In contemporary times, on such fare as PBS's *American Experience* and both the Discovery Channel and the History Channel, and to lesser extent, curiously, the Western Channel, the genre continues to find audiences in intriguing ways.

Do You Mean There Are Still Real Cowboys? (1988) was one of those airing on PBS's *American Experience*. Based on an idea and narrated by Glenn Close, this film, focusing on the Wyoming town of Big Piney, where Close had property at the time, offered a modern-day take on an authentic American tradition: the life of the American cowboy and his family and of ranching, a threatened way of life. Several years later on that PBS series, Hector Elizondo narrated the dramatized 2006 documentary *Remember the Alamo*, weaving a rather compelling, and often overlooked, historical narrative with interesting interviews and stylish re-creations. It was written, produced, and directed by Joseph Tovares.

The ambitious five-part *American Experience* miniseries, *We Shall Remain* (2009), presented a dramatic look at the Native American from Pilgrim America in the 1600s through Wounded Knee in the early 1970s. Under the umbrella title "We Shall Return," it was narrated by Benjamin Bratt and reenacted by a host of solid performers. The director was Chris Eyre, a Native American with a number of well-received films on his résumé. "The series is not an exploration of the way Indians lived among themselves," the *Los Angeles Times* wrote, "but rather the way their way of life was put under stress by white interests and attendant, imported ideas about land, money, humanity and God—and the various ways the natives accommodated or resisted new political realities and continually rewritten rules."

The PBS *American Experience* periodically has offered hour-long documentary portraits of such Western legends as Buffalo Bill, Annie Oakley, Jesse James, Kit Carson, and in early 2010, Wyatt Earp, arguably the definitive frontier figure in American Western lore. These documentaries invariably have Old West historians—as "talking heads"—reconstructing the stories of these nineteenth-century sagebrush superstars who, at least in the case of Earp, lived on the edge as both outlaw and lawman. The historians on the PBS Earp documentary, narrated by Michael Murphy, continually used the term *cowboy* in a derogative sense as paid-for-hire bad guys and more or less agreed that Earp got involved with the territorial politics of the time (the republicans were the moneyed interest from back East—the railroad tycoons, the bankers, the silver mine owners—and the democrats the local townsfolk and homesteaders).

Wyatt ultimately, following the infamous gunfight at the O.K. Corral in Tombstone, gave up what those involved with the documentary called "lawing" and disappeared in the haze of Western history, only to end up years later in the Hollywood of the 1920s with his wife and/or companion of forty-seven years, Josephine Marcus, trying—according to the PBS *American Experience* version—to set the record straight and to sell the movies on the idea of what really happened and hoping to interest early Western star William S. Hart, unsuccessfully, to play him.

Dutch filmmaker Thys Ockersen, from childhood a Roy Rogers fan, hunted down the King of the Cowboys for a loving tribute—titled (what else?) *Roy Rogers: King of the Cowboys*—which premiered as an original television special on AMC in December 1992 (several months after a theatrical showing in the Netherlands). Rogers was part of the film, along with Dale Evans, Roy Jr., Rogers's granddaughter Mindy, the Sons of the Pioneers, Ruth Terry (another of Rogers's former leading ladies), Al "Lash" LaRue, director William Witney, and others. Much of the filming was done at the Roy Rogers Museum in Victorville, California.

On the Discovery Channel, there was *Ten Most Wanted Outlaws of the Old West* in July 2003, and during 2006–2007, in conjunction with the BBC, there was a sterling, multi-episode documentary series *The Wild West*—in which, for instance, the fabled Gunfight at the O.K. Corral was again staged.

TBS's hour-long, three-part series in the early nineties, *The Untold West*, was about "Outlaws, Rebels and Rogues," narrated by Lou Diamond Phillips; "The Black West," narrated by Danny Glover; and "Hot on the Trail," narrated by Keith Carradine and Dee Hoty—who together starred on Broadway in *Will Rogers Follies*. Below the headline "Shattering the Legends of West's Pistol Packers," the *New York Times* said of the first one in the series, "Even if such revelations do not knock off your ten-gallon hat, they are presented engagingly, with plenty of clips of old movies, some harmless reenactments and amiable asides by Old West historians, who agree that the famous bad men and women of pulp and celluloid were all 'outlaws of the imagination.'" The second in the series offered an account of the role that blacks played in Western lore (including Mary Fields, who is said to have ridden for the Pony Express when in her seventies). The third was about (among others) Calamity Jane and a cavalry vamp named Mrs. Noonan who turned out to be a man.

Kris Kristofferson was the narrator of the six-part *Adventures of the Old West* series in 1993 on the Disney Channel. Included were such episodes as "The 49ers and the California Gold Rush," "Great Chiefs at the Crossroads," "The Trailblazers," "Pioneers and the Promised Land," "Frontier Justice: The Law and the Lawless," and "Texas Cowboys and Trail Drives." These are all available in a DVD package along with one other, "Scouts of the Wilderness," also produced and directed by Steve Purvis.

Big Guns Talk: The History of the Western (1997) was an entertaining two-hour TNT documentary, narrated by James Garner, that examined a number of themes, and as the network press release said, "explored through the years in Westerns: its myths, legend, heroes, stars, history and impact on culture. The installments include: 'A Liar's Frontier,' which focuses on the conventions, lies and delusions of the genre; 'The Hanging Tree' looks at the moral lessons taught in Westerns; 'Western Whitewash' reveals racial distortions in Western movies." Among the several participating in the show as "talking heads" were Charlton Heston; Clint Eastwood; Sam Elliott; Kris Kristofferson; Anthony Quinn; Tom Selleck; Carrol Baker; Katharine Ross; Jane Seymour; Richard Widmark; Ernest Borgnine; Robert Culp; Bruce Dern; Mario Van Peebles; native American actors Rodney Grant, Irene Bedard, Wes Studi; directors Budd Boetticher and Burt Kennedy; and others associated with the genre. Heston, in the documentary, sums it up: "The true Western hero is the true American—a decent man who will not give up, cheat or not keep his word. And he'll finish what he started."

Another early nineties Western-themed documentary was *Legends of the West*, hosted by veteran cowboy actor Harry Carey Jr. along with his pal, rodeo-rider-turned-leathered-actor Ben Johnson (they'd done some John Ford movies together). Writer/director Marino Amoruso, who had filmed documentaries on sports figures like Joe DiMaggio and Rocky Marciano and cultural personalities ranging from Elvis to Ol' Blue Eyes to Dean Martin, offered this one.

Ben Johnson, himself, was the subject of a documentary tribute called *Third Cowboy on the Right*, just after his death in 1996. It was filled with affectionate words from Charlton Heston, James Coburn (who narrated), Peter Bogdanovich, Timothy Bottoms, Harry Dean Stanton, Harry Carey Jr., and many others who had worked with him through the years. "This hand-crafted docu takes an unusually detailed look at the career of one of Hollywood's longtime leading character actors," *Variety*'s critic wrote. "True to the ingratiating personality of its subject and steeped in the world of the Western, this winning piece of specialized film history is a natural for fests, public TV and movie-oriented cable outlets."

Clint Eastwood on Westerns, narrated by Hal Holbrook, was among writer/critic Richard Shickel's star documentaries for TMC in 1992, and *Sam Peckinpah's West: Legacy of a Hollywood Renegade*, with narrator Kris Kristofferson, premiered on Starz! in 2004. On the BET, there was *That's Black Entertainment: Westerns*, a 2002 documentary narrated by Mario Van Peebles, with a look into the B Westerns produced for African American theaters in the 1930s and 1940s. It aired on Starz! Encore Entertainment.

Keith Carradine hosted and narrated the two pilot episodes in August 2003 and the first season of the History Channel's *Wild West Tech*. David Carradine took over during the following season in a poker game sequence in the second season opener "Six-Shooter Tech," in which Keith loses the hosting job to his brother David! The show ran from 2003 to 2005. Entertaining and interesting—and revisionist in many ways—it showed what really happened as compared to what we have been told occurred through books and film. The Carradines (first Keith and later David) introduced various characters, such as quick draw artists or bullwhip masters, and allowed them to demonstrate their respective arts of the Old West. Throughout were commentaries by a group of Western historians and students who would give their take on the "technologies" and events of historical record.

Rough Riders and Black Cowboy Legends was a 2004 documentary with insights from thirties and forties African American cowboy star Herb Jeffries, black rodeo champion Bill Pickett, and contemporary actors Glynn Turman, Reginald T. Dorsey, Obba Babatunde, and others telling the story of the black cowboys and the contribution they have made to the country's success.

The History Channel broadcast the two-hour *When Cowboys Were King*, narrated by, among others, Tom Selleck and Eli Wallach, in 2006, as well as a multipart series *Frontier: Legends of the Old West* in 1998 (Peter Coyote narrated). In 2000, the History Channel produced another one, *Frontier: The Decisive Battles of the Old Northwest*, presenting the story of four major battles that shaped the early history of the United States well into the nineteenth century.

In late 2009, *Cowboys and Outlaws*, a six-hour History Channel series, traveled back to America's Wild West past unveiling true stories of the post–Civil War years through the 1890s, considered the "golden era of the cowboy." The first episode, "The Real McCoy," was described this way by the cable channel's publicity machine: "At the dawn of the cowboy era, a mysterious disease threatens to derail the dreams of Texas cattlemen and their cowboys. One man vows to find a cure—and get fabulously rich at the same time. In a bold gamble, Joe McCoy, a nineteenth-century cattle baron, builds a city in the middle of nowhere: Abilene—the first 'cow town'—whose legacy would reshape the West."

This episode was followed by "The Real Wyatt Earp," taking him from upstanding lawman (looking like a caricature of actor Sam Elliott!) in Wichita and then Dodge City to Tombstone and the O.K. Corral gunfight, where he ultimately moved to the other side of the law. Earp then was pictured as fading into old age as a denizen of Hollywood in the late 1920s trying to sell his real story and meeting up, if very briefly, with author Stuart Lake, who immortalized him in ink. Along the way, as has become the norm in TV documentaries of this type, there were reenactments by real-life unnamed actors hazily acting out events, a number of Western "talking heads" historians discussing Earp and the Old West in general, and some brief insights into how the cowboy dressed, the type of weapons he used, the badges the lawman wore, the card games that were played, the saloon brawls, and so on.

Episodes titled "The Real Lonesome Dove," "The Real Billy the Kid," "Frontier Hit Man" (about notorious Tom Horn), and "Range War" rounded out this History Channel series.

Cowboys and Outlaws was a belated follow-up of sorts to the History Channel's 1992 Western documentary series that later was packaged for the DVD market and featured "The Real West: Buffalo Bill & His Wild West"; "The Real West: Outlaws—The Ten Most Wanted"; "The Real West: Legendary Cowboys"; "The Real West: The Law from behind the Tin Star"; "The Real West: The James Gang"; "The Real West: The Texas Rangers"; "The Real West: Wild Bill Hickok"; "The Real West: Guns That Tamed the West." Though brief, as narrator Kenny Rogers pointed out, the period of exploration and expansion known as the Wild West has long had a strong grip on the psyche of the American nation.

Also on the History Channel were dramatizations of significant events through the ages, mixed in subentries as "Time Machine" (the Little Bighorn, 2001); "The Plot to Kill . . ." (Jesse James, 2006); "Real Cowboys"

(Wyatt Earp, 2009); "American Bandits" (Frank and Jesse James, 2010), and others.

A&E Biography and later the Biography Channel through the years recreated hour-long profiles of Western legends, which included "Davy Crockett: American Frontier Legend," "Annie Oakley: Crack Shot in Petticoats," "Buffalo Bill: Showman of the West," "Wild Bill Hickok: Gentleman of the West," "The Earp Brothers: Lawmen of the West," "Sitting Bull: Chief of the Lakota Nation," programs on Calamity Jane and Doc Holliday, and in 1994, one on Roy Rogers and another on Gene Autry—can't leave those two fellas out.

And there have been television operas and ballets. No, not just Aaron Copland's *Billy the Kid* (periodically televised in whole or in part on prestigious showcases like *Omnibus* in the early fifties or on PBS), but Stewart Copeland's wry *Horse Opera*, dealing with, among others, Jesse James, Wyatt Earp, and Billy the Kid. This original from the nineties on BBC—an adaptation of Anne Caulfield's play *Cowboys*—was written by Copeland, the American musician who was the drummer of the famed rock group the Police, and British opera director Jonathan Moore. Copeland played Jesse, Moore was Billy, and British "alternative" comedian Rik Mayall was Wyatt—along with a substantial cast of "fill-in folk."

And lest we forget, Rodgers and Hammerstein's *Oklahoma!* belatedly came to television as a British-produced musical in 2003—only sixty years after it was created. Australian Hugh Jackman (pre-Wolverine) headed a multinational musical comedy cast as Curly, along with Scottish-born Josefina Gabrielle as Laurey, London stage actress Maureen Lipman as Aunt Eller, and (sole) American Shuler Hensley as Jud Fry.

CHAPTER ELEVEN

Western-Themed Series Episodes

Aside from drama anthologies, Western themes were incorporated through the years into assorted sitcoms and adventure series. Following is a small sample of them.

On *The Dick Van Dyke Show* (the last episode filmed), "The Gunslinger" had Van Dyke as Rob Petrie falling asleep in the dentist's chair and dreaming about being a swaggering sheriff in the Old West. In his dream, after being bushwhacked, Petrie engages in a showdown with nefarious Big Bad Brady (Carl Reiner in his Alan Brady guise).

Even Ozzie Nelson, on his long-running fifties series with Harriet, David, and Ricky, gets himself involved in a shootout with a popular TV cowboy (played by Western star Ben Johnson). In an April 1958 episode, Ozzie became "Six-Gun" Nelson for a supermarket contest in which he planned to be the fastest gun in town to win a teepee for the neighborhood kids. The episode was called "Top Gun."

A fifties *Superman* episode found Jimmy Olsen time-traveling back to the frontier, and it was up to the big guy with the red cape and the big red "S" on his chest to save Jimmy from harm.

On an *I Dream of Jeannie* episode in October 1966, titled "Fastest Gun in the East," Barbara Eden gives "master" Larry Hagman his fond wish of being a BMOC (big man on campus) in the Old West—and sends him there.

In a 1968 *Star Trek* episode, "Spectre of the Gun," Kirk, Spock, and company are sent to relive the gunfight at the O.K. Corral (but on the losing side!). Ron Soble guest starred as Wyatt Earp, Charles Maxwell and Rex Holman his brothers Virgil and Morgan, and Sam Gillman Doc Holliday.

The Mickey Rooney Show: Hey Mulligan (the official screen title for the 1954–1955 NBC series) offered up one Western-themed episode—"Bronc Buster"—which had the Mick dressed as an Old West cowboy complete with a two-gun holster and going to a pioneer days festival to rescue his girlfriend from a slick dude from Texas. The characters in the series are based in part on those created by Blake Edwards. Mickey Rooney was the executive producer and the show was filmed by Mickey Rooney Enterprises.

Hugh O'Brian, as Wyatt Earp, dropped in on Danny Thomas and family in the *Make Room for Daddy* episode "Wyatt Earp Visits the Williamses" in 1956. O'Brien also was Wyatt Earp on a 1960 CBS special hosted by Jackie Gleason, called *The Secret World of Eddie Hodges* (popular kid actor of the time who been in *The Music Man* on Broadway). And as his TV Earp character, O'Brian did a cameo in Bob Hope's theatrical Western *Alias Jesse James*, along with other TV cowboys and cowgirls.

On a 1955 episode of his long-running CBS comedy series, Red Skelton, as Sheriff Deadeye, faced down Clayton Moore as the Lone Ranger. About ten years later, Skelton as Deadeye crossed swords (pistols and bow-and-arrow?) with Bobby Darin as an Indian medicine man called Running Fever.

TV's "other" Lone Ranger, John Hart, donned the black mask once again in a confrontation with the Fonz on the 1982 *Happy Days* episode "Hi Yo Fonzie, Away!" A year earlier Hart as the Lone Ranger dropped in on klutzy superhero William Katt on *The Greatest American Hero* in an episode called "My Heroes Have Always Been Cowboys."

And on the imaginative early eighties time travel series *Voyagers*, in which a space cowboy and his young pal venture back and forth through time to try to "right" wrong history, there were at least two Western-themed episodes out of the twenty that aired: "Billy and Bully," about such disparate figures as Billy the Kid and Teddy Roosevelt (what did they have in common?), and "Buffalo Bill and Annie Oakley Play the Palace" (that's Queen Victoria's palace).

In "The Last Gunfighter," a 1992 episode of NBC's *Quantum Leap*, Scott Bakula, as quantum physicist from the future Sam Beckett, leaps into the life of eighty-two-year-old Tyler Means (in 1957), a onetime gunfighter. The old geezer makes a living doing Wild West reenactments—shootouts for tourists in the town of Coffin, Arizona—of what is reputedly his greatest achievement: cleaning up the town as a young man in a long ago showdown with the four infamous Claggett brothers.

Even the venerable *Simpsons* animated series did at least one Western-themed episode, albeit contemporary (in 2002), "The Lastest Gun in the West," with Dennis Weaver voicing former cowboy movie star Buck McCoy, who Bart convinces to make a comeback on "The Krusty the Clown Show."

One of the more intriguing Westerns, perhaps belonging in a category of its own, was as a segment of NBC's highly promoted but decidedly short-lived 1979 series *Cliff Hangers!* Each week the show offered a trio of twenty-minute serials (lumped together in a one-hour show), like the popular theatrical ones of an earlier day. The Western segment was called "The Secret Empire"—a reworking of sorts of a midthirties Gene Autry multi-episode serial titled *The Phantom Empire.* "The Secret Empire," which switched back and forth between sepia tone and color, starred Geoffrey Scott as Marshal Jim Donner, who, in 1880s Cheyenne, stumbles upon a vast technologically advanced, gold-seeking alien civilization in their underground city named Chimera, controlled by the evil emperor Thorval (Mark Lenard). This appears to be the rare Western serial on television—and unlike real movie cliff-hangers, it was never resolved since NBC yanked the show before concluding it.

CHAPTER TWELVE

Heading, Alas, Thataway

Trail's end on television effectively came with the conclusion of *Into the West* and the HBO series *Deadwood*—except for an occasional Western TV movie airing on the Hallmark Channel (generally produced by Larry Levinson) and, of course, the prestige of *The Virginian* in 2000 as well as *Broken Trail* in 2006, *Bury My Heart at Wounded Knee* in 2007, and *Comanche Moon* in 2008. And those assorted Western documentaries airing on the History Channel and PBS.

The trail vanished—and with it a huge chunk of American pop culture. It's now consigned to that big corral in the sky. Or TVLand or the Western Channel.

"Once," as Ed Weiner wrote in *The TV Guide TV Book* back in 1992, "they [cowboys] were as plentiful on the vast TV wasteland as were the buffalo they slaughtered on the real American prairie. Soon they were, like the Indians before them, pushed off their turf by the White Coats (doctor shows) and Blue Serge (lawyer shows), blown away like so many holstered and vested tumbleweeds."

But, as Jimmy Stewart once observed, "The Western is an original. An American feels 'This is ours!'"

Selected Bibliography

Books

Burlingame, Jon. *TV's Biggest Hits: The Story of Television Themes from "Dragnet" to "Friends."* New York: Schirmer Books, 1996.

Everson, William K. *The Hollywood Western: 90 Years of Cowboys, Indians, Train Robbers, Sheriffs, and Gunslingers and Assorted Heroes and Desperados.* Secaucus, NJ: Carol Publishing Group, 1992.

Goldberg, Lee. *Unsold Television Pilots, Volume 1: 1955–1976.* iuniverse, 2001.

Grossman, Gary H. *Saturday Morning TV.* New York: Delacorte, 1981.

MacDonald, J. Fred. *Who Shot the Sheriff? The Rise and Fall of the Television Western.* Westport, CT: Praeger, 1986.

Miller, Don. *Hollywood Corral.* New York: Popular Library, 1973.

Robertson, Ed. *Maverick: Legend of the West.* Beverly Hills, CA: Pomegranate Press, 1994.

Weiner, Ed. *The TV Guide TV Book.* New York: HarperPerennial, 1992.

Magazines and Newspapers

Gabler, Neal. "An Appreciation: Fess Parker's Davy Crockett Was a Hero When We Needed One." *Los Angeles Times*, March 20, 2010.

Goodman, Walter. "Shattering the Legends of West's Pistol Packers." *New York Times*, December 13, 1993.

Gould, Jack. "Musical 'Ruggles': Saga of the Gentleman's Gentleman Proves Disappointing in Channel 4 Version." *New York Times*, February 4, 1957.

———. "TV: Old West Updated; Authentic Look at 19th-Century America Narrated by Gary Cooper for N.B.C." *New York Times*, March 30, 1961.

James, Caryn. "How the West Was Lost (as a Staple of TV)." *New York Times*, September 15, 1996.

"James Arness: A Different View." *TV Guide*, February 24, 1979, p. 19.

Lloyd, Robert. "American Experience: We Shall Remain." *Los Angeles Times*, April 13, 2009.

"Manners and Morals: Kiddies in the Old Corral." *Time*, November 27, 1950.

O'Connor, John J. "Texas, All of It, According to Michener." *New York Times*, April 14, 1995.

"Radio and TV: The New Shows." *Time*, February 23, 1953.

Rosenberg, Howard. "*Brisco County* Full of Self-Mocking Spoofs." *Los Angeles Times*, August 27, 1993. articles.latimes.com/1993-08-27/entertainment/ca-28353_1_ brisco-county.

Shanley, J. P. "Television: 'Spectacular' Battle Begins; Judy Garland Debut on C.B.S. Sets It Off; Channel 4 Presents *Frontier* Premiere." *New York Times*, September 26, 1955.

Stang, Joanne. "Ponderosa Gold under a Painted Sky." *New York Times*, May 30, 1965.

Stanley, Alessandra. "'Broken Trail,' a Tale of Roping in Cattle and Rounding Up Girls." *New York Times*, June 23, 2006.

"Three New Series Say It's a Man's World." *New York Times*, October 6, 1956.

Websites

Broadcast Pioneers of Philadelphia. www.broadcastpioneers.com/bp3/aita.html

HistoryNet.com. www.historynet.com

Legends of America. www.legendsofamerica.com

Index

About the Author

Alvin H. Marill (1934–2010) was a graduate of Boston University and spent his career in direct marketing and the recording industry (for RCA Records and Columbia Records), in broadcasting (CBS Television), and in publishing, as editor of film and pop media books. For years, Marill was television editor for the publication *Films in Review* and wrote about television movies for Leonard Maltin's annual *Movie Guide*. He also was contributing editor for *Scarlet Street* magazine.

Among his many published books are *Samuel Goldwyn Presents, Robert Mitchum on the Screen, The Complete Films of Edward G. Robinson, The Films of Anthony Quinn, Big Pictures on the Small Screen, Sports on Television,* and books on Tommy Lee Jones, the Three Stooges, Tyrone Power, and Mickey Rooney. His books for Scarecrow Press include *Keeping Score: Film Music, 1988–1997* (1998); *More Theatre: Stage to Screen to Television, 1993–2001* (2002); and *More Theatre III: Stage to Screen to Television, since 2001* (2007). His five-volume *Movies Made for Television, 1964–2004,* commemorating the fortieth anniversary of the genre, was published in 2005, and a subsequent volume, *Movies Made for Television, 2005–2009,* was published in 2010.

Marill was a charter member of the Television Hall of Fame.